HARDY'S POETRY, 1860–1928

Dennis Taylor

Columbia University Press
New York   1981

Printed in Hong Kong

Library of Congress Cataloging in Publication Data

Taylor, Dennis, 1940–
  Hardy's poetry, 1860–1928.

  Bibliography: p.
  Includes index.
  1. Hardy, Thomas, 1840–1928—Poetic
  works.   I. Title.
PR4757.P58T3   821′ .8   80–20862

ISBN 0–231–05050–X

To Mary

Contents

List of Plates

Acknowledgements

The author and publishers wish to thank the following who have kindly given permission for the use of copyright material:

Faber and Faber Ltd. and Harcourt Brace Jovanovich Inc., for an extract from 'Quaker Graveyard in Nantucket' from *Poems 1938–1949* (in the U.S., *Lord Weary's Castle*), by Robert Lowell.

Faber and Faber Ltd. and Random House Inc. for an extract from 'On This Island' from *Collected Shorter Poems* (in the U.S., *Collected Poems*) by W. H. Auden, edited by Edward Mendelson.

Houghton Mifflin Company for an extract from 'Ars Poetica' in *New and Collected Poems 1917–1976*, by Archibald MacLeish.

The Trustees of the Thomas Hardy Memorial Collection in the Dorset County Museum for the extracts from the reels of *The Original Manuscripts and Papers of Thomas Hardy*.

Every effort has been made to trace all the copyright holders, but if any have been inadvertently overlooked the publishers will be pleased to make the necessary arrangement at the first opportunity.

Introduction

A man sits in an old church and sketches on a large architectural pad. He begins to muse about the many dead who lie buried there under stone effigies. He then thinks about the world outside the church, a world full of war and personal tragedy. He thinks also about himself and the gloomy setting of the church seems to harmonise with his reflections. Suddenly he looks up. His pencil and pad have slipped to the floor. It is much later. He feels stiff. He looks outside and discovers that the late evening fog has come up and engulfed the church.

This is a central type of experience in Hardy's poetry. As he meditates about the world, the world changes around him and intrudes on the meditation.

What happens in the course of a few minutes is the model for what happens in the course of years. A man walks along the beach and sees the woman he loves. She rides horseback and the rhythm of her riding and her singing blends with the rhythm of the tide. But a noise of waves jars the image. The ocean is all too real, the woman is dead, the man is forty years older than when he first saw her there.

The interruption of the reverie in the church is like the interruption of a forty-year-old habit of thought and feeling. The plot of the reverie, indeed, seems to repeat – recapitulate – the plot of a lifetime.

This is the plot I find most interesting in Hardy's poetry and whose implications for his development and his style of writing I find most fruitful. It is a plot which took Hardy a lifetime to develop. At the climax of this development, he could make brief moments of perception parallel the experience of years. We may be able to see the development quite dramatically in the following example. Perhaps as early as 1874 Hardy wrote the following stanzas:

> On the flat road a man at last appears:
> How much his whitening hairs
> Owe to the settling snow's mute anchorage,
> And how much to a life's rough pilgrimage,
> One cannot certify.

A second man comes by;
His ruddy beard brings fire to the pallid scene:
His coat is faded green;
Hence seems it that his mien
Wears something of the dye
Of the berried holm-trees that he passes nigh.

The snow-feathers so gently swoop that though
But half an hour ago
The road was brown, and now is starkly white,
A watcher would have failed defining quite
When it transformed it so.[1]

These lines are interesting in themselves but their implications are perhaps not fully clear. The speaker cannot discern two things: whether snow or age is whitening the hair of the first passer-by, and when the road changes from brown to white. What is the connection between these two questions?

In 1890 Hardy finished writing *Tess of the d'Urbervilles*. Describing a winter scene at Flintcomb-Ash farm, he wrote: 'Cobwebs revealed their presence on sheds and walls where none had ever been observed till brought out into visibility by the crystallizing atmosphere, hanging like loops of white worsted from salient points of the outhouses, posts, and gates.'[2]

In 1925 Hardy published 'A Light Snow-Fall after Frost'.[3] The poem contains a new stanza added some time after Hardy wrote the first three. It is possible that in rereading his novels Hardy noticed the image in *Tess* and added it to the poem where it clarifies and confirms the relation between the earlier stanzas. The new stanza becomes the second stanza of the poem:

The frost is on the wane,
And cobwebs hanging close outside the pane
Pose as festoons of thick white worsted there,
Of their pale presence no eye being aware
Till the rime made them plain.

Hardy has modified the *Tess* image so that not only do we look at the pattern of cobwebs, we look through it.

The addition of this image makes clear the relationship between the two questions by posing a third: when does the speaker realise that he is looking through cobwebs? The poem becomes a poem about realisations, realisations of changes taking place in the passers-by, in the road, and in the speaker. The parallels suggest a little allegory. The two passers-by are journeying two roads, the road outside the window, the road which is their pilgrimage through life. Their lives are changing. They seem to represent two stages of life, the one ruddy like the berried holm trees with which he shares a 'buried' life; the other with hair whitening from both age and snow, just as changes come mysteriously from both inside and outside. What is happening to the speaker in this half-hour parallels what is happening to the men outside. This parallel suggests the poem's ultimate question: when do we realise that our lives have changed, that we have grown old? This question is now implicit in the question about the scene: when do we realise that the scene in front of us has changed? The eye cannot see what is happening in front of it until something strikes the attention and reveals what has been changing for many moments. In a parallel way, a man ages and only at certain striking moments does he truly realise how many years have elapsed and how far he has come.[4] The cobwebs were there all along as we looked through the window, but their pattern only comes clear after a while. The window we look through is ultimately our own mind. In the small experiences, and in the larger ones, there are elements present, of whose 'pale presence' no eye is aware until nature's 'rime' makes them plain. Only then can they be quite defined.

I would suggest that this pattern of definition conditions Hardy's style of writing: his way of structuring his poems, his favourite images, his choice of words, his metres. The final definition of an experience is the poem. It is what Hardy called an 'expiation', a model of a late discovery, an imitation of a person coming to know himself within a reality which is much larger and more intricate than himself.

The gradual development of 'A Light Snow-Fall after Frost' is typical of the development of many of Hardy's poems. An initial impression is modified, abandoned, taken up again. It is influenced by what Hardy reads and what he has written. Gradually, its full import is realised after the experience and reflection of years.

'DEVELOPMENT'

The central issue in Hardy studies is what happens to an experience as it is made into literature, the experience remembered, the literature reread, a similar experience undergone, the whole made into more literature. While most of this book bears on this topic, the topic still needs much more exploration. At certain important moments in his poetic career, Hardy reread his works in order to prepare them for collected editions. He found it a tedious chore but at times, he said, a 'gleam of interest arises'.[5] Such major rereadings occurred for the Wessex Novels (London: Osgood, McIlvaine, 1895–6) shortly before Hardy resumed his career as a full-time poet; again for the Wessex Edition (London: Macmillan, 1912–14 with later volumes to be incorporated) which coincides with the major turning-point of Hardy's poetic career; then for the Mellstock Edition (London: Macmillan, 1919–20), as Hardy began his last decade of poetry. More rereading of the poems occurred for the collected editions of 1919, 1923, 1928 and even mysteriously 1930 – these last two incorporating changes Hardy made before his death and for the preparation of a last selected edition, *Chosen Poems*, not published until 1929.[6] So far these multiple collections have given work to those who have traced variant readings of individual lines; and the definitive variorum edition has now (after some delay) been published. But there also needs to be considered how the entire conception of new poems derived from multiple revisitations of old poems and novels. Hardy's last decade also saw him preparing his official biography, which entailed more reading of past works, as well as correspondence, diaries, etc. And at various stages throughout his career he reconsulted his notebooks. To follow an experience from its initial inception through these multiple revisitations and modifications makes for delight and discovery.

Development is a controversial word in discussions of poetry, and particularly in discussions of Hardy.[7] Several of the reviews in Hardy's collection, including Gosse's important *Edinburgh Review* article written with Hardy's help, assert some development, but in the vaguest of terms.[8] Hardy wrote many varieties of poems during each decade of his career and many of his later poems are like his earlier poems. His poetry does not display the obvious and clearly defined stages we find in certain other poets. Looking back over Hardy's poetry in 1922, Gosse decided that Hardy's talent had 'suffered very little modification in the course of sixty years' (*Sunday Times*, 28 May). This has remained the standard view. It is an unfortunate view because it reinforces other traditional views of Hardy's verse. A poet whose style is 'fixed' by the seventies and who continues to write poems for another sixty years can reasonably be thought of as a poet of 'perverse consistency', fixed ideas, cranky language habits, stereotyped plots, mechanical contrivances of metre. Success for such a poet is likely to be rare – a handful of the 900 poems – and will be due to 'escape from the governing frame', an overwhelming sincerity which is indescribable.

Nevertheless Hardy asserted that there was an important development in his poetry. Returning to poetry in 1897, 'he had found an awkwardness in getting back to an easy expression in numbers after abandoning it for so many years; but that soon wore off'.[9] Two years later he compared himself to Verdi who, according to the art histories, 'had only just arrived at maturity at the age of threescore and ten or thereabouts' (*Life*, 300). In an unpublished 1904 preface to the poems of 'Lawrence Hope' (Adela Nicolson), Hardy regretted the young writer's death and the relative immaturity of her poems, though he recognised 'their purely dramatic or personative character. But all such would have fallen naturally into their evolutionary place and value had they been succeeded by less wayward performances of larger scope and schooled feeling, such as would in the probable order of things have come from her hand if she had survived to philosophic years.'[10] In 1906 Hardy wrote: 'I prefer late Wagner, as I prefer late Turner, to early. . . . When a man not contented with the grounds of his success goes on and on, and tries to achieve the impossible, then he gets profoundly interesting to me' (*Life*, 329). In 1909, Hardy wrote in his preface to *Time's Laughingstocks*: 'As a whole they will, I hope, take the reader forward, even if not far, rather than backward.' In this same year he wrote to Henry Newbolt: 'Happily one can afford to dismiss the fear of writing oneself out, which we used to hear so much of.'[11] Hardy's practice refutes the romantic myth which says just the opposite. In 1917, the year of his supreme poetic volume, *Moments of Vision*, he reflected more deeply than usual over his career: 'I was quick to bloom; late to ripen'; 'I was a child till I was 16; a youth till I was 25 [the year he wrote 'Amabel']; a young man till I was 40 or 50 [the latter being the year he wrote 'Thoughts of Phena']' (*Life*, 378). In 1920 Hardy said: 'The value of old age depends upon the person who reaches it. To some men of early performance it is useless. To others, who are late to develop, it just enables them to complete their job.'[12] The year before Hardy had dictated: 'Speaking generally, there is more autobiography in a hundred lines of Mr. Hardy's poetry than in all the novels' (*Life*, 392). In a sequence of letters in 1920 Hardy re-asserted his perennial claim that his poetic fancies were 'impressions of the moment', 'impressions that frequently change'.[13]

It is important to connect Hardy's theory of 'impressions' with the other remarks he makes about the autobiography and development in his poetry. An impression for Hardy is not exactly a 'relative' or arbitrary point of view – though this may apply to some of his philosophic fancies. An impression, as applied to the bulk of his poetry, is more properly an impression of the autobiographical moment. It reflects a period of the life, and as the life changes, the nature of Hardy's impressions will change. By life I mean Hardy's mental and emotional life, which does not have a one-to-one correspondence with his external biographical experience whose import he might realise much later. An impression can be nurtured and preserved through the years until all of its significance is realised.[14] At that moment, a pattern emerges and a literary form is discovered.

In tracing Hardy's development, I have tried to be mindful of Ruskin's observation about his own development in *Praeterita* (I, 10):

> Some forces are failing while others strengthen, and most act irregularly, or else at uncorresponding periods of renewed enthusiasm after intervals of lassitude. For all clearness of exposition, it is necessary to follow first one, then another, without confusing notices of what is happening in other directions.

The ways in which Hardy's development takes place are numerous: in the growing economy and dramatic effect of the meditative poem, in the use of a favourite image of patterns, in the consistency of language and theme, in the technical and imitative possibilities of metrical rhythm, in choices of subjects and poetic forms which match stages of developing interest, in the synthesis of subjects and forms. At certain points, various of these 'forces' are realised together and at such points important advances in the lyric poem occur. Hardy illustrates the point well expressed by J. Hillis Miller in his introduction to *The Disappearance of God: Five Nineteenth-Century Writers*:

> The unity of a human life, like the unity of the writings which express it, is not something fixed and unchanging. A human life is a dynamic process which moves through various phases, while returning often to earlier ones, in the search for a full comprehension of its 'organizing principles.' Only through development can the nature of these principles be gradually revealed, for they cannot be completely expressed in any single form.

In Hardy's case, the sequence of phases is not merely dialectical; its chronological points can be specified as well. The development Hardy illustrates is consistent with his philosophy of meaning as that which develops slowly but reveals itself at certain dramatic instances, so that it illuminates the entire lifetime's work.

Since Hardy revisited his novels in order to write more poems, I have also occasionally considered how certain aesthetic elements in the novel receive their consummate development in the poem. In several cases, the vantage-point of the poems can make us see an interesting development through the novels.

PRÉCIS

I suggested above that at the end of a long process in Hardy's development a remembered impression is exhumed, a pattern is realised, and a literary form is achieved. The first chapter of this book considers Hardy's most important literary form, the meditative lyric. I attempt to trace its development within a circumscribed number of poems and within a circumscribed period, roughly 1890 to 1917. The second chapter casts a wider net and traces throughout Hardy's works an imagery of patterns. The widespread occurrence of this imagery, which symbolises the way impressions develop, is a kind of symbolic matrix in which the meditative lyric is firmly lodged. The imagery links Hardy's interest in the meditative poem with many currents of nineteenth-century intellectual history. The third chapter considers Hardy's long career as a poet, from 1860 to 1928, and focuses on the paradox that he is a poet of developing memories. His career shows a remarkable consistency by which a memory lyric of 1866 can develop, by a series of traceable steps, into a grand war poem of 1921. Gradually Hardy discovers the deep connections between the plot of his life and the plot of Victorian life – both caught up in fifty-year-old dreams soon to be interrupted by the realities of 1912–14. Hardy's lyric vision climaxes in the image of a grotesque nightmare apocalypse haunted by a changed world. The Epilogue discusses a brief pastoral period in Hardy's career, a late contemplative revisitation of his past which he experiences in the 1920s.

Each of the chapters and epilogue can be seen as focusing on some aspect of Hardy's relation to the romantic literary tradition – to the romantic meditative poem and traditions of reverie, to romantic aesthetics and its connections with the Gothic Revival, to the romantic visionary sensibility and its relation to theories of the grotesque, to the romantic version of the pastoral ideal. In developing his poetry, Hardy develops these traditions in important ways. In his notebooks Hardy quoted from an article on Turner: 'An artist must be able to persuade himself either that he is carrying to completion something begun by his forerunner, or that it is his to denounce the fraud of his predecessor, and to discover afresh the secret of art.'[15] Many of the traditions which Hardy carried on or reacted against underwent important developments in the 1860s. Indeed the decade was a decisive stage in the evolution of architecture, in the growth of public art collections, in discussions of the grotesque, in the collecting of ballads, in the Victorian novel, in philosophy and epistemology, in philology and prosody, in archaeology and history, even in photography. These developments profoundly impressed Hardy's mind at a formative stage.

His poetry was 'fixed' in the sixties only in the sense that the sixties gave him enough to think about for a lifetime. The manuscript for this book originally included discussions of Hardy's language, metrics, and the dating of his poems. But these subjects proved too extensive for inclusion here. In this book I have generally relied on poems whose date of composition can be reasonably assigned to a given year or period. It is true that many Hardy poems derive from old notes and are given many revisions through the years. But when Hardy decided that a poem was substantially written at an early date or was substantially changed by subsequent revisions, he usually indicated this fact in a postscript. There are many poems which can, with reasonable probability, be assigned to a given year or period.

ACKNOWLEDGEMENTS

The lack of a good critical tradition for Hardy's poetry has long been a puzzle. He has been a striking example of a poet's poet, read and loved by dozens of major modern poets but subject to a generally lukewarm critical commentary.[16] This situation has improved only in very recent years with the appearance of some perceptive books on the poetry. But in America at least Hardy has yet to attract a reading public like that which most other major modern poets have enjoyed. The 1930 edition of the *Collected Poems*, which is the more accurate edition and includes the posthumous *Winter Words*, has never been published in America. The recent (1976) definitive edition of the *Complete Poems*, which in England sold out its first printing of 10,000 copies well within a year, could not find an American publisher. One reason for this astonishing[17] situation is that the process which has popularised other poets – namely their introduction to a large body of graduate and undergraduate students by the universities – has never worked for Hardy. In many college corridors I find a sense of bewilderment, among those who care about Victorian and modern poetry, about how Hardy can best be presented. It has remained difficult to resolve certain paradoxes about Hardy's poetry, its variety and consistency, its privacy and its learning, its uniqueness and its representative character, its sincerity and its reliance on literary sources, its sense of tradition and its break with tradition, its constant experimentation and its emphasis on memory.

At the same time, we have seen recently much interesting analysis, particularly of Hardy's habits of perception and his relation to romantic, Victorian, and modern poets. Many poems have been explicated. I have tried to avoid retracing these steps. Valuable studies using portions of Hardy's unpublished notebooks have been made. I am thinking especially of Wright on *The Dynasts*, Millgate on the novels, Beatty on the architectural notebook, Gittings on the life, and Björk's annotations on a portion of the notebooks. Helpful compendiums of background material for the poems have been made by Pinion, Bailey, and Gerber. Purdy's *Bibliographical Study* remains a model of care.[18] A collected edition of Hardy's letters is now being published and edited by Purdy and Millgate. I have included in this book additional background information and citations from the notebooks which are relevant to the poems. Much valuable work relevant to Hardy has also been done on the nature of romantic and modern meditative poetry, on Gothic and Pre-Raphaelite art, on the intellectual and philological backgrounds of the Victorian age, on the history and theory of metrics, on ballads, war poetry, photography and the grotesque. *The Life of Thomas Hardy* remains an extraordinarily rich resource where profoundly interesting insights are likely to go unnoticed in the rush of social detail. It represents Hardy's last major assessment of his life and work and I refer to it as such even though he let Florence Emily Hardy's name stand as the author's.[19] Hardy's mind is not the amateur affair which less well-read critics have made of it. It is enormously wide-ranging and synthetic. The *Life*, which occasionally cites Hardy's reading lists (48, 59, 203, 212, 230), in fact touches only the surface of what he read and copied. His unpublished letters and notebooks are still, as Purdy said in 1954, 'an incomparable mine for the student of Hardy' (Purdy, p. viii). Most of the notebooks have recently become available in microfilm.[20] Also important is a wide variety of uncollected material including prefaces, annotations in books, interviews and recollections, though the latter, when uncorroborated, must be treated cautiously. *The Variorum Edition of the Complete Poems*, edited by James Gibson, was published too late for full consideration here. It will, however, prove invaluable for further study of Hardy's language and metrics. In all cases of poems whose early dating is important, I have used the early versions as described in the *Variorum*. Therefore, the reader will find a few discrepancies between the versions quoted here and those given in the 1976 *Complete Poems*.

This book, which I began writing in the late sixties, has gone through a number of versions. Many colleagues have read portions of earlier versions, though by now they may have forgotten and will be surprised to find themselves listed. Yet many of their comments have haunted me for a long time. At Yale, Louis Martz, Dwight Culler, William Kinsley, and Ed Reno helped me with a 1965 dissertation. At the University of California,

Santa Barbara, Benjamin Sankey, Alan Stephens, Elizabeth Schneider, Frank Cousens, Fred Turner, Walter Davis; and at Boston College Anne Ferry and Paul Doherty read earlier versions of the present manuscript. George Goldsmith and the Audio-Visual Department at Boston College assisted me with the photographs. Portions of Chapter 1, in earlier form, appeared in *Victorian Poetry*, 11 (1973), and the *Colby Library Quarterly*, xi (1975). An early short version of Chapter 2 appeared in *English Literary History*, 42 (1975).

The Consortium libraries of Boston (especially those at Boston College, Brandeis, Boston University, and the Boston Public Library), the Boston Athenaeum, Houghton and Widener libraries, the libraries at Yale, Johns Hopkins and Colby College, the New York Public Library, the University of California libraries at Santa Barbara, Los Angeles, and Berkeley, the Huntington Library, the Dorset County Museum and the public library at Concord, Massachusetts, have provided vital assistance. I am grateful to the reference librarians at Bapst Library who wrote dozens of letters on my behalf. Only *The Book of Baby Pets* (cf. below, p. 147) eluded them and me. I am particularly grateful to James Gibson who assisted me with his encouragement in the final stages and who introduced me to Macmillan.

I had hoped to get my family, both sides, into a dedication by mounting their names on the ogees and mullions of the illustration of Gloucester Cathedral, in the manner of a Hardy pedigree (cf. Illustrations 3 and 4). But I cannot make them fit and they are much too alive to be so engraved. They also helped keep me alive during these several years. But I must acknowledge the contributions made by John, Frank Matthew, Kathryn Elizabeth, and Mary Rebecca, all of whom are younger than this book. My parents should know that an earlier version was dedicated to them but they will understand that the old order changeth and a man must cling to his wife.

1 The Development of Hardy's Meditative Lyric

A MATURE MEDITATIVE MODEL

Like many of Hardy's important poems, 'Copying Architecture in an Old Minster' is little known and never anthologised. It illustrates many of the supposed defects of Hardy's poetry. The choice of words seems *ad hoc*, ranging somewhat uneasily from the archaic to the commonplace. Many of the poem's climaxes are carried by seemingly stale formulas of expression: 'the speechless midnight and dawn', 'a world so ancient and trouble-torn', 'ardours chilled and numb'. The meditation is fitted to a metrical frame which often seems to force the language into an artificial pattern of rhythm. The situation is a stock one, with its sinister clocks and ghosts. The poem's final surmise seems to be the kind of obsessive conviction that early critics called pessimistic and later critics called doctrinaire.

But if we look more closely at the poem, the theme becomes intellectually impressive and the supposed defects are transformed when we see their organic connection with the theme. It takes time for this consistency to settle into the reader's consciousness:

> How smartly the quarters of the hour march by
>   That the jack-o'-clock never forgets;
>   Ding-dong; and before I have traced a cusp's eye,
> Or got the true twist of the ogee over,
>   A double ding-dong ricochetts.
>
> Just so did he clang here before I came,
>   And so will he clang when I'm gone
>   Through the Minster's cavernous hollows – the same
> Tale of hours never more to be will he deliver
>   To the speechless midnight and dawn!
>
> I grow to conceive it a call to ghosts,
>   Whose mould lies below and around.

Yes; the next 'Come, come,' draws them out from their posts,
And they gather, and one shade appears, and another,
    As the eve-damps creep from the ground.

See – a Courtenay stands by his quatre-foiled tomb,
    And a Duke and his Duchess near;
And one Sir Edmund in columned gloom,
And a Saxon king by the presbytery chamber;
    And shapes unknown in the rear.

Maybe they have met for a parle on some plan
    To better ail-stricken mankind;
I catch their cheepings, though thinner than
The overhead creak of a passager's pinion
    When leaving land behind.

Or perhaps they speak to the yet unborn,
    And caution them not to come
To a world so ancient and trouble-torn,
Of foiled intents, vain lovingkindness,
    And ardours chilled and numb.

They waste to fog as I stir and stand,
    And move from the arched recess,
And pick up the drawing that slipped from my hand,
And feel for the pencil I dropped in the cranny
    In a moment's forgetfulness.   (369)

In one of the best short discussions of Hardy's poetry, an anonymous reviewer in *TLS* (1 June 1922) said of another Hardy poem: 'there is no line, until you reach the last four, that stops you with its beauty; and you run through the beauty of the last four to reach the end; and then the beauty of the whole takes you and flows back through the whole poem.' Such a transformation happens here. The last stanza is surprising in the way it returns to the setting. Such a return is traditional in the romantic meditative lyric, but Hardy modifies it in a distinctive way. The suggestion is made that more time has passed than we had supposed. The eve-damps of stanza 3 have been replaced by the fog. When the architectural pad fell to the stone floor, its clatter was not heard. A hidden natural development has taken place, changing the outer world and conditioning the speaker in ways he did not realise. His conscious thoughts have gone one way, the hidden world has gone another.

In the light of this striking revelation, we find that the theme of the poem becomes more interesting. Time passes and will bury us all – yes, but here we see it happening in the forming of the poem. Even as we try to express and understand the nature of time, it ricochets and leaves our formulations behind. In the first stanza, Hardy says that the first quarter of the hour becomes the second quarter before he has 'traced a cusp's eye'. This statement becomes the hidden dramatic principle of the poem as Hardy begins to trace the meanings he finds in the minster. His tracing, or meditation upon the dead, is not, as we first thought, an open-eyed meditation about the scene in front of him. The meditation grows stealthily blinder to the scene. 'I grow to conceive it a call to ghosts' seems to initiate a highly self-controlled manipulation of a staged setting. Yet this is the point at which Hardy begins to enter his dark ghost-led reverie. Thus the phrase reread seems to mean: 'I grow into my conception, my conception abstracts me from the world around.' Such stale phrases take on a rich life. Similarly, the 'speechless midnight', the 'cavernous hollows', 'shapes unknown', the incredibly slight bony sound of the 'creak of a passager's pinion / When leaving land behind', suggest, on rereading, that larger hidden world ready to spring. This world becomes known only at the end when the train of thought is broken through.

This is not to say that the conclusions arrived at within the meditation are not true. The world *is* ancient and trouble-torn, intents *are* foiled, ardours *are* chilled by time. But the way we know such things is not exempt from the conditions which cause them. The consistency of what Hardy knows with the way he knows is the principle of his great lyric achievement.

This consistency transforms the way we 'grow to conceive' the nature of Hardy's language. Hardy writes out of a language which is centuries old. Its roots are like the 'shapes unknown in the rear'. Its images, its words, its phrasings, its rhythms, form a tremendous system of interpretation which Hardy has inherited. It enables him to express his experience and yet it also contains and limits his experience, binding him to conceptions which were evolved centuries earlier in human experience. Human beings can hardly perceive those limitations any more than they can perceive the eyes through which they see. It is Hardy's genius that he can suggest the potential rigidity and obsolescence in inherited language. Indeed the phrases grow more formulaic as the meditation climaxes. There is the conceived world, 'so ancient and trouble-torn, / Of foiled intents, vain lovingkindness, / And ardours chilled and numb.' And there is the real world where such things are more terribly true than the speaker can conceive. 'Chilled and numb' also suggests subliminally, I think, the chilled and numb ardour of the man who is about to wake both from the abstractions of his language and the abstraction of his reverie. Hardy suggests a deep connection between these two sorts of abstractions.

The language of the poem is deliberately chosen from many contexts and many ages, and from varying levels of abstraction and concreteness. The technical language of *ogee* and *cusp* and *quatre-foiled*, the archaism of *parle*, the obsolete usage of *passager* and *jack-o'-clock*, the poeticism *pinion*, are mingled with still standard words like *ail* and *intents* (standard at least at the time the OED was published). The result, one of the most original achieved by a lyric poet, is that we sense the ageing process which is taking place in language even as we speak.

Perhaps the most interesting transformation occurs in the poem's metre. The metrical form is a modified and extended form of common metre, a quatrain of alternating cross-rhymed tetrameter-trimeter lines in duple rising or iambic rhythm: $a^4b^3a^4b^3$ d.r. Hardy expands the form with an extra line and puts the whole in a predominantly triple rising or anapestic rhythm: $a^4b^3a^4c^4b^3$ t.r. The extra c line rhymes, like a recurrent clock chime, with similarly placed lines in the three following stanzas. This chime interlocking the stanzas is abandoned in the last three stanzas as the reverie leaves time behind and then comes unknit. Under cover of what more or less looks like a traditional form, Hardy achieves a very nice onomatopoeia. He imposes the pattern somewhat awkwardly and obtrusively at the beginning. The first stanza associates the metrical rhythm with the ricochet of the clock. Indeed the phrase, 'ding-dong', is deliberately crude, almost comical in its assertion that the clock is clanging *now* as it is being described. But the immediacy of this coincidence of language and reality will prove deceptive. The onomatopoeia becomes deliberately strained towards the end of the second stanza. The rhythm thuds heavily through 'Minster's cavernous hollows' and skips quickly through the poem's most difficult metrical line: 'Tale of hours never more to be will he deliver.'

Many Hardy poems have a line like this which keys us to the significance of the rhythm. We try to read it slowly according to its natural accents, but the rhythm strains to impose its pattern. The difficulty is functional for Hardy dramatises how his language and rhythm are being influenced by forces outside his control. The third stanza settles more easily into the rhythm and the clock hypnotises the speaker, drawing the ghosts out of their moulds: ' "Come, come" '. Thereafter we forget the clock but the clock, stamped in the established rhythm, does not forget us. It may be signified subliminally in the 'overhead creak' of the passager's pinion. The reference to time in the penultimate stanza is extremely abstract, but the reference to time in the last stanza is extremely concrete. The rhythm of time has drawn the speaker backwards into the spell of reverie and then brought him forward into collision with the present. Harvey Gross suggests that the function of metrical rhythm is to image human experience as it takes place in time.[1] The ingenuity of Hardy's rhythm is that it imitates two temporal processes, the movement of thought and the movement of time in the outer world, two movements which converge, diverge, and collide in the last stanza when consummation comes.

Once Hardy's idea of meditation is realised, the difficulties of his style drop away. He makes us glimpse the processes which turn fresh insights into archaic formulas, tentative expressions into rigid abstractions, spontaneous rhythms into repetitive patterns. The stiffness of these conclusions is transformed because we see in them their beginnings and the larger world in which they have taken shape. Hardy's ability to root his poetry so firmly and complexly in this world accounts, I think, for his famous 'sincerity' and 'transparency'. We can see how such virtues are achieved by a style which usually indicates their opposites.

THE ROMANTIC MEDITATIVE TRADITION

Hardy's meditative lyric has long been difficult to imitate and to place in a specific tradition. One explanation of its uniqueness is that Hardy rewrites the romantic lyric in a way that goes against the grain of the major tradition of that lyric. 'Copying Architecture in an Old Minster', for example, is a 'new' version of 'Frost at Midnight'. The owlet's cry becomes Hardy's clock chime, the extreme silentness vexing meditation becomes the cavernous hollows, the abstruser musings become a growing reverie, the high abstractions of 'eternity' and 'Spirit' become those of 'foiled intents', and the secret ministry of frost becomes the ministry of eve-damps and fog. However, the gentle breathing of Coleridge's infant, moulded into the verse rhythm, is not here. Rather we have the ricochet of the clock. The end of Coleridge's poem suggests that the ministry of mind and the ministry of nature are harmoniously joined: the frost forms its icicles as the mind forms its thoughts.[2] Hardy's imagery suggests instead the growing disjunction of mental and natural reality. Accepting its initial premise – a man seeking connections within a natural setting – Hardy rewrites the romantic meditation from within, leading it to a view of mind and language which is carefully limited.

This limitation connects Hardy's romantic meditations with much older traditions, both biblical and classical. In his copy of Jeremy Taylor's *Holy Living and Dying* (London, 1850, Colby College Library Collection), Hardy marked a passage from the paragraph in which the preacher

describes how 'the life of a man comes upon him slowly and insen-
sibly'. That is, a man realises the meaning of his life only after many years
of distraction – 'but by that time his soul is thus furnished his body
is decayed'. The passage Hardy marked illustrates the point by citing
the sun's stealthy progress during the day: 'And still, while a man tells
the story, the sun gets higher . . . and then he shines . . . and sets
quickly; so is a man's reason and his life.' While a man reads and thinks
and tells his story in Hardy, the world passes him by. The parallel of a
meditation and a life, and the ancient sources of this parallel, are alluded
to by Hardy in a motto he sent to the Wessex Society of Manchester in
1908:

> While new tongues call, and novel scenes unfold,
> Meet may it be to bear in mind the old. . . .
> Vain dreams, indeed, are thoughts of heretofore;
> What then? Your instant lives are nothing more.   (*Life*, 336)

Coming from such traditions and others we shall explore in Chapter 2,
Hardy uses the Romantic meditative structure but resists the mainstream
tradition which 'tries to overcome the secondary or elegiac aspect of
language by making language coterminous with life'.[3]

Backgrounds in the Novel

Hardy's version of romantic reverie partly results from his career as a
novelist and his use of dramatic irony to show his romantic dreamers
within an uncongenial natural setting. *A Laodicean* begins in the following
manner:

> The sun blazed down and down, till it was within half-an-hour of its
> setting; but the sketcher still lingered at his occupation of measuring and
> copying the chevroned doorway, a bold and quaint example of a
> transitional style of architecture, which formed the tower entrance to an
> English village church. The graveyard being quite open on its western
> side, the tweed-clad figure of the young draughtsman, and the tall mass
> of antique masonry which rose above him to a battlemented parapet,
> were fired to a great brightness by the solar rays, that crossed the
> neighbouring mead like a warp of gold threads, in whose mazes groups
> of equally lustrous gnats danced and wailed incessantly.
>   He was so absorbed in his pursuit that he did not mark the brilliant
> chromatic effect of which he composed the central feature, till it was

brought home to his intelligence by the warmth of the moulded stonework under his touch when measuring; which led him at length to turn his head and gaze on its cause.

Except for the chromatic effect of the warp of sun rays (an image we shall explore later) this passage is like the plot of 'Copying Architecture in an Old Minster'. Between the novel and the poem, however, occurs an artistic development which affects every element of Hardy's technique.

One of the recurrent characterisations of Hardy's main characters is that they are subject to reveries which abstract them from the world around. These reveries are subject to various types of interruption or intrusion, a fall from a church spire, the coming of dust, a skimmity-ride, a knock at the door, a collision with a mailcart, a smack on the ear, a policeman's query, footsteps on the stairs.[4] These reveries symbolise and promote the growth of a lifelong emotion and frame of mind, an 'introspective inflexibility' (*The Mayor of Casterbridge*, 12, p. 89). Their interruption forecasts the ultimate ending of the reverie-bound life: 'He felt like an awakened somnambulist who should find that he had been accessory to a tragedy during his unconsciousness' (*Two on a Tower*, 40, p. 296). Jude is subject to the most interrupted reveries, and it is appropriate that after this last novel Hardy turned to a major exploration of the subject in himself. Indeed there is an unanswered question about the novels. Where is Hardy the narrator in relation to the universal patterns of tragedy he describes? Are his impressions as narrator immune to interruption?[5] Is the convention of the narrator's immunity justified, given Hardy's views? What is the relation between his own imaginative workings and the processes of the larger world which destroy his characters? This question becomes the central question of Hardy's second career, as he begins the search for a more profound artistic consistency of form and vision.

The Development of Hardy's Meditative Poetry: Summary

It took Hardy many years to learn how to write 'Copying Architecture in an Old Minster' and scores of other similarly interesting poems. Though Hardy's development is often denied, we can in fact trace the specific stages by which Hardy evolved his mature meditative lyric.

The story begins with poems Hardy wrote in the nineteenth century and published in *Wessex Poems* (1898). He establishes his characteristic meditative speaker within a natural setting. But the meditative frame of the poem, the interaction of mind and setting, is not yet made fully consistent with the subject of the speaker's thoughts. At the turn of the century, in poems published in *Poems of the Past and the Present* (1902), Hardy develops the implications of the meditative frame and explores (a) how the setting conditions the speaker's thoughts in complex ways, (b) how a meditation lasting a few minutes can become the model of how an entire day is spent. In the following decade, in poems written *c.* 1904–12 and published in *Time's Laughingstocks* (1909) or *Satires of Circumstance* (1914), Hardy begins (a) to relate the subject of his philosophic speculations to the meditative frame of his poem, and (b) to link these meditative poems with another series of developing poems, those containing a lover's journey. This connection becomes an extremely fruitful one. A more ambitious analogy begins to develop: the way a man pursues a vision of the years is like the way a man pursues his thoughts during a meditation. The changing world of the lover's journey is like the changing setting of the lyric speaker. In 1912 the full implications of this analogy become clear to Hardy in a very direct and personal way. His wife dies and the 'Poems of 1912–13' which follow include some of his greatest achievements.

In 1919 Hardy will remark about a certain unsuccessful poet that he 'never got going, never "got his crisis" '.[6] Hardy seems to apply the comment both to the development of a poet's talent and to the success of the individual poem. With the crisis of 1912 the elements of Hardy's poetry come together in a mature and definitive way. The poem becomes the model of a man's life. The way the poem grows and develops in the mind recapitulates the way the mind has developed over a lifetime.[7] Once he has achieved this model, Hardy goes on to write his greatest sustained achievement: *Moments of Vision*, published in 1917. The model is applied to a wide range of experience, from the growth of the smallest perceptions to the evolutionary development of human consciousness itself. The poem becomes the model of centuries of human experience, these ancient patterns becoming the patterns of the poem, 'The Pedigree'.

NINETEENTH-CENTURY POEMS

Wessex Poems

'Nature's Questioning' (43) is one of Hardy's most famous nineteenth-century poems. It is a controversial poem whose virtues and defects become clear when we see it as the first great step in Hardy's development of the meditative reverie:

When I look forth at dawning, pool,
    Field, flock, and lonely tree,
    All seem to look at me
Like chastened children sitting silent in a school;

Their faces dulled, constrained, and worn,
    As though the master's ways
    Through the long teaching days
Their first terrestrial zest had chilled and overborne.

And on them stirs in lippings mere
    (As if once clear in call,
    But now scarce breathed at all) –
'We wonder, ever wonder, why we find us here.'

The 'children' then conjecture about their creator: is He 'some Vast Imbecility, / Mighty to build and blend, / But impotent to tend'? Or is He an 'Automaton' or 'are we live remains / Of Godhead dying downwards, brain and eye now gone' or 'is it that some high Plan betides . . . Of Evil stormed by good'?

Thus things around. No answerer I. . . .
    Meanwhile the winds, and rains,
    And Earth's old glooms and pains
Are still the same, and gladdest Life Death neighbours nigh.

Allen Tate made 'Nature's Questioning' a famous case of a poem marred by philosophy. Hardy took too seriously the 'explanations' offered by Victorian philosophic naturalists. The poem misuses imagery in its hurry to make doctrinaire speculations about the universe. The natural objects are compared to 'chastened children' but the objects are insufficiently particularised. Thus the vehicle, children, cancels out the tenor, natural objects. Then the children become philosophic mouthpieces and the 'schoolmaster' becomes an absentee God whose personality contradicts what he symbolises: the Unknowable or an Automaton, hardly 'equipped to teach a class'. Hardy's 'abstractions are thus somewhat irresponsible, since he can never quite show us the experience that ought to justify them'.[8]

Tate ignores certain fertile possibilities in this poem. In the last stanza, the impersonal realism of 'winds, and rains' breaks through the allegory of 'nature speaking'. The 'I' of stanza 1 re-emerges and returns us to the initial situation of the speaker confronting the Wordsworthian bareness of

'field, flock, and lonely tree'. The poem foreshadows what we shall see
fully developed in 'During Wind and Rain': conflicting motions, that of
the developing meditation and that of a developing storm which advances
stealthily upon the speaker. The first three stanzas of 'Nature's Ques-
tioning' suggest the brooding stillness which precedes a storm. The initial
silence stirs into 'lippings mere' (as of wind-stirred leaves), and finally we
are given the fact of 'winds, and rains'.[9] There is also the suggestion that
the dawning of the first stanza has crept into the gloom of the last. We
remember that in 'Copying Architecture in an Old Minster', the ghosts
first emerge 'as the eve-damps creep from the ground'. In 'Nature's
Questioning', the speaker is at first transfixed by the look (later gaze) of
pool and tree which evoke the shades of children, as the scene 'stirs in
lippings mere'. There follows a similar 'abstraction' and a similar, though
more muted, interruption: 'Thus things around. . . .' In both poems the
speaker advances unwittingly closer to the sharp intimation that Life and
Death are 'neighbours nigh' *for him*.

The frame of the poem – initial perception, surmise, abstraction,
interruption or return to the initial scene – is richer in its dramatic
potential than anything the children actually say. Indeed, what the
children say is a very abstract equivalent for what will later be the mature
tragic relation of man and world. The 'Vast Imbecility' of a God obscurely
objectifies that of human consciousnss which 'builds and blends', becomes
'impotent to tend', and so becomes subject to the hazardry of hidden
changes. Such are the foiled intents in 'Copying Architecture in an Old
Minster'. What Tate describes as the usurpation of tenor by vehicle can be
justified as the potential of a mature poetry which deliberately dramatises
such usurpation: an image usurps the setting and a second image usurps the
first in a growing entrapment. Tate's critical categories do not do justice to
Hardy because Hardy insists on a tragic disequilibrium between imagina-
tion and reality, abstractions and experience, and ultimately between the
poem itself and the world around.

'Nature's Questioning' is the most important philosophical meditation
of the pre-1900 period. There are other examples. 'A Meeting with
Despair' (34) asserts an ominous change in a setting which had initially
sparked the meditation, and this change jars the speaker, 'intent / On my
new reasoning': 'I looked. . . . Heaven's radiant show / Had gone. . . .'
'A Sign-Seeker' (30) ranges through subtle changes of scene, like those
which will later occur in 'Copying Architecture in an Old Minster': 'I see
the nightfall shades subtrude, / And hear the monotonous hours clang
negligently by.' 'The Impercipient' (44) sinks suggestively into a
concluding darkness: 'Enough. As yet disquiet clings / About us. Rest

shall we.' But these meditative motions and settings seem manipulated, asserted rather than experienced. The setting in 'Nature's Questioning', however, seems to intrude on the meditation with an unusually surprising vividness, as though by a happy stroke of genius on Hardy's part.

Nevertheless the frame of 'Nature's Questioning', like those of the other early poems, is more conventional and generalised than dramatic and immediate. The ending is less an interruption than a rhetorical generality: 'Meanwhile [i.e. any "while"] the winds, and rains [i.e. any winds and rains].' Hardy's primary interest is rather in the speculations themselves than in their phenomenology. Later, in discussing 'Nature's Questioning', Hardy will insist that he is more interested in the way speculations – 'impressions of the moment' – are formed as fancies than he is in their doctrinal content.

The other important meditative experiment of *Wessex Poems* is 'Friends Beyond' (36), which Hardy, according to one report, approvingly said was Swinburne's favourite poem from the volume.[10] The setting is elaborated in a much more interesting way. As in 'Copying Architecture in an Old Minster', ghosts seem to exude out of the setting into the speaker's mind. What we saw implied in 'lippings mere' is made explicit here: the ghostly whispering is derived from the ripplings of water:

'Gone,' I call them, gone for good, that group of local hearts and heads;
    Yet at mothy curfew-tide,
And at midnight when the noon-heat breathes it back from walls and leads,

They've a way of whispering to me – fellow-wight who yet abide –
    In the muted, measured note
Of a ripple under archways, or a lone cave's stillicide:

The poem had opened in a dramatic present tense which jars curiously with the subject: 'William Dewey, Tranter Reuben . . . lie in Mellstock churchyard now!' This sort of ambiguous existence – we are dead *now*, we are here and not here – seems to catch up the speaker in a strange way: 'They've a way of whispering.' Though he is a 'fellow-wight' who yet abides, he is drawn into empathy with their ghostly success of achieving 'a morrow free of thought'. Thus, 'ignoring all that haps beneath the moon'.

William Dewey, Tranter Reuben, Farmer Ledlow late at plough,
    Robert's kin, and John's, and Ned's,
And the Squire, and Lady Susan, murmur mildly to me now.

The poem's last line, repeating the 'now' of the first stanza, hints of a return to the 'murmuring', 'muted, measured note of a ripple'. We are set back down in the present with a sense that we have been momentarily invaded by the ghostly dissolution and by the scene's impersonality.

But we cannot press this point very hard here. There is merely a hint of a dramatic return to the setting, a hint later perfected in 1921 in 'Voices from Things Growing in a Churchyard' (580). 'Friends Beyond' is basically a comic *tour de force*. Hardy's main interest seems to lie in the ironic speeches of these wry ghosts. Moreover, the churchyard and the lone cave, the noon-heat and the archway ripple, do not make up one specified time and place in which the poem now unfolds, as in the mature manner. The images still have the hypothetical generality of 'Whenever I look forth at dawning, pool' and thus accompany, without seriously qualifying, the meditation proper.

'The Souls of the Slain' (62) was written in 1899. It is Hardy's first major meditative poem to maintain an elaborate and specific setting and to end the meditation by a deliberately concrete return to that setting. It was one of Hardy's favourite poems from his second volume of poetry.[11]

The poem gives us an elaborate ocean-led brooding which compels the speaker in the context of lapsing time ('The thick lids of Night closed upon me / Alone') and incessant change ('amid everlong motion / Of criss-crossing tides'). The patterns of these tides bind the speaker in obscure ways. The modifiers – 'Many-caverned, bald, wrinkled of face' – seem to blend 'me' and 'the Bill', mental caverns and sea caverns, in a manner we shall not find unusual in Hardy:

> The thick lids of Night closed upon me
>   Alone at the Bill
>   Of the Isle by the Race –
> Many-caverned, bald, wrinkled of face –
> And with darkness and silence the spirit was on me
>   To brood and be still.

The 'bent-bearded slope' in the next stanza continues the skilful strain of imagery, naturalising the human and humanising the natural. But the imagery ironically intimates an ominous and ultimate discontinuity between man and nature. The speaker's brooding binds him into himself and at the same time, in some mysterious way, into an ominous pattern growing outside. This drama transforms conventional phraseology like 'the spirit was on me / To brood': 'spirit' as psychological mood blends with what seems to be a rising breath of air (a whirr 'from out of the Southward') and then issues in a 'dim-discerned train / Of Sprites'. These spirits, half perceived and half imagined, 'seemed nearing'. They articulate out of the whirr as subtly as the voices from 'lippings mere' in 'Nature's Questioning' and the shades from the 'eve-damps' in 'Copying Architecture in an Old Minster'. And the spirits' activity is as subtle as that which is compared to the 'overhead creak of a passager's pinion' in 'Copying Architecture in an Old Minster'. Thus here: 'in softness and smoothness well-nigh beyond hearing / Of corporal things. . . . And I neared in my awe, and gave heedfulness to them / With breathings inheld.'

However, 'The Souls of the Slain' suffers from a similar immaturity of content that we saw in 'Nature's Questioning' and 'Friends Beyond'. The speeches take up a disproportionate amount of space for their interest. The stated theme is that war heroes do not win military fame but are, at best, remembered for common everyday things by their family and friends. The precise relevance of these 'foiled intents' of ambition to the speaker's own condition is not clear as it is in 'Copying Architecture in an Old Minster'.

Nevertheless, the end of 'The Souls of the Slain' represents an important discovery by Hardy. The ghosts disband, their speeches ended, and there also occurs an ominous unknitting of the speaker's abstracted state, a drowning into reality. We return to the setting which has grown even more portentous:

> That engulphing, ghast, sinister place –
> Whither headlong they plunged, to the fathomless regions
>   Of myriads forgot.

>   XVI
> And the spirits of those who were homing
>   Passed on, rushingly,
>   Like the Pentecost Wind;
> And the whirr of their wayfaring thinned
> And surceased on the sky, and but left in the gloaming
>   Sea-mutterings and me.

The last two lines suggest the breaking of an illusion which parallels, in an obscure way, the disillusion of the forgotten ghosts. 'Was it wise now / To raise the tomb-door / For such knowledge?' they had asked. But how this question relates to the speaker's own condition is not yet clear.

'A Commonplace Day' (78) achieves a consistency of frame and subject which we have not seen in Hardy's poetry. The scenic frame moulds

and guides the subject as in 'The Souls of the Slain', but the subject is also,
for the first time, consistent with the frame.

When F. R. Leavis attacked Hardy's major status in his influential
Southern Review article of 1940, his longest instance was 'A Commonplace
Day'. The poem begins:

> The day is turning ghost,
> And scuttles from the kalendar in fits and furtively,
> To join the anonymous host
> Of those that throng oblivion; ceding his place, maybe,
> To one of like degree.
>
> I part the fire-gnawed logs,
> Rake forth the embers, spoil the busy flames, and lay the ends
> Upon the shining dogs;
> Further and further from the nooks the twilight's stride extends,
> And beamless black impends.

Leavis writes:

> The effect is boldly idiosyncratic, but one's feeling that there has been
> something excessive, an unjustifiable violence, gets confirmation when,
> in the second stanza, 'the twilight's stride extends'. This produces a
> slow-motion effect that contrasts, in grotesque caricature, with the
> speed-up of 'scuttles' (the foot advances remorselessly to crush the day
> that scuttles to avoid it).

The scuttling day also contradicts, according to Leavis, the waning day of
stanza four. Leavis adds: 'the generally-reflective rest of the poem is poor
stuff, though the final two lines might have been the close of something
better.'

Leavis does not see the overall comparison which controls the individual
images, the stanza form, and the rhythm. Nor does he see the connection
between the frame and the 'generally-reflective' sections which are vivified
by this connection. Hardy is comparing the last flickering of day to the last
flickering of the fire. The day 'scuttles' in fits like the fire. The light of day
is also replaced, gradually and fitfully, by the light of the fire which makes
one notice the long shadows cast by the twilight into the nooks. As day is
extinguished and the fire flares up, so also does reflection flare up: 'while
Day's presence wanes, / And over him the sepulchre-lid is slowly lowered
and set, / He wakens my regret.' These expansions and contractions of the
firelight and consciousness are mimed by the expansions and contractions

of the verse. Once the imagery and rhythm are established, they carry over subliminally into Hardy's reflections. He regrets that he has wasted the day, and he speculates that somewhere there arose some intent

> Of that enkindling ardency from whose maturer glows
>   The world's amendment flows;
>
> But which, benumbed at birth
> By momentary chance or wile, has missed its hope to be
>   Embodied on the earth;
> And undervoicings of this loss to man's futurity
>   May wake regret in me.

The buried images in 'enkindling' and 'glows' connect the subject with the setting. Hope dies like the day, and regret stirs like the fire. The last two lines are so potentially interesting because in them we may hear perhaps the rising of the fire. 'Undervoicings' suggestively focuses both setting and subject in the final close.

In its movement, the poem is a model of the whole wasted day and, by a possible implication, the whole wasted life. Full realisation of the import of the day occurs as the day turns ghost. Reflection flares up belatedly, just as the fire flares up in the context of the 'beamless black'. The immediacy of the imagery, emphasised by the present tense, is a remarkable development at this point in Hardy's poetry.

At this stage, we see Hardy unconsciously evolving a new poetry. The 'return' in the last line is still only potential, not fully actualised. That the poem is a model of the connection between the course of a life and the course of a meditation is a possibility barely glimpsed. Hardy will not develop this principle fully until he writes 'At Castle Boterel' (292) in 1913. Another poem of this earlier period, 'His Immortality' (109), and two slightly later 'Night in the Old Home' (222) and 'The Flirt's Tragedy' (160), will use fire imagery like 'A Commonplace Day'. But the full potential of such imagery will not be realised until 'Logs on the Hearth' (433), 1915, and 'Old Furniture' (428), published in 1917. This whole fireside series develops brilliantly that aspect of the setting of 'Frost at Midnight' where the 'low-burnt fire' casts a 'film . . . Whose puny flaps and freaks the idling Spirit / By its own moods interprets'.

In general Hardy's career approaches the condition of his description of Swinburne, who composed 'Fresh-fluted notes, yet from a minstrel who / Blew them not naively, but as one who knew / Full well why thus he blew' (265).

POEMS OF 1904–11

Hardy's cosmology – the 'generally-reflective' portion of poems about God and the universe – is usually considered, in Leavis's phrase, 'poor stuff'. His cosmology can be more interesting than is supposed, at least where it allegorises the mind's complex relationship to nature. This allegory becomes clear when the cosmology is related to the way the speaker's mind works within the poem.

Many of Hardy's naive allegorical poems are grouped in *Poems of the Past and the Present* (76–93). Generally these poems develop the thematic material of 'Nature's Questioning'. Mother Nature is blind, Doom is indifferent, God is absent-minded. Speakers, representing these entities, debate the issues. In the light of the later development, it is interesting that two of the poems show Hardy returning for dramatic effect to the setting: the mountains and night tempests in 'Doom and She' (82), the dawn in 'God-Forgotten' (87).

In 1910 – 11, we can see an important development in such cosmological poems. The cosmology becomes more interesting as its implications are carried out in the poem's frame.

'Aquae Sulis' (308), for example, combines the frame of 'Friends Beyond' and the philosophising of 'Nature's Questioning'. It is a sort of evolutionary midpoint between these poems and 'Copying Architecture in an Old Minster'. In a place of 'bubbling waters' while the 'chimes called midnight', 'a warm air came up from underground, / And a flutter, as of a filmy shape unsepulchered'. The filmy shape is an old pagan goddess who complains that the new Christian god has usurped her place. At the end, these two shapes – 'images both – twitched by people's desires' – dissolve back into 'a gossamery noise fading off in the air, / And the boiling voice of the water's medicinal pour'. 'And all was suspended and soundless as before.' Thus do the beliefs of one age supplant the beliefs of an earlier age.

With similar elaboration, 'Spectres that Grieve' (268), also probably from this period, describes how spirits come out of a scene and into the poet's consciousness:

> The speakers, sundry phantoms of the gone,
> Had risen like filmy flames of phosphor dye,
> As if the palest of sheet lightnings shone
> From the sward near me, as from a nether sky.

The light in the setting focuses the meditation in a manner reminiscent of an image in 'The Souls of the Slain'. In the latter poem, the soul flames appear 'On the ledge by the turreted lantern, far-sighted / By men of the main'. The light is both an internal and external light, growing in ways that are harmonic and also dissonant. This image will be fully developed later in 'A Singer Asleep'. After complaining that history has mis-represented them, the spectres 'left me musing there. . . . Until the New-Year's dawn strode up the air'. As in 'Aquae Sulis', the interruption is less an interruption of the lyric speaker than of the ghosts and is purgative, 'medicinal', Tennysonian. Nevertheless, the paradigm has great potential.

If we put 'Aquae Sulis' and 'Spectres that Grieve' next to 'God's Funeral' and 'A Plaint to Man', we can see one further important development. The growth of an idea during the course of a meditation becomes the model of the growth of an idea during the course of history.

'God's Funeral' (267) and 'A Plaint to Man' (266) describe the growth of the idea of God. In his copy of George Eliot's translation of Strauss' *Life of Jesus* (2nd edition, London, Swan Sonnenschein, 1898, Colby Collection), Hardy marked the following passage from Otto Pfleiderer's introduction: 'the religious imagination gave birth to these illustrations after the manner of unconscious poetry, that is, without distinguishing between the poetic form and the essential truth of the idea' (p. xvi). In the poems, man slowly emerged out of 'shapeless slime', gained percipience and projected the image of God like 'a shape [later phasm] on a lantern slide'. Then 'the deicide eyes of seers' made the phasm dwindle. 'Rude reality / Mangled the Monarch of our fashioning, / Who quavered, sank.' The speaker in 'God's Funeral' ends by 'mechanically' following with the rest of the religious believers who, we learned earlier in the poem, 'creep and grope . . . toward our myth's oblivion, / Darkling and languid-lipped'. In 'Aquae Sulis' and 'Spectres that Grieve', Hardy is very close to finding, in the meditative structure itself, this process of groping toward a myth's oblivion. His lyric speaker is as potentially spellbound by his conjured images as is the religious believer: 'And what we had imagined we believed.' If religion tends to materialise itself in the fact,[12] so does the poetic imagination: both are subject to interruption, as Hardy is learning to dramatise. In this he was probably influenced by that dramatic moment in 'The Scholar Gypsy' when both the poetic myth of the gypsy and the lyric trance of Arnold are interrupted by hidden temporal change: 'But what – I dream! Two hundred years are flown.'

'A Singer Asleep' (265) is the climactic pre-1912 example of Hardy's meditative poem. Like 'The Souls of the Slain', it uses an elaborate oceanic reverie and explicitly emphasises a dramatic return to the setting at the conclusion. Like 'A Commonplace Day', it gains great immediacy by use of the present tense and treats a subject which – now explicitly and clearly – is consistent with the poem's frame.

'A Singer Asleep' adds one other important dimension of consciousness to Hardy's meditative poem. It shows Hardy's growing awareness of the profound manner in which his new meditative poetry modifies the literary tradition. He is in a sense announcing that his own poetry does indeed rewrite the romantic meditative lyric. The poem addresses itself to the traditional elegy as it had developed out of 'Lycidas' and been modified by 'Adonais'. It is hardly the 'weak, conventional elegy' it has been called.[13] It moulds the tradition into a form consistent with Hardy's own meditative purposes.

Swinburne is buried, Hardy says, in 'this fair niche above the unslumbering sea, / That sentrys up and down all night, all day, / From cove to promontory, from ness to bay.' Just as the sea swells now, Swinburne's power 'swells yet more and more' while the 'brabble and the roar' of Victorian criticism 'is spent like spindrift on this shore'. This sense of Swinburne's snowballing power leads Hardy into an elaborate surmise that Swinburne's muse was Sappho. The surmise takes on the compelling quality of a dream:

> And one can hold in thought that nightly here
> His phantom may draw down to the water's brim,
> And hers come up to meet it, as a dim
> Lone shine upon the heaving hydrosphere,
> And mariners wonder as they traverse near,
>   Unknowing of her and him.

This spectral fusion of mind and setting, phantom and pharos light, is soon cut off by a return to the setting of the present real ocean:

> So here, beneath the waking constellations,
> Where the waves peal their everlasting strains,
> And their dull subterrene reverberations
> Shake him when storms make mountains of their plains –
> Him once their peer in sad improvisations,
> And deft as wind to cleave their frothy manes –
> I leave him, while the daylight gleam declines
>   Upon the capes and chines.

Presumably the sea is still a classical sentry patrolling cove and promontory as in 'Lycidas'. If Milton's day-star flames like Lycidas, Hardy's constellations wake for Swinburne. Hardy's ending is strikingly like Milton's: 'And now the sun had stretched out all the hills, / And now was dropped into the western bay; / At last he rose.' Significantly the last stanza reverts to the *ottava rima* form of Milton's last stanza though Hardy shortens the last line.

However, there is a more ominous implication in Hardy's return to the present. The pharos lights of the vision are suddenly juxtaposed with and blanched out by the waking constellations. Hardy's stars emerge here with the sinister ambiguity and icy impersonality of Shelley's beaconing star. What Meyer Abram says of 'Adonais' – that its conclusion is an 'astonishing' transformation of the metaphorical wind into the 'violence of a literal storm of wind'[14] – might be applied to Hardy's conclusion. The real sea breaks through the literary convention, as Hardy suddenly refers to the very physical reverberations which shake the corpse of Swinburne in his grave. Milton's sense of a similar reverberation – Lycidas welters to 'the parching wind' – ultimately loses its sting in the pastoral convention and the melodious tear. Also, Milton's image of Orpheus whose 'gory visage down the stream was sent . . . to the Lesbian shore' is transformed by an ultimate resurrection myth in a way that Hardy's image of Sappho is not: 'she, the Lesbian . . . leapt, love-anguished, from the Leucadian steep / Into the rambling world encircling deep / Which hides her where none sees.' This encircling deep breaks out of its mythic setting in Hardy's last stanza and links up with the renewed dull reverberations of the unslumbering sea. This grating roar, an unslumbering present, washes away immortal poets and interrupts the mythic trances of their disciples. Swinburne's progress from swelling tide to spectral gleam to eclipse matches Hardy's biographical relation to Swinburne: from 'that far morning of a summer day' when Hardy first read Swinburne, to the end of this elegy: 'I leave him, while the daylight gleam declines. . . .'

Hardy is growing more conscious that the aesthetic shape of the poem evolves out of a long literary history as well as out of the life of the poet. After 1912 he will perfect this important sense of the way the poem, as poem, is placed in relation to a larger changing world.

The Lover's Journey

While Hardy is developing his meditative reveries in a series of poems from 'Nature's Questioning' to 'A Singer Asleep', he is also composing a series of poems about lovers who journey through landscapes. He does not seem to realise the close connection between these two series until 1904 when he writes 'The Revisitation'. Then he becomes aware of the striking similarities in the setting and the structure of both types of poem.

In the early love journey poems, the lover travels through a changing setting which makes an ironic comment upon the quality of his love. Usually love is unrequited in these poems. Desperately the lover tries to recreate the past while trees shed on him 'their rime and hoar' (27) or while 'dawning' slips into 'night-wind' (31). Early in his journey, the setting sometimes encourages the growth of his romantic fantasy: 'the swinging trees / Rang above me' (27).[15] The stages by which the fantasy grows are carefully detailed.[16] But the setting is also the place 'where Legions had wayfared' (31) or the 'Field of Tombs' (27) or the ruins of temples serving 'men's idolatries' (96).

These are curious and unsettling poems. It is unclear how Hardy assesses the tragedies of these strange lovers. Do we identify with them as idealists who are victims of circumstance? Or do we view them as neurotics who actively shun reality? This issue is like that which often faces us in the novels. Is man's tragedy primarily due to change and chance which undermine the healthiest of minds? Or is it primarily due to perversities of will? [17]

This ambiguity may result from the uncertain distance which Hardy maintains toward these characters and these journeying lovers. Their experience is not quite accepted as his. Only with the death of his wife will the full personal import of the lover's journey become stunningly clear. Then Hardy will realise that he has taken a forty-year lover's journey. He will also realise that the way his mind works in a self-engrossed meditation is like the way his mind has worked over a lifetime. In these early poems, however, certain elements in the writing style lack firm justification. I am thinking particularly of the grotesque elaboration of the stories and the artificiality of the style:

> 'Alive?' – And I leapt in my wonder,
>   Was faint of my joyance,
> And grasses and grove shone in garments
>   Of glory to me.   (31)

Does this poetic diction reflect a self-induced sentimental passion? Or is the love genuine but caught up in anachronisms like old words?

This ambiguity is not resolved in 'The Revisitation' (152). But the poem is nevertheless an important milestone in Hardy's career. As Ezra Pound said, looking forward to the great 'Poems of 1912–13', 'there had been passages in "Revisitation"'.[18] 'The Revisitation' is the first of the love journey poems to use a setting with the sophistication we have seen in the meditative poems. And in so emphasising the setting, Hardy's emphasis begins to move toward larger issues of change and age. The lover not only moves through a setting but the setting conditions his reveries, changes in hidden ways, and interrupts those reveries. That interruption enacts in a moment what is the setting's usual function in such poems, to be an ironic comment on the lover's belated dream. Thus the present reverie in 'The Revisitation' seems to recapitulate the lover's entire dream-led life.

The poem is a long and ungainly one. Hardy seems excited by the potential of his new lyric and he experiments with it at length:

> And as thus I brooded longer
> With my faint eyes on the feeble square of wansome window-frame,
> A quick conviction sprung within me, grew, and grew yet stronger,
>   That the night, too, was the same. . . .

With this the narrator is plunged into the past which he now hopes to relive by journeying to the 'once-loved ground'. Just as the reverie had snowballed, so the journey snowballs: 'a sullen thunder muttered / As I mounted high and higher.' After the landscape ('immemorial funeral piles') makes its comment, he sits on the sun-heated Sarsen stone, disturbing the peewits. Referring both to his journey and his reverie, the narrator says:

> And so, living long and longer
> In a past that lived no more, my eyes discerned there, suddenly,
> That a figure broke the sky-line – first in vague contour,
>   then stronger,
> And was crossing near to me.

This is Agnette also returning to their favourite meeting place: thus the well-beloved materialises. Renewing their dreamlike love at this midnight moment, 'we sank to silent thought . . . our rended lives reclasping, / And contracting years to nought. / Till I . . . Sank to slow unconsciousness'. The setting now changes in its hidden inexorable way: 'the brief warm summer night had slid when, to my swift surprise, / A red upedging sun . . . Was blazing on my eyes . . . Flinging tall thin tapering shadows' and revealing Agnette's age. 'Time's transforming chisel / Had been tooling night and day for twenty years' and now breaks the twenty-year-old vision and the present reverie. Agnette leaves and her image lessens like an image in memory: 'I saw her form descend the slopes, and smaller grow and smaller.'

We are still far from those economical poems of Hardy's maturity which show how a forty-year vision grows, in Philip Larkin's phrase, 'smaller and clearer as the years go by'.[19] Not yet has Hardy resolved the problem of how to indicate the unfolding drama of a lifetime in a short poem. In 'The Revisitation', there are too many different reveries. There is too much grotesque plotting which must be recounted awkwardly by the protagonist. The function of the prosody is not quite clearly conceived. The narrator's experience is still an ambiguous mixture of something determined through the years and something indulged in for sentimental reasons. In 'Poems of 1912–13', Hardy will purge all sentimental excess.

Nevertheless, 'The Revisitation's parallel between the lover's journey and the lover's reverie has great potential. The poem was originally entitled 'Time's Laughingstocks' until it became the head poem of the volume of that name. Of this volume Hardy wrote that it should 'take the reader forward'.

'POEMS OF 1912–13'

Emma's death was 'so unforeseen that I can scarcely realise it at times even now'. The tragedy of Hardy and Emma's marriage, like any such tragedy, had many complex causes. For purposes of our discussion, however, we can see a certain pattern in Hardy's understanding of that tragedy which had fruitful consequences for his poems. Three weeks after her death, Hardy wrote:

> In spite of the differences between us, which it would be affectation to deny, and certain painful delusions she suffered from at times, my life is intensely sad to me now without her. The saddest moments of all are when I go into the garden and to that long straight walk at the top that you know, where she used to walk every evening just before dusk, the cat trotting faithfully behind her; and at times when I almost expect to see her as usual coming in from the flower-beds with a little trowel in her hand.[20]

The shock of Emma's death was more than a shock to a settled manner of life which had established itself for the estranged couple. 'For Hardy custom had never staled the charm of the sweetheart in his first wife.'[21] At Emma's death, Hardy discovered to his personal horror that their life together had been controlled by a romantic image of themselves that was forty years old. In his novel, *The Well-Beloved*,[22] he had described the artist Pierston: 'His record moved on with the years, his sentiments stood still.' In 1926, less than two years before his own death, Hardy read an article on Proust by Denis Saurat and was struck by two quotations from Proust. Hardy noted:

> It appears that the theory exhibited in *The Well-Beloved* in 1892 has been since developed by Proust still further:
>   'Peu de personnes comprennent le caractère purement subjectif du phénomène qu'est l'amour, et la sorte de création que c'est d'une personne supplémentaire, distinct de celle qui porte le même nom dans le monde, et dont la plupart des éléments sont tirés de nous-mêmes' (*Ombre*, i, 40).
>   'Le désir s'élève, se satisfait, disparaît - - et c'est tout. Ainsi, la jeune fille qu'on épouse n'est pas celle dont on est tombé amoureux' (*Ombre*, ii, 158, 159).[23]

Years earlier, Edward Springrove in Hardy's first published novel, *Desperate Remedies* (1870), is credited with a similar theory in the passage beginning: 'He [Springrove] says that your true lover breathlessly finds himself engaged to a sweetheart, like a man who has caught something in the dark. He doesn't know whether it is a bat or a bird, and takes it to the light when he is cool to learn what it is . . .' (II, 3, p. 25). This is somewhat facile philosophising, however, on the part of the inexperienced Springrove. In *A Pair of Blue Eyes* (1873), Elfride's comparison of herself to *La Belle Dame sans Merci* in Chapter 7 is meant to be fanciful. But as is often the case in Hardy's career, what he had imagined is what eventually came true — 'In warranty of my rhyme' (399). Elfride quotes the Keats stanza beginning: 'I set her on my pacing steed, / And nothing else saw all day long.' Forty years later, these lines would evolve through literary history and through Hardy's personal life into 'The Phantom Horsewoman'.

I am suggesting then that Hardy discovered that the image of his early love had become a 'phantom horsewoman', a *personne supplémentaire*, which had persisted long after the couple themselves had changed. And the world had changed around them. Revisiting Sturminster Newton where he and Emma 'spent their happiest days' in 1876–8 (*Life*, 111), Hardy paused in front of a tree:

> Presently he exclaimed as if to himself:
> 'How it's grown! I planted that tree when I came here. It was then a

small thing not so high as my shoulder.'

He waited a moment as if thinking. Then:

'I suppose that was a long time ago. I brought my first wife here after our honeymoon. . . . She had long golden hair. . . . How that tree has grown! But that was in 1876. . . . How it has changed . . .' He paused, still staring at the tree – then remarked: 'Time changes everything except something within us which is always surprised by change.' [24]

One senses that in the later years of their marriage, neither Emma nor Hardy could see exactly what had changed or why the change had occurred. For Hardy, realisation came when a sudden shock exposed the sharp gap between present reality and the past image.

The shock comes and Hardy's consciousness is flooded. And the cruel law is revealed – that we know the state of reality best when that reality has ceased to exist. The full import of his life comes clear when '[a]ll's past amend, / Unchangeable. It must go' (277). In 'The Walk' (279), Hardy revisits the hill where he used to walk, '[n]ot thinking of you as left behind'. Now, however, the hill has the Proustian 'look of a room on returning thence'. The self has moved much further on that it had realised. 'I seem but a dead man held on end / To sink down soon' (277).

The death of Emma also provided Hardy with the final clarification of his art. In 1910 he had written his fifteen 'Satires of Circumstance' and in 1911 published them in the *Fortnightly Review*. In the light of 27 November 1912 (and of 4 August 1914) Hardy regretted the publication of these 'caustically humorous' productions: 'So much shadow, domestic and public, had passed over his head since he had written the satires that . . . he would readily have suppressed them if they had not already gained such currency' (*Life*, 367). In a letter of 1 December 1914 he wrote: 'Some, even many, of the pieces in the volume [*Satires of Circumstance*] do not precisely express my attitude to certain matters nowadays. . . . [T]hey seem to myself harsh beside the others.' [25] By contrast Hardy described 'Lyrics and Reveries', also in *Satires of Circumstance*, as 'some of the tenderest and least satirical verse that ever came from his pen' (*Life*, 367). Since satire of circumstance runs through all of Hardy's poems, what exactly did he mean by his changed 'attitude to certain matters'? His meaning becomes a little clearer in a letter he wrote to Gosse in 1914: 'The little group of satires cost me much sadness. . . . The scales had not fallen from my eyes when I wrote them, and when I reprinted them they had.' [26] We can see the scales fall in a concrete instance between 21 and 27 November 1912. On 21 November, Hardy wrote 'The Bird-Catcher's Boy' and later significantly put the exact month and day of composition in a postscript. 'The

Bird-Catcher's Boy' (809) sets out to expose the Wordsworthian surmise in 'Lucy Gray'. Where Wordsworth ends, 'Yet some maintain that to this day / She is a living child . . .' Hardy ends 'And the tide washed ashore / One sailor boy.' Six days later Emma died and the scales fell. The exposer became the exposed, and Hardy found himself waking into the intenser drama of his own life. The scales fell, and Hardy discovered the profound way in which a poem comes out of a man's life, as the final clarification and epitaph of an experience which has formed over the years. The satire of circumstance was implicit, Hardy discovered, in the inmost working of a lyrical sensibility.

An important distinction must be made concerning Hardy's 'veteris vestigia flammae' experience. It is sometimes associated with senti-mentalism, like that Hardy satirises in some of his characters. Troy, for example, after Fanny's death 'had no perception that in the futility of these romantic doings, dictated by a remorseful reaction from previous indifference, there was any element of absurdity' (*Far from the Madding Crowd*, 45, p. 358). Lionel Johnson called Troy's emotion 'the most like sincerity possible, of a theatrical conscience'.[27] 'To care for the remote, to dislike the near; it was Wildeve's nature always. This is the true mark of the man of sentiment. . . . He might have been called the Rousseau of Egdon' (*The Return of the Native*, III, 6, p. 254). Pierston is closer to Hardy, but his passion comes across as literary sentimentalism: 'The only woman whom I never rightly valued . . . and therefore the only one I shall ever regret' (II, 3, p. 73). Because the woman is inaccessible, she is now loved – a romantic irony captured nicely in Yeats's 'He Wishes His Beloved Were Dead'. Even Florence Hardy referred wryly to the 'late espousèd saint' and said: 'All the poems about her are a fiction, but a fiction in which their author has now come to believe.'[28] But the actual poems of 1912 and later suggest that Hardy is far removed from such luxurious indulgence. The poems seem to come out of his life in a way that Hardy called 'inevitable', as the belated clarification of an experience in which his very identity was involved. They were an 'expiation', as Hardy called them, rather than an indulgence.[29]

The discovery of a mature aesthetic was an enormously fertile one. 'The verses came; it was quite natural; one looked through the years and saw some pictures; a loss like that just makes one's old brain vocal!'[30] 'The poems of 1912–13', Pound said, 'lift him to his apex . . . all good, and enough for a lifetime.'[31] In these new poems Hardy brings together all the important elements of his past experimentation:

1. A man meditates within a setting while the setting changes:

Till in darkening dankness
The yawning blankness
Of the perspective sickens me!   (277)

Or is it only the breeze, in its listlessness
Travelling across the wet mead to me here? . . .   (285)

Soon you will have, Dear, to vanish from me,
For the stars close their shutters and the dawn whitens hazily.
(289)

2. A lover moves through a changing landscape in quest of the woman he once loved:

Why go to Saint-Juliot? What's Juliot to me?
I've been but made fancy
By some necromancy
That much of my life claims the spot as its key.   (288)

I see what you are doing: you are leading me on
To the spots we knew when we haunted here together. . . .
(289)

Yet again I am nearing
Castle and keep, uprearing
Gray, as in my prime.   (296)

He comes and stands
In a careworn craze,
And looks at the sands
And the seaward haze,
With moveless hands
And face and gaze. . . .   (294)

3. The structure of the man's meditation is the model of a life caught in the pursuit of a forty-year-old emotion:

Thus I; faltering forward,
Leaves around me falling,
Wind oozing thin through the thorn from norward
And the woman calling.   (285)

The critical moment for the fusion of these elements occurs in March. Hardy makes a personal revisitation to Cornwall where he had courted Emma forty years previously. He drives to the spot where they had once picnicked on the slope. It was 'dry March weather' at that time, but this

March it is raining. They had climbed the dry road beside a chaise, but this March he drives alone on a waggonette. These two journeys proceed together in his mind, the journey he is taking now, the journey he took then and has been taking in imagination for forty years. This double plot becomes the subject of Hardy's great poem, 'At Castle Boterel' (292). The poem is the final form of these two conflicting journeys, the last journey repeating and yet effacing the tracks of the earlier one. The mind moves slowly through the poem, etching the picture of the past with increasing clarity against the backdrop of the rain: 'I look behind at the fading byway, / And see on its slope, now glistening wet, / Distinctly yet // Myself and a girlish form.' The picture becomes most clear just as it reaches the point of extinction:

> I look and see it there, shrinking, shrinking,
> I look back at it amid the rain
> For the very last time; for my sand is sinking,
> And I shall traverse old love's domain
>   Never again.

This is a great moment in English poetry. The poem is perfectly integrated with the life, both the life and the poem developing alike and coming to parallel conclusions. Just as 'Time's unflinching rigor' has undermined and yet clarified the substance of a forty-year love, so the present rain undermines and clarifies the 'phantom figure' of the poet's meditation. Was Dylan Thomas thinking of this poem when he praised Hardy's 'long, slow-lined, beautifully contrived, technically masterly evocations of the loves of the sand-sinking past'?[32]

As Hardy succeeds in making the poem the climactic model of the life, the structure and language and rhythm of his poems become beautifully consistent with their subject. The stylistic potential of the earlier poems is fulfilled, and the earlier ambiguities are resolved. We can see this new assurance in 'The Phantom Horsewoman' (294), which is Hardy's climactic lover's journey. The ambiguities we saw in Hardy's authorial detachment from his earlier lovers are here dramatically overcome. The poem seems on first reading to be narrated by an objective observer. Curious and detached, he describes a man who journeys to the sea to find his well-beloved. There the man described 'sees as an instant thing . . . [a] phantom of his own figuring'. The narrator is cautious and catechetical: 'And what does he see when he gazes so? . . . They say he sees. . . .' But there is something peculiar about this narrator, with his unusually intimate knowledge of the man described: 'Not only there / Does he see this sight, / But everywhere / In his brain – day, night. . . .' How would the narrator know? Also there is something curiously haunting about the poem's rhythm. The Swinburnian intensity of the last line, for example, seems to reveal a hypnotic anapestic current. This current seems to jar the quaint columnar formality of the poem:

> A ghost-girl-rider. And though, toil-tried,
>   He withers daily,
>   Time touches her not,
>   But she still rides gaily
>   In his rapt thought
>   On that shagged and shaly
>   Atlantic spot,
>   And as when first eyed
> Draws rein and sings to the swing of the tide.

We eventually grow to conceive that the narrator *is* the man he describes, and that his description is the final articulation of a forty-year-long vision which has unconsciously monopolised his life.[33] His detachment now is a symptom of that tragic separation between his conscious mind and the spell of the vision. That vision, seemingly timeless ('Time touches her not'), has increased in power through the years just as it is doing now as he walks along the beach. All the while, hidden changes were – and are – preparing the surprise of obsolescence: 'He withers daily.' Once the poem is so exposed, we feel strongly the hypnotic syncopated rhythms of the short lines and behind them we may hear the Arnoldian sound of 'that shagged and shaly / Atlantic spot'. The poem's rational structure and architectural verse form now seem the skeleton outline of a once visionary music. The quaint formality of this music indicates its age.

As a series, 'Poems of 1912–13' shows Hardy gradually realising the implications of his new aesthetic discovery.[34] The sequence of poems corresponds to the growing stages of Hardy's awareness between December 1912 and April 1913. Most of the poems were written in this period and they are roughly arranged (with some exceptions to emphasise the pattern) in chronological order. The arrangement shows that Hardy's first reaction to Emma's death was a shock that reverberated through every level of his emotional and intellectual life. The shock was followed by a variety of desperate reactions: the desire to blame himself, the desire to blame her, the desire to recapture the past and live it over, the terrible puzzlement that human beings can waste such happiness, the terrible despair. This variety of reactions eventually gives way to a more persistent theme: an increased fascination with the early image of their love. This image grows in intensity and binds the mind once again. As it grows in intensity, however, its phantom character becomes more and more clear, until the great poetic breakthrough occurs. Hardy sees that the mental process he is undergoing in these months of 1912–13 is like the process which has been taking place for forty years. This final vision tends to transcend the bitterness and recriminations though their echoes are still heard. But the tragedy of marital bitterness has been placed in the larger perspective of time and human blindness.

'The Going' (December 1912) begins the series. It may have been Hardy's first poetic reaction to Emma's death. Each stanza starts up a theme which will be expanded upon in the following months. Out of stanzas 1 and 5 ('Why did you give no hint that night? . . . Why, then, latterly did we not speak? . . .') spring the bitter recriminations of 'Your Last Drive' (December 1912) and 'Without Ceremony'. Out of stanza 4 ('You were the swan-necked one. . . .') spring the fanciful myths of 'Rain on a Grave' (January 1913), 'I Found Her Out There', and 'The Haunter'. The greatest achievements eventually develop out of stanzas 2 and 3. As he moves through the present setting he sees 'morning harden upon the wall, / Unmoved, unknowing / That your great going / Had place that moment, and altered all'. He is now caught up in an expanding *and* obsolescing vision: 'Why do you make me . . . think for a breath it is you I see / At the end of the alley of bending boughs . . . in darkening dankness!' As January grows into March, this paradox is more and more deeply felt – in 'The Voice', 'A Dream or No', 'After a Journey', 'At Castle Boterel', and 'The Phantom Horsewoman'. The visions in these poems, so belatedly vivid, then stale into the diminished images and rhythms of 'St. Launce Revisited' and 'Where the Picnic Was':

> Now a cold wind blows,
> And the grass is gray,
> But the spot still shows
> As a burnt circle – aye. . . .

The 'veteris vestigiae flammae' have burnt themselves through forty years and through this present series of poems into 'stick-ends, charred'. Like Shakespeare in the sonnet Hardy quoted in *The Well-Beloved* (iii, 1, p. 144), Hardy is consumed by that which he was nourished by.

'Poems of 1912–13' thus recapitulates the life and, in arranging the series so, Hardy seems to announce that this has become the principle of his mature lyric poetry.

MOMENTS OF VISION, 1917

'There is absolutely no observation too minute, no flutter of reminiscence too faint, for Mr. Hardy to adopt as the subject of a metapysical lyric,' Gosse wrote in his *Edinburgh Review* article, 'and his skill in this direction has grown upon him.' In turning from 'Poems of 1912–13' to *Moments of Vision* (1917) we find that Hardy applies his new principle of dramatic reverie to a whole range of experience and, indeed, to human life itself which Hardy had earlier defined as 'an existence, an experience, a passion, a structure of sensations' (*Tess of the d'Urbervilles*, 14, p. 115). In 1917 Hardy described his lyric aesthetic in a newly definitive way:

> I believe it would be said by people who knew me well that I have a faculty (possibly not uncommon) for burying an emotion in my heart or brain for forty years, and exhuming it at the end of that time as fresh as when interred. (*Life*, 378)

This principle, first discovered in memories of Cornwall of 1870, now applies to hearing an old psalm tune, seeing an old violin, living with old furniture, mourning the death of a sister. *Moments of Vision* constitutes the central body of Hardy's poems.

The greatest poem in *Moments of Vision* is probably 'During Wind and Rain'. It is a superbly economical poem which imitates the development of human life itself. The memory pictures shared by Hardy and Emma (many of which come from her *Recollections* which he read after her death) become representative of universal human experience. Hardy achieves this ultimate objective poetry only as a result of his previous experiments with the meditative reverie and the lover's journey.

The myth that Hardy's poetry does not develop in specific and important ways is clearly refuted by 'During Wind and Rain'. As is the case with many Hardy poems, unless we see the development we may miss the rich complexity of the finished work. For example, one representative Hardy critic complains that in the last line of 'During Wind and Rain' the 'formulaic has taken hold again'. Hardy has trundled his tombstones on stage once more. This kind of misreading results from the view that Hardy 'is an obsessional poet'. His poetry 'revolves around a small number of *idées fixes*'. Indeed if a body of poetry does not mature over a period of half a century, it is natural to conclude that the poet lacks 'self-criticism'. His consistency is 'almost perverse'.[35]

The last line of 'During Wind and Rain' is in fact a surprising line. It undermines any conventional expectation of the 'formulaic'. We discover that the relation between the storm images and the memory images is more concrete than we had supposed.

Hardy was delighted to find one reviewer who seemed to have discerned the principle of 'During Wind and Rain'. The reviewer made the poem typical of Hardy's work and wrote that in Hardy's poetry 'there is quite a strong probability that he will actually find himself in a churchyard where the natural inclemency of the weather is reinforced by the rain-worn cherubs on the tombstones, the half-effaced names, the dripping moss and the direct reminders of the dead'.[36] In 1922 Hardy would point out that churchyards were often used in his poems, not because of their gloom, but because he 'used to spend much time in such places sketching, with another pupil, and we had many pleasant times at the work'.[37] He thus had much time to observe how a concrete setting, which happened to be a churchyard, could modify one's reflections.

The situation of 'During Wind and Rain', therefore, is a very specific one. The speaker looks out at a graveyard during the advancing stages of a storm; and he remembers the advancing stages of a human lifetime.[38] The storm begins with the rising of the wind, then the fleeing of the storm-birds, then the beginning of a gale (strong enough to rip the rotten rose from the wall), and finally the coming of rain. At the same time the life remembered advances from childhood (the first scene, with its nursery rhythms, experienced as though by an impressionable child), through youth (associated with elders and juniors and their shared project), into the time of courtship and finally into the prosperous years of adulthood:

> They sing their dearest songs –
> He, she, all of them – yea,
> Treble and tenor and bass,
>   And one to play;
> With the candles mooning each face. . . .
>   Ah, no; the years O!
> How the sick leaves reel down in throngs!
>
> They clear the creeping moss –
> Elders and juniors – aye,
> Making the pathways neat
>   And the garden gay;
> And they build a shady seat. . . .
>   Ah, no; the years, the years;
> See, the white storm-birds wing across!
>
> They are blithely breakfasting all –

Men and maidens – yea,
Under the summer tree,
    With a glimpse of the bay,
While pet fowl come to the knee. . . .
    Ah, no; the years O!
And the rotten rose is ript from the wall.

They change to a high new house,
He, she, all of them – aye,
Clocks and carpets and chairs
    On the lawn all day,
And brightest things that are theirs. . . .
    Ah, no; the years, the years;
Down their carved names the rain-drop ploughs.   (441)

We discover that we have been following two journeys, both con-ditioned and interrupted by the changing elements. The smaller experience of the speaker caught in an evolving reverie recapitulates the larger experience of a lifetime caught in an evolving life-style. The reverie is periodically interrupted by the advancing storm just as the life remembered is periodically interrupted by the advancing years. And the final unknitting of the reverie is like the final unknitting of the life itself. Moreover, the reverie and the life are interrelated in an interesting way. When the speaker sees the sick leaves reeling down, he then remembers a scene where they cleaned up and tamed these leaves: 'Making the pathways neat . . . And they build a shady seat.' When the speaker sees the white storm-birds wing across, he then remembers a scene where 'pet fowl come to the knee'. When the wind beats against the wall, the speaker then remembers a scene where they 'change to a high new house'. In its choice of images, the reverie tries to tame nature and halt the inexorable processes of time. But nature plays the last trick on the reverie. When the speaker remembers the '[c]locks and carpets and chairs / On the lawn all day', nature intrudes with the present reality of other things on the lawn – gravestones down which the rain is ploughing. One of Hardy's drawings in *Wessex Poems*, illustrating 'Her Death and After', had captured well this eerie confusion (see Illustration 1).

The style of the poem is beautifully consistent with this drama of reverie and time. That style may strike us at first as very curious with its surprising use of the present tense ('they sing their dearest songs'), its stark formality ('Elders and juniors', 'Men and maidens'), its touch of stiltedness ('He, she, all of them – yea'). But the style reflects the quality of the remembered scenes: they bind the mind as though they still exist and yet they have grown old-fashioned and brittle over the years, like photographs in an old family album. In contrast to the remembered scene, the final line of each stanza surprises us with its concreteness. If we had supposed that the image of storm-bird and rotten rose were dictated by a conventional ballad formula, we discover to our surprise by the end of the poem that these are very real objects which the speaker now sees.

Meanwhile, during wind and rain, a life and a reverie reach parallel conclusions which have grown '[s]maller and clearer as the years go by': a name etched out on a tombstone, the poem itself. The poem is the reverie's final definition, carved out into letters on the page.

In tracing Hardy's development of the meditative poems from 'Nature's Questioning' to 'During Wind and Rain', I have necessarily focused on the high points. Overlooked are a complex of related poems which affect the development of our examples. In concluding this chapter, I would like to correct this over-simplification in the case of 'During Wind and Rain' by considering it as not merely the climax of a series of major examples written since the 1890s. The poem also develops and brings together a number of poetic possibilities which Hardy explores separately in poems written shortly before, or about the same time as 'During Wind and Rain'. When we consider these more recent tributaries, as well as the larger stream, the economy of 'During Wind and Rain' seems an extraordinary achievement indeed.

'Lament' (283) is a poem of 1912 – 13 and was influenced, like the two following poems and 'During Wind and Rain', by Emma's *Recollections*. It repeatedly contrasts memories of the past with the reality of a present grave:

> How she would have loved
> A party to-day! –
> Bright-hatted and gloved,
> With table and tray
> And chairs on the lawn
> Her smiles would have shone
> With welcomings. . . . But
> She is shut, she is shut
>   From friendship's spell
>   In the jailing shell
>   Of her tiny cell.

Some of these images (i.e. 'chairs on the lawn') and the clipped dimeter rhythms will be used in 'During Wind and Rain'. But a great distance still separates the two poems. There are no surprises in 'Lament'; the memory images are not structured in a dramatically progressive fashion; the graveyard is merely alluded to, not actually seen by the dramatic speaker.

'The Change' (384) was written in January–February 1913. Here Hardy explores how the past casts a hypnotic spell and comes alive stage by stage in the speaker's consciousness. Each stanza, as in 'During Wind and Rain', is punctuated by a mournful ballad refrain: 'Who shall spell the years, the years!', 'Who shall unroll the years O!'

> Out of the past there rises a week –
>   Who shall read the years O! –
> Out of the past there rises a week
>   Enringed with a purple zone.
> Out of the past there rises a week
>   When thoughts were strung too thick to speak,
> And the magic of its lineaments remains with me alone.

The speaker then goes on to remember the successive stages of a love relationship. Two images, the 'candles flinging / Radiance' and the 'white owl', may look forward to the candle-lit scene and white storm-birds of 'During Wind and Rain'. However, while the memory images of 'The Change' are more structured than those in 'Lament', the final import of those memories is unclear. A mysterious 'doom that gave no token' and led to a broken heart hounded the lovers and left the speaker only 'sweet reverberances'. In 'During Wind and Rain', the nature of the doom is entirely clear and its reverberances are universal.

'The Interloper' (432) was published in *Moments of Vision*. Using a dramatic present tense, 'The Interloper', like 'During Wind and Rain', begins with a description which seems to make present what is actually past. These memory images now binding the mind are stated with a suggestive vagueness and starkness so that they seem like photographic frames: 'There are three folk driving in a quaint old chaise. . . . Next / A dwelling appears by a slow sweet stream',

> Where two sit happy and half in the dark:
> They read, helped out by a candle-gleam,
>   Some rhythmic text;
> But one sits with them whom they don't mark,
>   One I'm wishing could not be there.

This last memory and others ('I discern gay diners in a mansion-place,' 'People on a lawn – quite a crowd of them. Yes. . . .') forecast specific moments in 'During Wind and Rain'. But unlike the latter, these memories follow no coherent plot and are shadowed by a phantom presence whose import is obscure. Indeed Hardy tried to clarify the poem with an unidentified epigraph referring to 'the figure and visage of madness'. Professor Purdy thinks this a reference to Emma's growing derangement of mind. But the reference is not clear. When asked in conversation to define 'that under which best lives corrode', Hardy indeed answered 'Madness'. But when told that the line had been interpreted as referring to 'no definite thing, but a sort of undermining rot which destroys everything', Hardy replied: 'That was a remarkably good guess. He got as near it as one possibly could.' Hardy then reread the poem and suggested that 'Insanity' might be a better word than 'Madness': 'I wonder how I could make it clear.' The relation of madness to an undermining rot that destroys *everything* is indeed unclear. Perhaps Hardy is referring to insanity in some broad sense, related to his continuing interest in minds spellbound by images and undermined by time. In his *Literary Notes*, I, Hardy paraphrased Comte's description of 'Madness . . . always characterized by excess of Subjectivity' in which 'the recollections become more vivid and distinct than the sensations'. This indeed is relevant to Emma's specific neurosis. At any rate, this series of poems shows Hardy in the process of making what he means 'clear'.[39]

'The Five Students' (439) may be the latest in this series if Hardy identifies the poem's 'dark She' with his sister who died in November 1916. The poem skilfully contrasts nature's progress and the human progress. Man lives out the scenes of his advancing life and these are juxtaposed with natural scenes which begin in spring and go through summer, autumn, and finally winter:

> Icicles tag the church-aisle leads,
> The flag-rope gibbers hoarse,
> The home-bound foot-folk wrap their snow-flaked heads,
> Yet I still stalk the course, –
> One of us. . . . Dark and fair He, dark and fair She, gone:
> The rest – anon.

The poem makes explicit what 'During Wind and Rain' more deftly suggests: the deceptive stability of the human scene, the stages of man which advance nowhere, and the tortoise and the hare effect where man runs but nature creeps and overtakes: 'The leaf drops: earthworms draw it in / At night-time noiselessly.' The grotesque puppet-like pronouns will also be used in 'During Wind and Rain' where, again, one's entire identity as a human being is vulnerable before nature's plough. What 'During Wind and Rain' will add to 'The Five Students' is the style of remembering of 'The Change' and 'The Interloper'. The result will be that the nature contexts of 'The Five Students' will be juxtaposed with richly developed human scenes still lived in memory and embodied in spare, present-tense images. The human scenes in 'The Five Students' are more abbreviated and grotesque: five students striding down a road and gradually dropping away.

In 'During Wind and Rain', Hardy will consider anew the question which has inspired him, as we saw, since the scales fell from his eyes in 1912. Where is the lyric speaker now? How precisely does his poetic utterance relate to his present situation? In answering these questions, 'During Wind and Rain' achieves an immediacy and vividness not felt in the other poems. What gave Hardy the hint for this new degree of immediacy may have been 'The Wind's Prophecy'.

'The Wind's Prophecy' (440), Hardy says in his postscript, is '[r]ewritten from an old copy'. As other evidence suggests, this means that while Hardy used an old draft, he rewrote and expanded it quite considerably. The poem's subject is presumably Hardy's 1870 journey to Cornwall when he was about to meet Emma and leave his girl-friend, Tryphena. The full implications of the journey did not come clear until much later.[40] The three major journey poems of *Moments of Vision*, 'The Five Students', 'The Wind's Prophecy', and 'During Wind and Rain', are placed together forming a triptych at the centre of the volume.

In 'The Wind's Prophecy', the speaker's reverie is periodically interrupted by a storm which grows in violence and seems to oppose his romantic vision of Tryphena. When Hardy was rewriting 'The Wind's Prophecy' he may have noticed how the journey of a speaker through a present storm-driven scene is like the journey of man through an entire time-driven life in 'The Five Students'. This dramatic principle, which works on a small and a large scale, is what 'During Wind and Rain' manages to comprehend.

'The Wind's Prophecy' is a flawed poem. Its ominous import is obscure and its descriptions seem out of proportion to its subject. Nevertheless its influence on 'During Wind and Rain' was probably critical. The speaker is placed in a concrete present scene which conditions his reflections; and this dramatic placing has profound implications for the speaker's entire life. 'During Wind and Rain' is a kind of reverse image of 'The Wind's Prophecy'. In the latter poem, the speaker's interrupted reverie forecasts his future; in the former it recapitulates his past.

Finally, 'The Wind's Prophecy' may have contributed to the peculiarly dramatic effect of the last line of 'During Wind and Rain': 'Down their carved names the rain-drop ploughs.' Here the outline of a life still lived in memory is suddenly transformed into the rain-etched outline of names on a grave. Nature's impersonal pattern emerges from and replaces man's personal pattern. What was fresh and alive turns out to be obsolescent and skeletal. An analogous transformation occurs at the end of 'The Wind's Prophecy'. The outline of the speaker's romantic vision ('My eyes now as all day / Behold her ebon locks of hair!') is replaced by nature's impersonal outlines: 'gulls shine out like silver flecks / Against a cloud. . . . [C]lots of flying foam / Break from its muddy monochrome, / And a light blinks up far away.' Intimidated by this eerie illumination in the scene, the speaker desperately insists on his interior illumination: 'there shine's the star for me!' Nature rebuts by an image ('The all-prevailing clouds exclude / The one quick timorous transient start'), and the silver-grey contrasts in the scene deepen into the stark black-white contrast of the spectral pharos-shine:

> Yonder the headland, vulturine,
> Snores like a giant in his sleep,
> And every chasm and every steep
> Blacken as wakes each lighthouse-shine.

Is not the shock we feel at seeing this emergent light like the shock we feel in seeing the emergence of carved names in 'During Wind and Rain'?

Thus when Hardy came to write 'During Wind and Rain', he was prepared to include several elements: the contrast between Emma's life and her present grave as in 'Lament'; the stages of their love relationship, each stage punctuated by a ballad refrain as in 'The Change'; the vivid present-tense description of a still lived past as in 'The Interloper'; the contrast between the stages of man and the changes of nature as in 'The Five Students'; and the interruption of the speaker's reverie by an advancing storm as in 'The Wind's Prophecy'. Amazingly, 'During Wind and Rain' is able to comprehend all of these elements and yet is shorter than any of these other poems. What Hardy did was:

(1) make the stages of Emma's life and his own symbolise the stages of all human life,
(2) make this human life the subject of the speaker's reverie, and make the reverie advance stage by stage like the life,
(3) contrast human life with nature by contrasting the speaker's reverie with the present scene,

(4) make the interruption of the speaker's reverie seem like the interruption of a life, and

(5) use the ballad refrain as the connecting link between the memory images and the intruding scene.

The subjective working of the mind is beautifully fused with the objective working of the world. The poem seems to be a direct imitation of human life, both 'transparent' and 'sincere'.

Thus 'During Wind and Rain' did not spring fully formed out of Hardy's head. It is the product of a number of elements which is more than the sum of their parts. The poem is a fine example of Hardy's patient genius and is a culminating clarification of his life and poetic technique.

What we have seen happen in 'During Wind and Rain' is typical of Hardy's habits of compositions. The great poems illuminate all the poems; and all the poems contribute to the great poems. Once we see Hardy's evolution, we may respond to his poetry not in an excessively restrictive way but like Dylan Thomas ('I like all his poems') or like Philip Larkin: 'may I trumpet the assurance that one reader at least would not wish Hardy's Collected Poems a single page shorter, and regards it as many times over the best body of poetic work this century so far has to show.'[41]

2 The Patterns in Hardy's Poetry

As, in looking at a carpet, by following one colour a certain pattern is suggested, by following another colour, another; so in life the seer should watch that pattern among general things which his idiosyncrasy moves him to observe, and describe that alone. This is, quite accurately, a going to Nature; yet the result is no mere photograph, but purely the product of the writer's own mind.   (*Life*, 153)

One of the obvious characteristics of Hardy's *Complete Poems* is its enormous variety of 'feelings and fancies written down in widely differing moods and circumstances, and at various dates. It will probably be found, therefore, to possess little cohesion of thought or harmony of colouring. . . . I do not greatly regret this,' Hardy continued in his preface to *Poems of the Past and the Present*. 'Unadjusted impressions have their value, and the road to a true philosophy of life seems to lie in humbly recording diverse readings of its phenomena as they are forced upon us by chance and change.'

However, another obvious characteristic of the *Complete Poems* is its consistency of vision and coherence of sensibility. This paradoxical variety and unity of Hardy's poetry presents a great challenge to the critic. Hardy's account of the seer whose idiosyncrasy moves him to observe a pattern may apply to the individual poem which is unique in itself. Yet it may also apply to the general character of all the poetry which is based on a consistent idiosyncrasy throughout. Hardy was keenly aware of this paradox. In his poem 'Rome. The Vatican: Sala Delle Muse' (70), Hardy confesses that he is in love with many different kinds and aspects of poetry. Yet he worries: the 'lover of all . . . is a fool to whim'. The poem, however, suggests that there is a figure in the carpet. The Muses' Hall grows still, 'the chiselled shapes . . . combine in a haze of sun', and the figure of unity appears. She is the central Muse whom Hardy projects, 'an essence of all the Nine', and the various literary forms are but 'phases' of her.

If there is a unity in the *Complete Poems*, then, it must be consistent with great diversity. If Hardy is not a naively under-organized poet, neither is he

39

an obsessively over-organised one. In a famous and well argued essay by R. P. Blackmur, Hardy became the example of the latter type of poet. Hardy's poetry reveals an 'absolutist, doctrinaire . . . totalitarian, frame of mind'. 'If you had the pattern, everything else followed right. Pattern was the matrix of experience. If you could show experience as pattern, you showed all that could be shown.' Such patterns – having to do 'with love, time, memory, death and nature' and their mechanical fatality – become 'rigid frames to limit experience'. 'Some of these obsessions . . . lost the pattern-character of ideas and became virtually the objects of sensibility rather than the skeleton of attention.'[1]

Blackmur is writing in the tradition of those early critics who objected to Hardy's pessimism. With Blackmur, this objection has become more sophisticated and focused on the form rather than the content of Hardy's pessimism, namely its doctrinaire rigidity. This kind of charge in the early reviews in turn provoked Hardy's claim that there was little cohesion of thought in the poetry. The critical problem is: how can we describe the cohesion of Hardy's achievement while avoiding Blackmur's charge and being true to the wide variety of experience Hardy expresses?

The pattern we need to find is one which organises a vast amount of experience and yet lets experience develop according to its own organic laws. In describing this pattern, we may take a hint from Blackmur. It is true that Hardy's impressions are sometimes 'rigid frames', 'objects of sensibility'. But his impressions become such only at the final stage of their development. In other words, Hardy dramatises how impressions develop: they begin as rich experiences controlled only by what Blackmur calls the 'skeleton of attention'. They evolve and grow stealthily older until they end as 'rigid frames', exposed skeletons, jarred by the changing world. Blackmur does not see the interesting figure in his own critique of Hardy. In a deeper and more tragic sense than Blackmur sees or can accept,[2] Hardy fulfills Blackmur's demand that the good poet should reveal 'the pattern *in* the flesh'.

A number of such pattern-plots can be traced in various dimensions of Hardy's poetry, in his meditative structures, language, and rhythms. In this chapter, I wish to trace another kind of pattern which serves as a signature in many Hardy poems. Here I am not speaking of pattern in some general sense. Throughout his poetry, Hardy is interested in the idea and image of a pattern itself. A visual pattern is a constant image which symbolises the way a typical impression develops. The use of this image is a good example of what Hopkins calls the 'underthought' in a lyric passage, as distinguished from the 'overthought' or paraphraseable content. The underthought, Hopkins says, is

. . . conveyed chiefly in the choice of metaphors etc used and often only half realised by the poet himself, not necessarily having any connection with the subject in hand but usually having a connection and suggested by some circumstance of the scene or of the story.[3]

Visual patterns can be found in every corner of Hardy's world. There are patterns in the branches of trees, in window lattices, in lines on a hand, in veins on a leaf. When some fateful complication in human life is revealed, the revelation is compared to the moon lighting up a pattern of branches. This visual pattern is more than a cliché for the classical pattern of fate. It embodies what Hardy sees as the tragic relation of mind and reality. This relation begins as a unity and ends in a shocking discord. The pattern symbolises both the way we realise our world and what happens to that realisation: it grows in somewhat unconscious ways, it obsolesces in ways we do not immediately see, it is belatedly exposed. Richard Wilbur was perhaps thinking of Hardy when he wrote in 'Years-End':

> These sudden ends of time must give us pause.
> We fray into the future, rarely wrought
> Save in the tapestries of afterthought.

In an unpublished notebook, Hardy copied: 'We live forward, we understand backward.'[4] The statement comes from a passage in William James which concludes: 'concepts, being so many views taken after the fact, are retrospective and post mortem.' The visual image of a pattern symbolises this paradoxical relation of consciousness and life. We come to know the shapes of our lives most clearly when those shapes have become obsolescent. 'His brain . . . like the brain of most people . . . was the last part of his body to realise a situation' (Life, 224). Since our consciousness is bound by these old patterns, we are destined for tragedy in a world where 'nothing is permanent but change'.[5] What we 'think the real to be', the pattern motivated by our 'passions, prejudices, and ambitions', becomes subject to the 'gradual closing in of a situation' (Life, 186, 120). 'Rigidity' characterises one stage of the pattern. The development itself of the pattern, with its intimation of the larger life conditioning it, is interesting, organic, and complex.[6]

In this chapter I will be discussing the way in which a visual pattern symbolises different stages of an experience, symbolises the intricate relation of mind and reality, works through a variety of concrete images, produces a *gestalt* effect which links visual art and literary experience, illustrates Hardy's development as a poet, and defines his unique aesthetic.

I will also be considering another aspect of Blackmur's charge. Like Tate, Blackmur suggests that Hardy's sensibility rigidified because it had been 'violated by ideas', especially big Victorian ideas. Hardy's intellectual life, however, is much more interesting than is usually supposed. The breadth of his interests, and the originality of his synthesis of those interests, can be seen in his use of the visual pattern image. In this chapter, for example, we will see that Hardy's patterns are derived from, and synthesise, patterns of Gothic architecture, Pre-Raphaelite theories of design, nineteenth-century pattern images used in evolutionary, epistemological, poetic, and novelistic contexts, light and shade techniques in various visual arts, biblical images, and the Keatsian aesthetic tradition. The chapter assumes that some of the intellectual history of the century can be traced in the root metaphor of a pattern;[7] and that Hardy represents an important development of this metaphor.

Branches

Hardy's most common image embodying a pattern is that of interlacing branches. He develops the image most strikingly as a result of the surprise of Emma's death.

> The twigs of the birch imprint the December sky
>   Like branching veins upon a thin old hand;
> I think of summer-time, yes, of last July,
>   When she was beneath them, greeting a gathered band
>   Of the urban and bland.
>
> Iced airs wheeze through the skeletoned hedge from the north,
>   With steady snores, and a numbing that threatens snow,
> And skaters pass; and merry boys go forth
>   To look for slides. But well, well do I know
>   Whither I would go!   (735)

The pattern signals both the beginning and the end of the experience. The beginning is vague and undefined – Emma is remembered underneath the summer birch trees. But the pattern was quietly working even then and it is finally seen in all its stark clarity, just as one finally sees the summer greenery transformed to bare winter branches imprinting the sky. Hidden changes have cut not only into the outer world of July but the inner world of the lovers, and both worlds are joined in one life pattern. This interdependence of inner and outer worlds, seen in the comparison of twigs to branching veins, drives the speaker inexorably towards the belated

realisation that he has aged and his life is gone. The image of iced airs
wheezing through the skeleton hedge captures perfectly, and night-
marishly, this inevitable blending of human and natural patterns. Mean-
while the rest of the world, the bland and the merry, go forth in blithe
unconcern. The pattern of their lives has not yet come clear.

In the poem he wrote on Hardy, Robert Lowell seems to glimpse this
fundamental imagery in Hardy:

> No longer to lie reading 'Tess of the d'Urbervilles,'
> while the high, mysterious squirrels
> rain small green branches on our sleep!   ('The Lesson')

The poem ends: 'cold slices the same crease in the finger, / the same thorn
hurts. The leaf repeats the lesson.'

Throughout Hardy's poetry there are numerous hints of an interlacing
branches image which every now and then becomes explicit, its meaning
forcefully asserted:

> The bushes that veiled it once have grown
>   Gaunt trees that interlace,
> Through whose lank limbs I see too clearly
>   The nakedness of the place.   (392)

> I am sure those branchways are brooding now,
> With a wistful blankness upon their face,
> While the few mute passengers notice how
> Spectre-beridden is the place.   (544)

In the previous chapter we quoted from Hardy's reflections on revisiting
Sturminster Newton after his wife's death: 'How that tree has grown! . . .
How it has changed. . . . Time changes everything except something
within us which is always surprised by change.' The slow intertwining of
natural and personal growth, their unsynchronised relationship, the subtle
life-long preparation of a final surprise, the symbol of a tree with its
spreading pattern of leaf and branch − all are signs of a new lyric. Emma
Hardy's life had 'shut like a book' while Hardy had taken 'light notice'.
Now, 'ten years since / I saw her on the stairs', the belated realisation, the
tragic enthralment by the past, has grown in Hardy, shutting him in the
pattern:

> And the trees are ten feet taller,

> And the sunny spaces smaller
> Whose bloomage would enthrall her.   (691)

Once seen, the pattern seems present from the beginning like the 'skeleton of attention'. When Hardy now remembers Emma, he instinctively places her '[a]t the end of the alley of bending boughs' (277). These overhanging branches masked what now reveals itself 'in darkening dankness', namely '[t]he yawning blankness, / Of the perspective'. That perspective was secretly preparing itself as Hardy 'saw morning harden upon the wall . . . unknowing / That your great going / Had place that moment, and altered all.' Hardy now remembers even further back when he first met Emma in Cornwall and he 'followed her on / By an alley bare boughs overspread'. Here he explicitly defines the pattern as fate: 'a Plan of the past . . . was in working at last.' He did not 'foreshadow what fortune might weave / From beginnings so small'. 'I was bound to obey' (360). A little later they caressed '[u]nder boughs of brushwood / Linking tree and tree / In a shade of lushwood' just as they would end: 'Under bents that quiver / There shall rest we' (515). When the romantic image ceases to correspond to the reality of an embittered marriage, Hardy images the tragic fixation in a familiar way: 'What now I see before me is a long lane overhung / With lovelessness, and stretching from the present to the grave' (323). The beloved now lies 'white, straight, features marble-keen', and so Hardy looks back to that 'old romance' conducted when 'the wide-faced moon looked through / The boughs at the faery lamps of the Larmer Avenue' (862).[8]

So closely is the pattern of his love identified with that of his consciousness that Hardy gradually sees himself as a man who has become a 'phantom', 'so bare a bough / As Nature makes of me' (387): 'faltering forward, / Leaves around me falling, / Wind oozing thin through the thorn from norward . . .' (285). Bare-branched and thorn-like, he strongly identifies with a tree in 'The Tree and the Lady':

> I'm a skeleton now,
> And she's gone, craving warmth. The rime sticks like
>   a skin to me;
> Through me Arcturus peers; Nor'lights shoot into me;
>   Gone is she, scorning my bough!   (485)

Such a background of implications makes a poem like 'At Day-Close in November' so extraordinarily rich in meaning. The branching pattern symbolises his own conscious life, one whose patterns of awareness flourish until they become blind to the larger flux of things:

Beech leaves, that yellow the noon-time,
　　Float past like specks in the eye;
I set every tree in my June time,
　　And now they obscure the sky.

And the children who ramble through here
　　Conceive that there never has been
A time when no tall trees grew here,
　　That none will in time be seen.　(274)

Cobwebs

Hardy's art gives depth to those cobweb images which we might too quickly pass over as clichés. A romance dies for reasons the speaker does not yet understand at the time of 'the yellowing leaf; at moth and gnat / And cobweb-time' (579). An old ecstasy endures in a man now 'cobwebbed, crazed' (571). At a remembered 'House of Hospitalities', 'the mole now labours, / And spiders knit' (156). 'Where once we danced . . . The floors are sunken, cobwebs hang, / And cracks creep' (660).

Web lines and crack lines are often associated in Hardy. This is because the lines of the pattern become the cleaving[9] lines of its dissolution. Such images, then, are more than conventional images of decay. They connote the subtle intertwining of nature and mind in a common death-bound motion. A woman cannot awake from the dream that her lover has died: 'Yet stays this nightmare too appalling, / And like a web shakes me' (314). The approach to death takes place '[t]hrough vaults of pain, / Enribbed and wrought with groins of ghastliness' where 'garish spectres moved my brain' and pain is 'blent / With webby waxing things and waning things' (122). As the frost wanes, 'cobwebs hanging close outside the pane' become visible, '[o]f their pale presence no eye being aware / Till the rime made them plain' (702). This image, from 'A Light Snow-Fall after Frost' (discussed in the Introduction), is associated with a range of inner and outer experiences. Hardy closely associates the image with workings of the imagination: 'these creatures of the imagination [i.e. ghosts] are uncertain, fleeting, and quivering, like winds, mists, gossamer-webs' (*Writings*, 202). Perhaps E. A. Robinson was influenced by Hardy when he described human wisdom as

　　　　a web that error weaves
　　On airy looms that have a sound
　　No louder now than falling leaves.　('Hillcrest')

These patterns of realisation are like those 'outward forms' of Truth which Wordsworth describes in 'Mutability': they 'melt like frosty rime, / That in the morning whitened hill and plain / And is no more'.

Miscellaneous Images

Once attuned, we can find different kinds of images for Hardy's mind-nature patterns. The 'everlong motion / Of criss-crossing tides' encourage the speaker to 'brood' in 'The Souls of the Slain' (62). The 'target circles' of rain which 'quivered and crossed', 'imprinted the step's wet shine' where the speaker lives out a determining episode in his life (478). Ghosts cast a spell over the speaker because they have 'imprinted / Their dreams' on the walls of a house (537). A bitterly remembered day 'glossed the thrums / Of ivy, bringing that which numbs' (603). Men pursue their spasmodic pleasures like larks singing in the 'latticed hearse' of their cages (918).[10] One of the most suggestive examples is 'The Ghost of the Past' (249) where the speaker keeps a 'spectral housekeeping' with 'the Bygone there – / The Present once to me'. As time passes and the Bygone continues to usurp the present, 'its form began to fade'. Now,

> It looms a far-off skeleton
>   And not a comrade nigh,
> A fitful far-off skeleton
>   Dimming as days draw by.

Can one resist the suggestion that as the past fades, Hardy fades, his own self dimming within the skeleton of what was his 'present' reality, a 'Bygone' pattern?

Indeed Hardy sees his mind as a network of memory grown quaint and brittle in the present:

> Do they know me, whose former mind
>   Was like an open plain where no foot falls,
> But now is as a gallery portrait-lined,
>   And scored with necrologic scrawls,
> Where feeble voices rise, once full-defined,
>   From underground in curious calls? (666)

He is one among 'scathed and memoried men' (359);[11] his heart is inscribed with 'graving', with 'quaint vermiculations' (391). He is '[e]nchased and lettered as a tomb, / And scored with prints of perished hands, / And chronicled with dates of doom' like the 'ancient lands' in which he lives (75). Since life 'has bared its bones' to Hardy, he refuses to visit America where the tragic patterns have not yet ripened: their 'riper times have yet to be' and they are still free of those tears which 'peoples old in tragedy / Have left upon the centuried years' (75). In one of his most skilful poems about meditative patterns, Hardy gazes at the patterned lines of his pedigree till 'the tangles troubled me'. 'The branches seemed to twist into a seared and cynic face' until Hardy feels forestalled by the hereditary past patterning his 'every heave and coil and move': 'I am merest mimicker and counterfeit!' (390) For a moment Hardy seems to see the patterns working through him from the distant past. His realisation seems dictated from without (by the globing moon) and from within (the moon then compared to a dolphin's eye seen within a wave). The images make play on the intersections of inner eye and outer world, seeing and being seen, receiving and reflecting light like the moon. At the end of the poem, the vision of the pattern finally disappears: 'The cynic twist of the page thereat unknit / Back to its normal figure, having wrought its purport wry.' Hardy's reaction is a complex of relief (is he now free from the confining pattern he saw in dream?) and regret (for a moment he had seen the drift of his life).

One of the paradoxes of Hardy's patterns is that they grow more clear as they grow more obsolescent; the outlines of the pattern grow sharper and simultaneously skeletal until the final definitive pattern is an epitaph of the experience in which it grew. Hardy's patterns seem to grow in on themselves, become indrawn, and emerge as engraved epitaphs on the mind or nature.[12] When the patterns of experience begin, they are '[c]ommonplace, scrawled / Dully on days that go past' (587). Then they sharpen in retrospect. 'My full script', Hardy says, 'is not confined / To that stone space, but stands deep lined / Upon that landscape' (633). Hardy and his friends knew 'not what lay behind' their early experience and now the friends are ghosts and Hardy is 'brow-lined' (760). On a later anniversary day, the old tree has become wind-cracked, a 'multitude of white stones' has emerged on the garth, and the man's eyes are 'so sunk that you saw the socket-bones' (407). Such is the shock which strikes us at the end of 'During Wind and Rain', stunning us with the last markings of once real people *and* with the obsolescent outline of those people carved in Hardy's brain: 'Down their carved names the rain-drop ploughs'. Hardy's poetry contains many skeletons and 'tersely lined' tombstones which are suggestive in this manner.

HARDY AND THE GOTHIC REVIVAL

'Pattern was the matrix of experience,' Blackmur said of Hardy. 'View the matrices rather than the moulds,' Hardy said after he toured English cathedrals in 1911.[13] Hardy's first period as a creative artist was not as a poet but as a Gothic Revival architect. Here, as in so many other ways, the 1860s moulded Hardy's sensibility. The patterns which fascinated him derive partly from the patterns of Gothic architecture, and his patterns gain much of their profundity from their roots in this art. It is important therefore to understand the critical artistic moment which the 1860s represent. In *Jude the Obscure*, Hardy asserted that the stone yard, with its 'new traceries, mullions, transoms, shafts, pinnacles, and battlements', was 'a centre of effort as worthy as that dignified by the name of scholarly study within the noblest of the colleges' (II, 2, p. 98). Hardy is not only exalting humble workmen; he is exalting the art and study of architecture, and his comment still rings with excitement that was widespread in the sixties.

Much has ‚been published on the Gothic Revival, and Hardy's architectural background is well known.[14] But the significance of the connection still needs to be examined. Moreover the influence of Gothic Revival theorists on Hardy's literary sensibility has not, to my knowledge, been explored. Hardy's response to such theorists represents an important interpretation of the implications of Victorian Gothic and its relations to the other philosophical and aesthetic currents of the age.

The status of the architect as an artist and a professional had been slowly growing in the nineteenth-century.[15] The 1860s represent a high water point. In 1866 the Institute of British Architects (founded in 1834) became the Royal Institute of British Architects. It included most of the eminent Victorian architects (though only a small proportion of all architects) and sponsored important publications in architectural scholarship.[16] The decade was also the climax of the Gothic Revival. In 1872 Charles Locke Eastlake wrote its eulogy, *A History of the Gothic Revival: An Attempt to Show How the Taste for Mediaeval Architecture Which Lingered in England During the Two Last Centuries Has Since Been Encouraged and Developed* (Longmans, London). This book remains the standard treatment of the subject, though Kenneth Clarke's more critical *Gothic Revival* (1928) is perhaps better known. Eastlake discussed the cooperation of literature, art, antiquarianism, church groups, and architects in building public support for the movement. The high points are Horace Walpole's Strawberry Hill, the Gothic novel, Scott's novels and ballads, Pugin's buildings and books, especially *Contrasts: or, a Parallel between the Noble Edifices of the Middle Ages, and Corresponding Buildings of the Present Day; Shewing the Present Decay of Taste* (1836, 1841), the *Ecclesiologist* journal started in 1841 to promote medieval church architecture as a way of promoting High Church religion, Ruskin's *The Seven Lamps of Architecture* (1849) and *The Stones of Venice* (1851–3), and Gilbert Scott's 700-plus buildings in a Gothic style. In the 1860s, the 'Battle of the Styles' between Classical and Gothic was being decided generally in favour of the latter.

'During the last ten years,' Eastlake wrote, 'to which this history extends, viz. from 1860 to 1870, the list of Gothic architects has reached an extraordinary length, while the number of buildings partaking more or less of a Mediaeval character which have been erected within that period is probably double that of the preceding *decennium*.'[17] The 1860s saw the completion of the Oxford Museum, the Manchester Assize Courts, Balliol College (fictionalised as Biblioll College in *Jude the Obscure*), and the Houses of Parliament (whose burning in 1834 marks a significant date in *Desperate Remedies*, III, 1). The 1860s also saw the beginning of the Albert Memorial, the London Law Courts, and the St Pancras Station and Hotel. These buildings illustrate the success of the movement in spreading from churches to public buildings and domestic architecture.

The period in which Hardy worked as an architect, 1856 to 1872, represented the triumph of the creative architect and high Victorian Gothic. When he left the architectural profession, a lull, as Hardy said in *A Laodicean*, had 'come over the study of English Gothic architecture, through a re-awakening to the art-forms of times that more nearly neighbour our own', that is, 'Jacobean, Queen Anne, and kindred accretions of decayed styles' (I, 1, pp. 5–6).[18] In an irony Hardy would have appreciated, Eastlake's 1872 eulogy was practically the movement's epitaph.

Also contributing to the success of the Gothic Revival was the Pre-Raphaelite movement in painting and poetry. The 1850s were the triumphant years of Pre-Raphaelite painting, climaxing in the great 1857 exhibitions and the Oxford Murals, which were soon to fade. Though 'The Blessed Damozel' was published in 1850, the 1860s might be considered the triumphant decade of Pre-Raphaelite poetry, with an audience growing for important publications by Morris, the Rossettis, Swinburne, and others. In *Desperate Remedies* Hardy writes that Cytherea 'leant out upon the sill like another Blessed Damozel, and listlessly looked down upon the brilliant pattern of colours formed by the flower-beds on the lawn' (v, 2, p. 71). In 1912, Hardy quotes apparently from the sentence in Morris' 'The Art of the People', where Morris writes: 'Many a grin of pleasure . . . went to the carrying through of those mazes of mysterious beauty.'[19]

The connections linking these two great movements were, generally, medieval symbolism and the emphasis on intricate design, especially designs following the foliation principle of vegetable Nature.[20] Ruskin, who defended the Pre-Raphaelite movement so successfully in 1851, defined in *Elements of Drawing* (1857) the first law of landscape drawing as 'organic unity; the law, whether of radiation, or parallelism, or concurrent action, which rules the masses of herbs and trees, of rocks, and clouds, and waves'. The second law is 'the individual liberty of the members subjected to these laws of unity'.[21] Faithful rendering of unique detail, minute and careful patterning, characterised both the art and architecture in their respective modes. Both groups drew upon Owen Jones's *The Grammar of Ornament* (1856, revised in 1865). Jones's pictures of designs from all over the world found their way into neo-Gothic reliefs, windows, carpets, tapestries, furniture and wallpaper designs, and perhaps 'the leafy pattern of china-ware' on Hardy's chalice of memory in 'Under the Waterfall' (276). Such designs were promoted by William Morris, who in 1861 founded his firm of decorators with its famous purpose of 'reinstating decoration, down to its smallest details, as one of the fine arts' (*DNB*). (Morris had worked in 1856 for the high Victorian architect George Street, who designed the London Law Courts as well as Denchworth School, Berkshire, which Hardy sketched in his notebook.)[22] Owen Jones's 'General Principles' state: 'The general forms being first cared for, these should be subdivided and ornamented by general lines; the interstices may then be filled in with ornament, which may again be subdivided and enriched for close inspection. . . . In surface decoration all lines should flow out of a parent stem. Every ornament, however distant, should be traced to its branch and root.'[23]

I have cited the above details because they profoundly influenced Hardy. From 1856 to 1861 he worked for John Hicks, a Dorchester architect and church restorer, and in this setting debated with his fellow apprentices the High Church principles in which he had been brought up (*Life*, 29). In 1862 he went to London 'to pursue the art and science of architecture on more advanced lines' (*Life*, 35). He worked until 1867 for Arthur Blomfield as a 'Gothic draughtsman who could restore and design churches and rectory-houses' (*Life*, 36). Eastlake cites Blomfield as one of those

> . . . who began to design under advantages which were unknown to the previous generation, who have learnt by degrees to distinguish between the faults and merits of Pointed architecture, and who, having studied the style with respect to its local and national characteristics, are

enabled to attain an individuality of treatment to which their predecessors could not aspire.[24]

Hardy's architectural notebook still exists and has been published and finely introduced by C. J. P. Beatty. The unpublished notebooks contain many other drawings.[25] The published notebook is full of the intricate detail one might expect and exemplifies, as Beatty notes, many of the currents of the 1860s: the application of Gothic to domestic architecture, the use of ironwork (which Ruskin attacked but Blomfield used), designs copied from Owen Jones, echoes of Pugin, whom Hardy continued to praise in his later years,[26] Morris's Arts and Crafts Movement, Ruskin (Hardy also refers, in the *Life*, 193, to Ruskin's description of St Mark's, probably the one in *The Stones of Venice*), and examples of both English and French Gothic. Eastlake discusses these competing styles of the 1860s and in *A Laodicean* Hardy refers to 'the days of the French – Gothic mania which immediately succeeded to the great English-pointed revival under Britton, Pugin, Rickman, Scott, and other mediaevalists' (i, 1, p. 6). In 1862, according to Beatty, Hardy became a member of the Architectural Association (founded in 1847 to promote dialogue among young architects), which sponsored the tour of Westminster Abbey by Gilbert Scott which Hardy attended (*Writings*, 211). Hardy was proposed by Blomfield, who had become president of the Association in 1861. 1863 was indeed Hardy's *annus mirabilis* in architecture. In 1863 he considered 'becoming an art-critic for the press, particularly in the province of architectural art' (*Life*, 47). In the same year he wrote a prize essay on architectural materials for the Royal Institute of British Architects and received the medal 'from the hands of Sir Gilbert Scott' (*Life*, 42, 404). (Hardy may be confusing this occasion with another – cf. Purdy, p. 293.) Blomfield would become vice-president of the RIBA in 1886. Also in 1863, Hardy's design for a country mansion won a prize, awarded by William Tite, then president of the RIBA, who had helped defeat Scott's French–Gothic proposal for the Whitehall government offices.[27] Hardy took himself very seriously indeed as a Gothic architect and associated with some of the movement's most prominent practitioners. He was also influenced by its most prominent theorists.

In 1867 Hardy returned to Dorchester and did some work for Hicks. In 1869, after Hicks's death, G. R. Crickmay took over the practice and Hardy worked for him, preparing 'church-drawings' (*Life*, 63). He did this intermittently until 1872 and also returned to assist Blomfield for short periods. In 1872 he helped design schools for Roger Smith who, Hardy notes, was later professor of architecture at the RIBA (*Life*, 87).

In 1872 he also assisted Raphael Brandon, whom Hardy described as

> . . . a man who interested him much. In collaboration with his brother David [sic]²⁸ he had published, several years before, the *Analysis of Gothic Architecture* . . . and . . . *Open Timber Roofs of the Middle Ages*. Both these works were familiar to Hardy, having been quite text-books for architects' pupils until latterly, when the absorbing interest given to French Gothic had caused them to be superseded.²⁹   (*Life*, 76–7)

Eastlake celebrated Brandon's Apostolic Church in Gordon Square as 'one of the grandest and most effective modern churches which have marked the Revival' (p. 241). Brandon's *Analysis*, according to Eastlake, played a major role in promoting work in medieval design. Though Blomfield liked French Gothic and though Hardy's notebook contains French Gothic designs, Hardy agreed with Brandon's preference for the less 'muscular' English Gothic. Hardy called Brandon a 'literary architect',³⁰ and Brandon's *Analysis* shows his enthusiasm for the Gothic style, 'so transcendently beautiful, so perfect in itself' (quoting F. A. Paley on p. 2). Brandon's *Open Timber Roofs* opens with the statement which Hardy's passage on the stone-mason's yard in *Jude* may reflect and which these pages on Hardy's Gothic background have assumed: 'The historian, whose task it may be to . . . trace the progress of intellect, the improvements and revolutions in learning and science . . . will probably find few that are more gratifying . . . than the important change which has happily occurred in the matter of Ecclesiastical Architecture.'

During his years as an architect, Hardy kept at his writing, first as a poet, then as a novelist. He came to regret the monotony of architectural drawing (a monotony reflected in the notebook) as opposed to 'actual designing' (*Life*, 46). In 1872 he finally made the switch from professional architect to professional writer by refusing a generous offer from Smith (*Life*, 91). Occasionally, however, he would do architectural work in later years. Indeed in 1893–4, as he composed his last novel and planned to resume poetry, he did a major restoration at West Knighton Church.³¹ Throughout his life he was consulted about planned restorations. He never got over a regret at leaving architecture. He continued to haunt cathedrals in his later years.³²

FROM ARCHITECT TO POET

The powerful influence of Gothic architecture on Hardy's imagination did not end when he turned to literature. Many readers, most notably Proust, have discussed the influence of architectural training on the 'structure' of the novels.[33] In the poems, Gothic architecture provides a massive background for:

'Heiress and Architect' (49), dedicated to Blomfield, which progresses through four types of architecture which seem to be: English Pointed, Crystal Palace, Pre-Raphaelite Chamber, and Early English Gothic Tower;

'A Man' (123), about an architect who died rather than dismantle a Tudor Gothic;

'Architectural Masks' (130), which contrasts domestic Gothic architecture with a cheap modern villa;

'The Church-Builder' (139), about a man who hangs himself in the Perpendicular Gothic church he had constructed;

'The Spell of the Rose' (295), in which a man gives his beloved a Strawberry Hill rather than the rose of his heart;

'The Abbey Mason' (332), dedicated to Hicks,

'In Sherborne Abbey' (726).

These last two are the most important.

'The Abbey Mason' describes the creation of the Gloucester Cathedral's south transept. The poem represents Hardy's interesting response to an issue which was frequently discussed in his architectural years, namely the stages of Gothic architecture and the manner in which they had evolved.[34] Hardy valued churches which illustrated 'two or three styles' and regretted their destruction in the name of uniformity (*Writings*, 205). Stinsford Church, for example, was 'an interesting old church of various styles from Transition-Norman to late Perpendicular' (*Life*, 9). One of Hardy's drawings for *Wessex Poems* captures vividly the sense of transition in the thick Norman columns and the Gothic arcades. (See Illustration 2.)

Gloucester Cathedral is the most vivid example in England of the co-presence of architectural stages. (It also contains the most striking example of intricate network tracery.) In 1911 the issue of Gothic origins still interested Hardy so much that he journeyed to Gloucester to investigate the origin of English Perpendicular, 'which he ascertained to be in the screen between the south aisle of the transept – a fact long known probably to other investigators, but only recently to him'.[35] The south transept is a peculiar problem for architectural historians because the records claim it was built decades before the period of Perpendicular Gothic was supposed to begin.[36] In composing his poem, Hardy was probably influenced by memories of what he had read and he may have reviewed his

Gothic theorists when he returned from Gloucester. He had known well and copied from Frederick Apthorp Paley's *A Manual of Gothic Mouldings* (1845). In Paley he read that 'in Gothic moulding all the links in the process of formation are connected and complete, from the first and rudest origin to the most elaborate development; and the steps are so natural, the transition so easy'. Brandon's *Analysis of Gothic Architecture* followed the description established by Thomas Rickman and traced the stages, Norman, Semi-Norman, Early English, Decorated, Perpendicular. These are the stages Paley also followed and Hardy copied down his terms in his notebook. Nevertheless, Brandon added, 'it is impossible to fix with absolute and preemptory certainty where one stage of art left off, and where another began'.[37]

Given this qualification, Brandon traced how the lancet style of Early English evolved into the complex traceries of Decorated. The older lancet windows and mouldings with their 'bold projections and deep hollows . . . gave way to a system of grouping, richer and far more beautifully blended', of mullions and tracery: 'shafts ceased to stand detached . . . and became instead firmly compacted into a mass.' In this Decorated style, 'the principal lines of the composition verged pyramidically, rather than vertically [as in Early English] or horizontally [as in Norman]'. With the last Perpendicular stage, 'the outline of window-tracery began to show a tendency to adapt itself to the vertical bearing of the mullions, instead of branching off from them in flowing undulations'. The principle of the 'equilateral triangle' was the basis of this long development which thus ended with the 'last gorgeous style' of the Perpendicular with its sharp right angles. In 1905 Francis Bond published his *Gothic Architecture in England* (London, Batsford) which discussed the Gloucester south transept in phrases very similar to those Hardy used in 'The Abbey Mason'.[38]

In describing the formation of the transept, Hardy constructs an imaginative theory by which the Norman stage and the late Perpendicular stage literally flow into each other. The architect was building an Early English-style abbey 'roundabout the Norman core' but the problem of the transept puzzled him: how to make the upper archmould meet the lower tracery curves. Despairing, he left his architectural diagram out in the rain and the rain solved the architectural problem. The water made the drawn lines stream 'in small white threads / From the upper segments to the heads / Of arcs below, uniting them / Each by a stalactitic stem'. The hint is taken. 'Templates were cut . . . And the work swelled and mounted higher . . . Here jambs with transoms fixed between . . . There little mullions thinly sawn / Where meeting circles once were drawn . . . [t]he ogee arches transom-topped – / the tracery-stalks by spandrels stopped.'

Thus the new style is born and its 'symmetries salute the sun'. Such is Hardy's strikingly literal version of the artist waiting 'upon nature for his cue'. (See Illustration 3.)

Pound called 'The Abbey Mason' Hardy's personal aesthetic.[39] Indeed Hardy said he wrote the poem because he was 'so much impressed by the thought that the inventor's name, like the names of the authors of so many noble songs and ballads, was unknown'.[40] Ten years later, when Hardy published 'Barthélémon at Vauxhall' (519), he used very similar phrasing to describe the spread of a musical style: 'And then were threads of matin music spun / In trial tones. . . . [T]ill, caught by echoing lyres, / It spread to galleried naves and mighty quires.'

'The Abbey Mason' presents the development of a pattern whose coherence only emerges after much unconscious evolution. The final pattern reveals where the earlier styles were tending. The matrix underlying the various mouldings seems to be that equilateral triangle Brandon cites. 'View the matrices rather than the moulds' means, for Hardy, not only viewing the abstract pattern but perceiving its surprising emergence at the end of a dark historical development.

It is fitting therefore that Hardy also associated his architectural patterns with pedigree patterns whose lines and tangles interconnect '[w]ith offspring mapped below in lineage' (390). Many interesting connections can be made between 'The Pedigree' and 'The Abbey Mason'. Just as Hardy had gazed at the lines of the south transept, he would gaze at the lines of family trees:

> The pedigrees of our county families, arranged in diagrams on the pages of county histories, mostly appear at first sight to be as barren of any touch of nature as a table of logarithms. But given a clue – the faintest tradition of what went on behind the scenes, and this dryness as of dust may be transformed into a palpitating drama. . . . [A]nybody practised in raising images from such genealogies finds himself unconsciously filling into the framework the motives, passions, and personal qualities which would appear to be the single explanation possible of some extraordinary conjunction in times, events, and personages that occasionally marks these reticent family records. (*Writings*, 24)

Hardy compiled his own pedigree with painstaking care.[41] He is at the bottom centre of the diagram where the various stalactitic stems tend to converge – thus creating the impression that the matrix of the pedigree is an inverted triangle. Of course, the bare lines of the triangle are subdivided and 'the interstices . . . filled in with ornament, which may again be subdivided'. But the diagram follows the *dictum* that 'all lines should flow out of a parent stem. Every ornament, however distant, should be traced to its branch and root.' These are Owen Jones's terms, of course, which influenced neo-Gothic tracery and Pre-Raphaelite design. I am suggesting that Hardy extended the principle to a great variety of patterns, including the pattern of personal identity unfolding in time.

Perhaps the most interesting connection of all is that which can be made between the mason's rain-blotted diagram and Hardy's sketch of Emma in 'The Figure in the Scene' (416):

> But I kept on, despite the drifting wet
> > That fell and stained
> My draught, leaving for curious quizzings yet
> > The blots engrained.
>
> And thus I drew her there alone,
> > Seated amid the gauze
> Of moisture, hooded, only her outline shone,
> > With rainfall marked across.

When Hardy defined the central principle of his poetry as that of exhumed memory, one of the four poems he quoted as examples was 'The Figure in the Scene'. This brings us to the key issue, how the visual patterns of Gothic art influenced the imaginative patterns of the poetry. Hardy pointedly asserted the influence: 'he carried on into his verse, perhaps in part unconsciously, the Gothic art-principle in which he had been trained – the principle of spontaneity, found in mouldings, tracery, and such like' (*Life*, 301). This oft-quoted statement is usually interpreted as meaning merely the 'principle of spontaneity'. But the reference is more specific, and the Gothic art-principle includes more than just spontaneity. When Hardy vigorously defended the principle of 'organic form and symmetry' in literature and 'the well-knit interdependence of parts',[42] he also did so not only in a generic sense but in a specific sense, for it was Gothic design which had early captured Hardy's imagination. To understand the implications of this, we need to consider the central issue of the Gothic Revival.

The Gothic form, Hardy said, was an 'aesthetic phantom' (*Writings*, 214). It was a style of the past, its origins were obscure, it had developed by imperceptible stages, its monuments were subject to decay. The stones out of which its patterns were constructed were imbued with 'memories, history, fellowship, fraternities'.[43] 'To restore the grey carcases of a mediaevalism whose spirit had fled' (*Writings*, 7) was a forlorn hope. The results of Gothic Revival were often grotesque combinations of old and new materials, old and new forms. 'Nobody', Hardy said in 1896, 'but those who have had to carry [restorations] out knows the difficulties of such problems – whether to preserve the venerable *lines*, or the venerable *substance*, when you cannot do both.'[44] There thus 'arises a conflict between the purely aesthetic sense and the memorial or associative. . . . [T]he architect . . . is pulled in two directions – in one by his wish to hand on or modify the abstract form, in the other by his reverence for the antiquity of its embodiment.' Hardy made these last remarks in a paper delivered before the Society for the Protection of Ancient Buildings. The Society had been founded by William Morris in 1877 as part of a reaction against some of the ravages of ancient buildings carried out under the influence of Gilbert Scott.[45] Hardy regretted the part he had played in these ravages (*Life*, 31) but also saw the problem as ultimately insoluble: what was not restored would often eventually disintegrate. Both antiquarian and restoration architect were faced with the fact that the Gothic substance perished while the form remained, and remained only in the architectural sketchbook or the renewed monument.

Many of Hardy's later observations about his architectural work carry with them this combined sense of the delicate intricacy of Gothic design and its fast perishing nature. In the *Early Life*, he remembers his 1870 work at St Juliot church and cites 'his drawings of the highly carved seat-ends and other details that have disappeared'.[46] Just before the old chancel-screen disappeared, 'Hardy had made a careful drawing of it, with its decayed tracery, posts, and gilding, marking thereon where sundry patchings and scarfings were to be applied' (*Life*, 79). For the year 1873 the *Early Life* records that he 'walked to Tintagel Castle and sketched there a stone altar, having an Early-English ornamentation on its edge; which altar in after years he could never find' (*Life*, 91). Similarly Hardy will talk about trying to find old quadrilles (*Life*, 43). In a letter of 1914, Hardy wrote: 'When I was young French architecture of the best period was much investigated, and selections from such traceries and mouldings as those at Rheims were delineated with the greatest accuracy and copied by architects' pupils – myself among the rest. It seems strange indeed now that the curves we used to draw with such care should have been broken as ruthlessly as if they were a cast-iron railing replaceable from a mould.'[47] Brandon had enthusiastically proclaimed the new creative possibilities of Gothic architecture: 'The day is surely coming when it will no longer be studied as a dead language.'[48] But for Hardy as for Jude, 'mediaevalism was as dead as a fern-leaf in a lump of coal' (*Jude the Obscure*, II, 2, p. 99) and he sadly attended Brandon during his decline (*Life*, 77). Hardy's great admiration for Scott's *Marmion* (*Life*, 49), which has surprised many, can be understood if we see that Hardy valued the poem for its evocation of a lost world. *Marmion* indeed was singled out by Eastlake (p. 115) for its influence on the medieval revival:

> It will not be – it may not last –
> The vision of enchantment's past:
> Like frostwork in the morning ray,
> The fancied fabric melts away;
> Each Gothic arch, memorial-stone,
> And long, dim, lofty aisle, are gone;
> And, lingering last, deception dear,
> The choir's high sounds die on my ear.
> Now slow return the lonely down,
> The silent pastures bleak and brown. . . .
>
> (Canto First, Introduction)

Ainsworth's *Rookwood*, to which we shall return, also exploits such Gothic contexts, for example the broken arches and piers of Davenham Abbey, with its 'great marigold, or circular window, which terminated the chapel, and which, though now despoiled of its painted honours, retained, like the skeleton leaf, its fibrous intricacies entire'.[49] Ainsworth's description draws on the traditional parallel of Gothic patterns to wood patterns. But the description, like Hardy's comments, makes us realise that Gothic architecture is like organic nature, not perhaps in its origins, but in its decay. Hardy intimately associated such an effect with poetry: 'the lichened colleges . . . had done nothing but wait, and had become poetical' (*Jude*, II, 2, p. 98). Later he will make a similar remark about the King James Bible:

> They translated into the language of their age; then the years began to corrupt the language as spoken, and to add grey lichen to the translation; until the moderns who use the corrupted tongue marvel at the poetry of the old words. When new they were not more than half so poetical. So that Coverdale, Tyndale, and the rest of them are as ghosts what they never were in the flesh.   (*Life*, 385)

Hardy would also have appreciated Richard Wilbur's beautiful assessment of the Pre-Raphaelite tradition in 'Merlin Enthralled'. The Arthurian dream ends:

Their mail grew quainter as they clopped along.
The sky became a still and woven blue.

The rich aesthetic, historical, and tragic associations of Gothic patterns were not lost upon Hardy when he turned to the novels and the poems. And it was natural for him to use the Gothic pattern as a signature for certain tragic human plots. His theme, he said in a 1912 postscript to *Jude*, was 'the forced adaptation of human instincts to rusty and irksome moulds that do not fit them' (*Writings*, 35). Thus Hardy's visual patterns, complex, antique, can symbolise tragic human patterns, those rigid yet frail moulds into which lives fall until they become a phantom of what they have been.[50] This is what makes 'In Sherborne Abbey' the most interesting of the previously listed poems in which the architectural setting plays a major role. It is also probably the latest of the series.

The architectural patterns and personal patterns of Hardy's life came together in the same period and place. It was at St Juliot that Hardy met his wife and the tragic pattern of his life began. Remembering their visit together to Tintagel Castle he would later define his great poetic principle of exhumed memory (cf. Chapter 3). In 1912 he used an interesting image to describe memory: 'our imperfect memories insensibly formalize the fresh originality of living fact – from whose shape they slowly depart, as machine-made castings depart by degrees from the sharp hand-work of the mould' (*Writings*, 22). Ruskin had said that 'in the Gothic vaults and traceries there is a stiffness analogous to that of the bones of a limb, or fibres of a tree'. Hardy associated this characteristic in turn with the historical growth and decay of these forms, and then with the insensible formalising of memory. The Gothic pattern, so beautiful in its synchronic form, so plaintive in its diachronic growth, could thus be associated with the larger pattern of life and mind. The Gothic pattern, unconsciously evolved by the abbey mason, growing in persuasive power over the years, seen in its full import when its substance has begun to decay, retrieved only in belated re-creation – such a pattern is a basic 'underthought' in Hardy's poetry.

THE INTELLECTUAL AND LITERARY TRADITIONS

In considering the original synthesis that Hardy's patterns represent, there is another tradition that we must take into account. The image of a pattern occurs at striking moments in the intellectual and literary traditions which influenced Hardy. In his early years, the Pre-Raphaelite painter, Holman

Hunt, had drawn 'geological and astronomical diagrams' and they had seemed to him 'full of poetic suggestions'.[51] This kind of poetic suggestion powerfully affected Hardy. In the 1860s and thereafter, pattern images from science, philosophy, and art, which had drawn upon ancient traditions, began to interact in various novel ways. Hardy as a poet holds a key position in this crossing of the ways of pattern imagery.

When Hardy read Darwin in 1859, he read his description of the tree of life which 'fills with its dead and broken branches the crust of the earth, and covers the surface with its ever-branching and beautiful ramifications'. Darwin takes the conventional landscape pattern and sets it moving, enclosing us in sometimes dizzying ways. We are somewhere in the midst, among life-forms 'produced by laws acting around us'. What we know about this world is like what we know about ourselves: 'We see nothing of these slow changes in progress, until the hand of time has marked the long lapse of ages.' Darwin's actual diagram of diversifying species and genera had, I suspect, a powerful influence on Hardy's imagination and helped him connect his Gothic patterns with his pedigree patterns.[52]

Darwin's diagram traces the development of a present existing variety, for example *a 14*, back through a series of past varieties, *a 14* to *a 1*, out of an original species, *A*. The other capital letters on the bottom row represent related species of a common genus. The space between each horizontal line from *a 1* to *a 10* may represent 'a thousand generations'. The space just above *a 10* (between Row X and Row XI) represents a 'great number of generations' so as to get us up to recent history. What we see now in 1859, namely the horizontal line containing *a 14* to *m 14*, is a number of varieties which represent different stages of development out of the original species, *A*. The only other ancient species to survive to the present are *F* which has remained relatively unchanged and *I* which has evolved into the present existing varieties, *n 14* to *z 14*. (Where a dotted line meets a horizontal line marks the point at which a variety becomes 'sufficiently distinct' to be recorded as a new variety. Where a dotted line stops without meeting a horizontal line marks the point where a variety becomes extinct.)

The letters on the top row, therefore, are the remains of the primordial genus. To reconstruct that genus, and thus understand the proper nature and relationship of the survivors, we need to climb back down the historical tree. The picture we now have of the pattern of nature is very incomplete and based on much hypothetical reconstruction. Only a few of the marked varieties on the diagram may actually have been found. Thus many of the letters on the diagram represent hypothetical or starred forms, and the space between each horizontal row represents transitional forms of which we know nothing. Moreover the current survivors are changing their nature or becoming extinct in ways we cannot see until the process has taken place.

Once we have grasped this picture, Darwin then adds: 'In the diagram, each horizontal line has hitherto been supposed to represent a thousand generations, but each may represent a million or hundred million generations, and likewise a section of the successive strata of the earth's crust including extinct remains.'[53] This temporal expansion takes the breath away. The varieties *a 1* to *a 14* convert into species and *A* converts from a species into a genus. At the same time, the temporal stratification converts like a *gestalt* diagram into a spatial stratification, the layers of the earth on which we live and which we will soon become part of.

Thus the evolutionary record we are left with is the barest matrix of an inconceivably rich history. The beginnings of that history (the vertical dotted lines below the bottom horizontal line) was the end of another huge history, perhaps converging toward some 'origin of species' which is lost to our scrutiny and probably to our imaginations. This aspect of Darwin's diagram had, I suspect, a lingering influence on Hardy which climaxed when he brooded on another kind of diagram, that of his family tree. He then wrote 'The Pedigree', in which he feels controlled by a long history whose nature he cannot penetrate because its ultimate source he cannot see.

Darwin and Gothic architecture were thus complementary influences on Hardy. Whether the pattern existed on the naturalist's drawing-board or on the Gothic Revival architect's sketching-pad, it represents a pattern which has evolved subtly through the ages and whose mature character is just now seen. In both cases, the pattern is seen belatedly. Moreover, the pattern once seen is subject to hidden obsolescence because, for the architect, the old Gothic structures may be on the verge of disintegration and because, for the naturalist, new discoveries may render the old diagram scientifically obsolete.

Perhaps this dramatic connection between Gothic and evolutionary patterns may have struck Hardy when he read Herbert Spencer in the 1860s. Spencer made patterns the generating principle of every activity, from the development of art to the development of organisms. An 'indefinite, incoherent homogeneity' evolves into a 'definite, coherent heterogeneity' which eventually hardens and becomes brittle like a bony structure.[54] I think Hardy was remembering this image of a ramifying network against the background of the 'unknowable' when he said of Spencer: ' "*First Principles*" . . . acts, or used to act, upon me as a sort of patent expander when I had been particularly narrowed down by the events of life. Whether the theories are true or false, their effect upon the imagination is unquestionable, and I think beneficial.'[55] Hardy's final description of the abbey mason's work is: 'Petrified lacework – lightly lined / On ancient massiveness behind. . . .'

Other aspects of Hardy's patterns were influenced by other thinkers whom he read. Henry Maudsley (1835–1918) was an English physician and professor at University College who wrote *Natural Causes and Supernatural Seemings* (London: Kegan Paul, 1886). The book shows the obvious influence of Darwin and Spencer. Hardy copied extensively from it in his unpublished notebooks. In the following passage (which Hardy did not copy), Hardy may have noticed the way a pattern can symbolise mental activity:

> . . . once an idea not entirely false has obtained settlement in the mind, it becomes . . . a centre to which associations form gradually . . . the unrelated thus becoming by degrees more and more related, and in the end, perhaps, the centre of a group of relations that prove to be of the greatest service in bridging a chasm of thought between separate groups of ideas. It is like bringing into complete and regular intercommunication, by means of a new railway with its suitable network of branches, separate parts of the country.[56]

Maudsley's image is like certain eighteenth-century images of the human organism as a web-like network. The most telling example is perhaps Diderot's elaboration of the image in *D'Alembert's Dream*, which Hardy would have known through his careful reading of Morley's *Diderot and the Encyclopaedists*.[57] Behind Diderot's images stretches the vast complex of images associated with the great chain of being, and behind them the classical image of webs of fate.

The web of fate image is used most notably in Aeschylus' *Agamemnon* which Hardy cited more than any other Greek play.[58] The image is later used in striking contexts by Gibbon, Shelley, Swinburne, Tennyson, Carlyle, Schopenhauer, Pater, and Symonds.[59] Hardy copied from Symonds: 'Each act, as it has had immeasurable antecedents, will be fruitful of immeasurable consequents; for the web of the world is ever weaving.' In *The Revolt of Islam*, from which Hardy often quoted, Shelley uses pattern images – pines weaving shades, mists entwining their woof, wreaths of budding foliage, nets of iron, mazes of waterways – as a recurrent motif.[60] In Shelley such patterns can symbolise beauty and harmony and creativity; conversely they can symbolise mental chains and submission to circumstance. This ambiguity, that a pattern can be either a liberation or a prison, profoundly impressed Hardy, who saw the alternatives as a sequence: what begins as a subjective pattern created by the mind ends as an objective pattern controlling the mind. Pater's use of the image combines the Greek insight with the new insights of Victorian science. 'Necessity', he wrote, '. . . is a magic web woven through and through us, like that magnetic system of which modern science speaks.' His famous 'Conclusion' to *The Renaissance* uses the pattern image as a way of uniting the subjective impression and the objective world: each individual weaves an image of himself which is a 'design in a web, the actual threads of which pass out beyond it'.

Many other images from Victorian science and industry influenced Hardy. He recommended the field of electric engineering to a friend (*Writings*, 69). New currents and systems were being discovered within reality ('every heave and coil . . . [w]ithin my brain' 390) and were being imposed on the landscape without. In 'Lonely Days' (614) the pattern of '[t]ramlines' and 'electric ropes' expresses the pattern of modern life which has passed the lady by and left her 'thinner wrought'. Maudsley's last sentence reminds us that this age of rapidly expanding railway and roadway systems is also an age of maps. Hardy had mapped Wessex and in 'The Place on the Map' (263) the new varnished map 'lined' with shires and rivers becomes the 'charted coast' of memory. The outer map of the landscape becomes the inner map of the mind. Hardy probably knew the famous scene in Leslie Stephen's 'A Bad Five Minutes in the Alps' (*Fraser's Magazine*, 1872), which may have been the model for a similar scene written very soon thereafter in *A Pair of Blue Eyes* (Chapter 22). Stephen, reflecting in the midst of a geological fissure into which he has fallen, speaks suggestively of the 'innumerable scratches and cross-hatchings' made upon the mind as it ages. And Dickens, in *Dombey and Son* (23), compares the figure to memory: 'Patterns of carpets faded and became perplexed and faint, like the memory of those years' trifling incidents.'

Hardy therefore holds a key place in a long nineteenth-century exploration of the proper relation between mental patterns and world patterns.

But of all the thinkers whose use of a pattern image had an influence on Hardy, George Eliot was perhaps the most influential. Eliot uses the pattern image as a constant reference point for many dimensions of experience in *Adam Bede* and, most originally, in *Middlemarch*. Dr Lydgate, a model for Hardy's Dr Fitzpiers, sees the body 'as consisting of certain primary webs or tissues', a concept which shows 'new conceptions and hitherto hidden facts of structure'. And character too, Eliot adds, 'is a process and unfolding'. In her first scene with Lydgate, Rosamond had 'woven a little future' and their love starts as a 'gossamer web': 'And

Lydgate fell to spinning that web from his inward self with wonderful rapidity.' Meanwhile the social web grows around him, as he increasingly feels 'the hampering threadlike pressure of small social conditions, and their frustrating complexity'. This web is partly objective, partly subjective, for we make up 'our most inward life' partly out of the 'fabric of opinion' we think others have of us. Every ego organises events like a candle organising the scratches on a pier-glass into 'a fine series of concentric circles'. So Eliot is taught, she says, by an 'eminent philosopher', perhaps Herbert Spencer. Every person sees his own figure in the carpet, has his own point of view 'as various as the faces to be seen at will in. fretwork or paperhangings'. Such egoism can become ingrown and quiver 'thread-like in small currents of self-preoccupation' as with Casaubon, or become 'a close network aloof and independent' as with Rosamond, or become incrusted with sophistry 'perpetually spinning . . . into intricate thickness, like masses of spider-web, padding the moral sensibility', as with Bulstrode. Meanwhile the job of the novelist consists 'in unravelling certain human lots, and seeing how they were woven and interwoven'. At the same time the novelist is limited. He can only concentrate on a 'particular web'.[61]

Eliot, Hardy noted, was once mistaken as the author of *Far from the Madding Crowd*. Hardy thought of her as 'that great thinker − one of the greatest living, he thought, though not a born storyteller by any means' (*Life*, 98). Where Eliot cites the patterns that control both life and art, Hardy dramatises their actual working in 'the locality and scenery of the action' (cf. discussion of *The Woodlanders*, below p. 83). In his poetry Hardy goes further and dramatises their actual workings in his own perceptions. What Eliot made the subject of philosophical speculation, Hardy will show conditioning the act of speculation.

When Hardy contemplates his branch and lattice and tracery patterns, he connects them with his personal life and with a vast tradition of pattern imagery. We can say that in a sense Hardy synthesises the two dimensions of a pattern, its synchronic and diachronic dimensions. A pattern is not only a present aesthetic organisation of an impression. It is also an historical development in the relation between mind and world. According to Philip Appleman, these were two dimensions, the aesthetic impression and the Darwinian perspective, which Pater could not reconcile.[62] Hardy, however, dramatises how a pattern defines a moment of experience and a long temporal process; its lines organise the poem and yet extend far beyond and behind the poem.

THE PATTERN *GESTALT*: GOTHIC LIGHTS

'[T]he seer should watch that pattern among general things which his idiosyncrasy moves him to observe. . . . This is . . . a going to Nature; yet the result is no mere photograph. . . .' (Cf. Epigraph.) In watching a pattern with Hardy, we find that the pattern changes and is realised differently at different moments in its development. To dramatise this change of realisation, Hardy uses an interesting *gestalt* effect which depends on light and shade and outline. A number of sources influenced Hardy in his development of this effect: architectural theories and facts of light values, late Gothic novels, and painting's experiments with shadow and outline and framing effects. After noting these influences and some of their specific effects in Hardy, I will turn to his favourite evocation of the *gestalt* effect, in the imagery of light and branch and shadow.

Hardy's architectural notebook shows his technical interest in light and colour combinations. He would have read Owen Jones's account of the way colours change in different contexts: 'When two different colours are juxtaposed, they receive a double modification; first, as to their tone (the light colour appearing lighter, and the dark colour appearing darker); secondly, as to their hue, each will become tinged with the complementary colour of the other.' Paley's *Manual* explains that 'we read and peruse, a Grecian moulding by its lights, and the Gothic by its shadows'. He also noted that Early English Gothic had developed the 'deep rounded hollow . . . by which the contrast of light and shade was obtained'. Ruskin describes the difference between Greek and Gothic styles in terms which suggest a *gestalt* change: 'there are two marked styles . . . one in which the forms are drawn with light, upon darkness, as in Greek sculpture and pillars; the other in which they are drawn with darkness upon light, as in early Gothic foliation.' In *Modern Painters*, Ruskin had also described the way mouldings change dramatically in their value 'according to their position and the time of day. A moulding which is of value on a building facing south, where it takes dark shadows from steep sun, may be utterly ineffective if placed west or east.' In *Seven Lamps*, Ruskin urged young architects to develop the habit of 'thinking in shadow, not looking at a design in its miserable liny skeleton; but conceiving it as it will be when the dawn lights it, and the dusk leaves it'.[63]

Hardy's architectural notebook shows his concern with the proper positioning of a house toward the sun (Beatty, 108). He was extremely sensitive to the way a structure is realised differently at different times of day and in different kinds of light. Visiting Stonehenge in 1897, he wrote: 'The misfortune of ruins – to be beheld nearly always at noonday by visitors, and not at twilight' (*Life*, 296). Describing Stonehenge two years later, he wrote: 'In the brilliant noonday sunlight . . . the scene is . . . garish and depressing. In dull, threatening weather, however . . . its charm is indescribable. . . . [C]olours are revealed on the surfaces of stones. . . . [O]n moonlight nights it is at its finest . . .' (*Writings*, 200). In 1883 Hardy had applied a related notion to the way we realise the depths of an individual's character, for example, the Dorsetshire labourer: 'As, to the eye of a diver, contrasting colours shine out by degrees from what has originally painted itself of an unrelieved earthy hue, so would shine out the characters, capacities, and interests of these people to him' (*Writings*, 170).

Hardy's childhood reading of Victorian Gothic novels helped open his imagination to the dramatic possibilities of light and Gothic architecture. Indeed these late Gothic novels were influenced by the growing interest in Gothic architecture which the early Gothic novels had helped promote. S. M. Ellis and Hardy talked about Ainsworth and James Grant in April, 1913, at which time Hardy said that Ainsworth was 'the most powerful literary influence of his boyhood, and *Old Saint Paul's* his favourite romance'. After the visit, Ellis sent Hardy an illustrated copy of Ainsworth's *Windsor Castle*, and Hardy wrote back: 'I am much obliged. . . . In looking over it I am carried back to the days of my boyhood.' Ellis also remembered Hardy's claim that Grant's *The Scottish Cavalier* 'was one of his favourite books in boyhood, and seventy years later he still retains vivid memories of the scenes and characters in this picturesque romance'.[64]

Old Saint Paul's, published in the same year as the important second edition of Pugin's *Contrasts* (cf. below, p. 85), counterpoints its action with the dramatic shadows and moon-lit patterns of St Paul's Cathedral. *The Scottish Cavalier* opens with scenes of flickering lights and shadows playing against the surfaces and silhouettes of windows, mansions, and Gothic towers. *Rockwood*, with its strong parallels to *The Woodlanders*, opens with candle-lit figures thrown 'into darkest relief', takes place in a densely foliaged wooded area (where the falling branch of a mystery tree portends the death of one of the noble family), and carefully describes various lighting effects. For example, as the sun 'sank behind the hall, its varied and picturesque tracery became each instant more darkly and distinctly defined against the crimson sky' (I, 7, p. 51). Such forms are intimately connected, in these novels, with the tragic human action and serve as a signature for what is to come. Thus the third chapter of Book II of *Rookwood* begins: 'Lights streamed through the chancel window as the sexton entered the churchyard, darkly defining all the ramified tracery of the noble Gothic arch'. Hardy's 'The Church-Builder' begins: 'The church flings forth a battled shade / Over the moon-blanched sward. . . .'

HARDY AND ART

There is another important source of Hardy's interest in the symbolic possibilities of light and shade. Here again his experience in the 1860s formed his sensibility. Like many other phenomena which influenced Hardy, the development of public art collections had had a late start in England. Founded in 1824 and moved to its Trafalgar Square building in 1838, the National Gallery made dramatic strides with the appointment of its first director, Sir Charles Lock Eastlake (uncle of the author of *History of the Gothic Revival*), in 1855. During Eastlake's ten-year term, the early Italian collection was greatly expanded, the huge Turner bequest was received (in 1856, the year in which the National Portrait Gallery was established), and Queen Victoria made a contribution of Italian, Nether-landish, and German paintings (1863), which added to the great Krüger collection which had been received in 1854. By 1888, the number of paintings had grown (from 149 in 1838) to 926. Meanwhile, the Royal Academy had moved, in 1869, to Burlington House, where the first summer exhibition drew over 300,000 attendance. Public awareness of the value of art was increasing so fast that in the 1860s auction prices soared.[65]

The son of a master-mason without access to private collections, Hardy was no longer largely confined, like many writers before him, to occasional auction rooms and holiday exhibitions. James's hero in *The Princess Casamassima* is similarly placed: 'some of the happiest moments of his life had been spent at the British Museum and the National Gallery' (XVII). In art as in architecture Hardy was singularly positioned to benefit by a major new avenue of creative inspiration.

The *Life* records that during his years in London his 'interest in painting led him to devote for many months, on every day that the National Gallery was open, twenty minutes after lunch to an inspection of the masters hung there, confining his attention to a single master on each visit, and forbidding his eyes to stray to any other' (*Life*, 52). By this method, Hardy said, a young person 'would insensibly acquire a greater insight into schools and styles . . . than from any guide-books'. Hardy himself was a water-colourist in these years and he would later supply his own drawings for *Wessex Poems*. In 1862 we find him listening to, and commenting on, Ruskin's *Modern Painters*, the last volume of which had appeared in 1860 (*Life*, 38). F. B. Pinion has listed an enormous number of Hardy's references to paintings in his novels, and Alistair Smart, in his important article on the novels, has found yet others: 'The influence, for example, of Hogarth upon Fielding, or of Guercino upon Stendhal, was a far more superficial and limited thing than the profound and far-reaching effect exerted by the whole heritage of European art upon Hardy's thought and sensibility.'[66] Hardy's surprising admiration for Scott's *The Bride of Lammermoor* ('an almost perfect specimen of form' – *Writings*, 121) may be due to the fact that the tale is an explication of a painting. The painter, Dick Tinto, who claims that a novel should use words like colours, has painted a scene: 'The light, admitted from the upper part of a high casement, fell upon a female figure of exquisite beauty. . . .' The viewer, he says, should gather 'from the position, attitude, and countenance of the moment, not only the history of the past lives' but their present and their future as well. Tinto's manuscript of notes on the scene are then sorted out by the narrator who 'wove it into the following Tale, in which, following in part . . . Tinto's advice, I endeavoured to render my narrative rather descriptive than dramatic' (Chapter 1).

Hardy's notebooks also contain many entries on painting which are copied from periodicals and books over a period of many years. Part of his extremely detailed notes of 1863, entitled 'Schools of Painting', also exists. The notes on the Italian Schools reveal that Hardy read carefully Luigi Lanzi's multi-volume *The History of Painting in Italy*, which Hardy either quotes or paraphrases, though he adds the most interesting observation himself.[67] He probably read Lanzi in the South Kensington Museum (*Life*, 38).

Hardy seemed to like paintings and etchings which emphasised chiaroscuro, the dramatic and symbolic effects of light and shade. He cites a 'Dureresque' effect in one of the Rainbarrow hill scenes in *Return of the Native*: 'Shadowy eye-sockets, deep as those of a death's head, suddenly turned into pits of lustre' (I, 3, p. 18). The sharp outline of a face against a dark-tanned background is compared to an effect of Rembrandt (II, 6, p. 161). He admired Gérôme's painting of the Crucifixion (exhibited at the Royal Academy in 1870): 'The *shadows only* of the three crucified ones are seen. A fine conception' (*Life*, 76). The memory of this painting stayed with Hardy, for in 1888 he remembered it again when commenting on the original insights achieved by a group of religious enthusiasts: 'They open fresh views of Christianity by turning it in reverse positions, as Gérôme the painter did by painting the *shadow* of the Crucifixion instead of the Crucifixion itself.'[68]

Hardy also liked paintings which associated such dramatic light effects with skeletal patterns:

The birds were crossing and recrossing the field of the glass in their flight hither and thither between the Strassburg chimneys, their sad grey forms sharply outlined against the sky, and their skinny legs showing beneath like the limbs of dead martyrs in Crivelli's emaciated imaginings. (*A Laodicean*, v, 1, pp. 329–30)

Similarly, when Angel Clare returns home in *Tess*: 'You could see the skeleton behind the man, and almost the ghost behind the skeleton. He matched Crivelli's dead *Christus*. His sunken eye-pits were of morbid hue, and the light in his eyes had waned'.[69] In one of his later poems Hardy will compare himself to a 'rag drawn over a skeleton, / As in El Greco's canvases . . . Whose cheeks have slipped down, lips become indrawn' (666).

Hardy also admired Hobbema's 'The Avenue' (*Life*, 120), with its picture of a human figure framed in the middle of a long receding avenue of trees. He mentioned the picture in 1878 and in 1883 cited Hobbema's vision of 'a straight open road, bordered by thin lank trees, all sloping away from the south-west wind-quarter' (*The Romantic Adventures of a Milkmaid*, IX, p. 360). Some time later, at the Wallace Collection, Hardy might have seen a similar vista by Aelbert Cuyp, 'The Avenue at Meerdervoort'. In 1878 Hardy had coupled Hobbema's painting with Boldini's 'The Morning Walk' (sic) which relies on a somewhat similar effect of lines which converge in the background.[70] These two paintings are perhaps the respective models for two of Hardy's own drawings in *Wessex Poems*: the country road, the distant figures, and interlacing branches drawn for 'Her Death and After'; the gentleman on the square-faced avenue flanked by receding buildings with their narrow windows, drawn for 'The Burghers'. In the first drawing Hardy completes the pattern by joining the overarching trees; in the second, he sharpens the pattern by stressing the outline of the windows. (See Illustrations 7 and 8.)

Hardy is interested in the coalescence of these various effects, the patterns of light and shade, the patterns of the ageing body, the perspective patterns of a changing and receding outer world in the midst of which we take our journey through life. On 3 January 1886 he says: 'My art is to intensify the expression of things, as is done by Crivelli, Bellini, etc., so that the heart and inner meaning is made vividly visible' (*Life*, 177). Again, the meaning of this remark is more specific than is usually supposed. The previous entry in the *Life*, for 2 January, connects the human and natural patterns within a temporal perspective: 'Cold weather brings out upon the faces of people the written marks of their habits, vices, passions, and memories, as warmth brings out on paper a writing in sympathetic ink.'

It might also be noted here that Hardy admired the stark etchings of William Strang (Purdy and Millgate, *Letters*, 275, 284), though his enthusiasm seemed to wane in later years (Collins, *Talks*, 61). Strang composed on extraordinary number of portraits of Hardy – at least ten – made over a twenty-eight-year period, 1892–1920. Strang's etching, 'The Crucifixion' (1914), imitates Gérôme's device of giving the 'shadows only' of the crucified one; and perhaps Hardy discussed the effect with him. Hardy would surely have known Strang's noted etching of 1889, 'The End', in which Death looks through a window patterned with cobwebs.[71] In 1882 Hardy had observed: 'A skeleton – the one used in these lectures – is hung up inside the window. We face it as we sit. Outside the band is playing, and the children are dancing. I can see their little figures through the window past the skeleton dangling in front' (*Life*, 157).

From his background in painting and Gothic architecture, Hardy brings to his literary work the desire to create a literary equivalent for a pictorial effect, so that the manner by which a reader processes a poem in time will be equivalent to the manner by which a viewer processes a painting in space. Alastair Smart says of the Gérôme painting that only when the 'viewer has had time to recognize the significance of the three long shadows in the foreground' does he become 'aware, with startled surprise, of the nature of the event that is being presented to him'.[72] In his poetry, Hardy will try for a similar effect, drawing the reader's imagination into contemplation of a pattern whose implications will surprise him. In describing the Gérôme painting, Hardy, we saw, compared a reversal in one's estimation of a religious phenomenon to a reversal in one's realisation of a painting, both producing a sense of imaginative deepening and new understanding.

To make this link between pictorial realisation and growing awareness, Hardy explores the process by which one pattern of light and shade reverses or changes to the opposite pattern. Perhaps the most interesting image which Hardy found in the Gothic novels of his childhood was one from Grant's *The Scottish Cavalier*. Walter is in his dungeon cell where 'a single ray of sunlight . . . penetrating the cobwebs and dust of the prison window, radiated through its deep embrasure, and threw the iron gratings in strong shadow on the paved floor'. Later in the day:

> The shadow of the grating on the floor grew less and less distinct, for as the light faded, his vaulted prison became darker, until all became blackness around him. Anon the pallid moon rose slowly into its place, and from the blue southern sky poured a cold but steady flood of silver

light into the cheerless room, and again, for a time, the shadow of the massive grating was thrown on the discoloured floor.   (I, p. 79)

In his own novels Hardy gives such change a clearly *gestalt* character. At a critical moment in *Desperate Remedies*, when the church burns, 'the square outline of the church tower, on the other side of the way, which had hitherto been a dark mass against a sky comparatively light, now began to appear as a light object against a sky of darkness. . . .' (X, 3, p. 196). Another such effect is described at the beginning of *A Pair of Blue Eyes*:

> The dusk had thickened into darkness while they thus conversed, and the outline and surface of the mansion gradually disappeared. The windows, which had before been as black blots on a lighter expanse of wall, became illuminated, and were transfigured to squares of light on the general dark body of the night landscape as it absorbed the outlines of the edifice into its gloomy monochrome.   (2, pp. 7 – 8)

'In Her Precincts' (411) clearly relates such a *gestalt* to a change in consciousness. The poem describes a lover who journeys to his girl-friend's home, 'the square of each window a dull black blur'. But he is deceived in her, she is partying: 'The black squares grew to be squares of light. . . .' One of Hardy's drawings in *Wessex Poems*, illustrating 'Leipzig', seems to catch such an effect. A fiddler stands at dusk outside the lit windows of a tavern, just at the point when the lighted windows begin to dominate the scene. Two other drawings, one for 'San Sebastian' and another for 'Leipzig', catch the moment when the dusk changes to evening and tiny gimlets of light from windows begin to punctuate the surroundings. (See Illustration 11.)

A description in the *Life* captures the moment when dark leaves against a daylight background begin to change to moon-lit leaves against a dark background: 'We sat down by daylight, and as we dined the moon brightened the trees in the garden, and shone under them into the room' (122). The reverse effect, a rich night-time pattern blanching into a day-time pattern, is described in *The Hand of Ethelberta*. When the curtains are opened and the day is revealed, the brilliant shapes of the ballroom metamorphose: 'the hitherto beaming candle-flames [were] shining no more radiantly than tarnished javelin-heads, while the snow-white lengths of wax showed themselves clammy and cadaverous. . . . The leaves and flowers which had appeared so very green and blooming by the artificial light were now seen to be faded and dusty' (5, p. 43). I think Lowell suggests a somewhat similar effect in his poem on Hardy as he looks

through the window of memory to contemplate the Hardy landscape:
'Perhaps the trees stopped growing in summer amnesia.' But the window
becomes blanched: 'Ah the light lights the window of my young night, /
and you never turn off the light' ('The Lesson').

Light and Branch

Night lights and branching patterns enable Hardy to achieve his most
interesting lighting effects and relate them to the development of a pattern
in the mind and in the world. The moon for example makes the ghostly
pattern emerge, just as the outline we never saw during the day we now see
at night: [73]

> And through the thin thorn hedge, by the rays of the moon,
> I can see the tree in the field, and beside it the mound –
> Now sheeted with snow – whereon we sat that June. . . .   (827)

'I looked back as I left the house, / And . . . The moon upsidled through
the boughs' (902). 'A bough outside is waving, / And that's its shade by
the moon' (537).[74] In these cases, a betrayal of love that still traumatises
the speaker, a sundering of lovers in ways they did not realise at the time,
the imprint of a ghostly vision on the living – all contribute to the fulling
pattern. 'In Sherborne Abbey' (726) links the moon's irradiation with the
'insistent'[75] Gothic pattern:

> The moon has passed to the panes of the south-aisle wall,
> And brought the mullioned shades and shines to fall
> On the cheeks of a woman and a man in a pew there.
>
> . . . .
>
> Forms round them loom, recumbent like their own,
> Yet differing; for they are chiselled in frigid stone.

But the living and dead forms are not so different after all. The living forms
which emerge out of the dark into the patterned moonlight will assumed
their engraved fate:

> And a cloud comes over the moon:
> The print of the panes upon them enfeebles, as fallen in a swoon,
> Until they are left in darkness unbroke and profound,
> As likewise are left their chill and chiselled neighbours around.[76]

'A Hurried Meeting' (810) is Hardy's most elaborate narrative example of this symbolism. The poem, about an unwed mother, describes an 'August moonlight' setting where 'elms . . . [o]utscreen the noon and eve', and where a mansion 'mute in its woodland wreathing' casts a 'faint irradiation' on the slope. The woman slips '[t]o the moonshade' and keeps brushing the 'gossamer-web' off her naked neck, but it keeps clinging to her as closely as her sad fate. At the end, 'she emerged from shade to the moonlight ray'. Thus the 'sweet allure' of a 'witching' love draws to its 'heart-outeating' conclusion. In 'The Harbour Bridge' (742) the bridge's 'lines of rope and spar / Trace themselves black as char'. Through them we see the 'cut black-paper portraits' of people including a couple who face a tragic separation:

> They go different ways.
> And the west dims, and yellow lamplights shine:
> And soon above, like lamps more opaline,
> White stars ghost forth, that care not for men's wives,
>   Or any other lives.

A similar emergence of light marks a new and ominous experience in 'The Wind's Prophecy': 'every chasm and every steep / Blackens as wakes each pharos-shine' (440).

Both these last poems focus on the transition between dusk and dark and make this period symbolise the setting in of a future life pattern. 'The Revisitation' (152) focuses on the transition between dawn and day and makes this transition symbolise the realisation of a past life-pattern.[77] The speaker begins the process of realisation with his 'faint eyes on the feeble square of wan-lit window frame'. The poem is full of ominous light changes, as when the peewits reveal 'their pale pinions like a fitful phosphorescence / Up against the cope of cloud'. The obsolescence of the pattern is fully revealed when the harsh 'upedging sun' blanches the space around and reveals the lines of age in the well-beloved. He then watches her form 'smaller grow and smaller'.

Thus the light and pattern image can represent various stages of development and realisation. It can give a rich tragic weight to the slightest moment. As an 'enthralled' lover journeys home in 'First Sight of Her and After' (361), 'the pattern grows / Of moonshades on the way'. In retrospect Hardy saw his life as dominated by the image. At the beginning of a life or a love or a vision, and at their skeletal conclusions, the pattern presides in 'At Moonrise and Onwards' (517):

>   – How many a year
>   Have you kept pace with me,
> Wan Woman of the waste up there,
>   Behind a hedge, or the bare
>   Bough of a tree!
>
>   No novelty are you,
>   O Lady of all my time,
> Veering unbid into my view
>   Whether I near Death's mew,
>   Or Life's top cyme!

Since the moon in this poem is a 'furtive feminine shape' and 'reluctantly' reveals itself 'nude of cloud', the moon's pattern is elusive, hidden, belatedly revealed. It leads the heart and mind into their expansions (here an inflorescence peaking in a cyme) until the pattern twists into a coil in which the mind finds itself mewed up. To this parallel of nature and Gothic architecture images, I shall return in a moment.

Finally, in 'A Cathedral Façade at Midnight' (667), Hardy applies the waxing-waning light paradox to the 'development' of old ideas and beliefs, symbolised in the old statues:

> The lunar look skimmed scantly toe, breast, arm,
>   Then edged on slowly, slightly,
> To shoulder, hand, face; till each austere form
>   Was blanched its whole length brightly
> Of prophet, king, queen, cardinal in state,
> That dead men's tools had striven to simulate;
> And the stiff images stood irradiate.

Irradiated, the obsolescence of the images is exposed – as though the moon-lit pattern had cooperated with 'the sure, unhasting, steady stress / Of Reason's movement, making meaningless / The coded creeds of old-time godliness'.

It is typical of Hardy's coherent sensibility that he believed Salisbury's 'graceful cathedral pile was the most marked instance in England of an architectural intention carried out to the full' (*Life*, 295). His essay, 'Memories of Church Restoration', shows that he was thinking primarily of the west façade as seen from the north-east corner of the Close (*Writings*, 214). On a visit there, shortly before composing 'A Cathedral Façade at Midnight', he wrote:

Salisbury. Went into the Close late at night. The moon was visible through both the north and south clerestory windows to me standing on the turf on the north side. . . . Walked to the west front, and watched the moonlight creep round upon the statuary of the façade – stroking tentatively and then more and more firmly the prophets, the martyrs, the bishops, the kings, and the queens. (*Life*, 296).

The Salisbury façade, reproduced in Illustration 12, was one of three examples Hardy cited when he discussed Gothic architecture's 'aesthetic phantom without solidarity' (*Writings*, 214; cf. above, p. 56). During his lifetime Hardy returned again and again to this cathedral (*Life*, 420 and *passim*).

Biblical Shadows

In dramatising the relation between the synchronic and diachronic dimensions of a pattern, Hardy went back to the book that influenced him before most others. His patterns, for example, work not only like a Darwinian evolutionary pattern but like the pattern of God's judgement in the Old Testament. There is a strong biblical echo in Darwin himself. Nature's laws are 'silently and insensibly working' over a period whose length 'impresses my mind almost in the same manner as does the vain endeavour to grapple with the idea of eternity'. In present history however, 'we only see that the forms of life are now different from what they formerly were'.[78] In the biblical passages Hardy loved, he found a similar process at work. God's judgement works quietly for years and ages, and suddenly the form of that judgement is revealed: 'Thou sweep'st us off as with a flood, / We vanish hence like dreams.'[79] In each case, the pattern grows in darkness and the mind cannot follow it. Yet when the pattern's final form is revealed, the process seems, to our minds, to have occurred with spectral speed. A similar paradox can be found in the Greek version of the fates – Clotho slowly spinning the thread, Atropos suddenly cutting it. Both ancient images fitted well with the geological uniformitarianism of Lyell and Darwin. Describing Troy's discovery of his own true nature in *Far from the Madding Crowd*, Hardy wrote:

The suddenness was probably more apparent than real. A coral reef which just comes short of the ocean surface is no more to the horizon than if it had never been begun, and the mere finishing stroke is what often appears to create an event which has long been potentially an accomplished thing. (46, p. 364)

Hardy also carefully read Gibbon and surely enjoyed Gibbon's vision of the epochs of human history which proceed as stealthily as the epochs of an individual life:

> We imperceptibly advance from youth to age, without observing the gradual, but incessant, change of human affairs, and, even in our larger experiences of history, the imagination is accustomed, by a perpetual series of causes and effects, to unite the most distant revolutions. But, if the interval between two memorable areas could be instantly annihilated; if it were possible, after a momentary slumber of two hundred years, to display the *new* world to the eyes of a spectator, who still retained a lively and recent impression of the *old*; his surprise and his reflections would furnish the pleasing subject of a philosophical romance. (XXXIII)

If Gibbon's last phrase suggests Hawthorne rather than Hardy, Hardy would also explore the spell of reveries which can last moments or lifetimes and even bind generations. Gibbon is here referring to an earlier form of the Rip van Winkle motif – that of the Seven Sleepers who fell asleep in a pagan age only to wake two hundred years later in a Christian one. Hardy would not miss the Gibbonesque irony: the sleepers 'related their story, and at the same instant peaceably expired'.[80]

Thus the growth of a pattern in Hardy's poetry is often accompanied by a shadow which moves with imperceptible slowness and then suddenly extends itself, its import fully revealed. 'Shades far extend / Like lives soon to end' (675). Death is imminent when 'evening shades are stretching out' (660). The sun throws 'a shade to where / Time travelled at that minute. . . . Little saw we in it' (484). Shadows attend a chapel-organist's suicidal plot (the patterned light of the 'lowering sun peering in at the window-pane' throws 'shades from the boys of the chore / In the gallery, right upon me'). At the end of the poem, 'the sun lowers and goes; shades deepen; the lights are turned up' (593). A woman sings the same early love-song 'when in afteryears / The shades stretched out, / And paths were faint' (532). 'The shadows of the evening are stretched out', Hardy marked in *Jeremiah*. He made note of this 'beautiful chapter' on the same day he described the visits to Salisbury and Stonehenge cited above (*Life*, 296). He also made note of Psalm 109: 'I am gone like the shadow when it declineth.'[81] We have already cited the growing 'pattern' of 'moon-shades' in 'First Sight of Her and After' (361). We seem to miss the intermediate stages of our directioned lives just as Hardy misses the summer in 'Before and after Summer' (273). In February he sees a radiant

1 Hardy's graveyard drawing for 'Her Death and After'

2 Hardy's drawing for 'Her Dilemma'

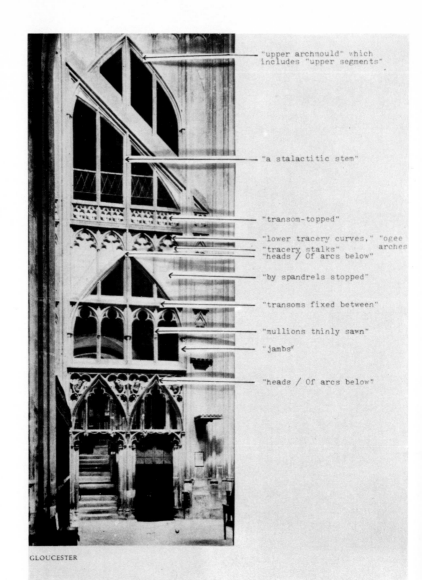

"upper archmould" which
includes "upper segments"

"a stalactitic stem"

"transom-topped"

"lower tracery curves," "ogee
"tracery stalks"   arches
"heads / Of arcs below"

"by spandrels stopped"

"transoms fixed between"

"mullions thinly sawn"

"jambs"

"heads / Of arcs below"

GLOUCESTER

3 'The Abbey Mason' and the Gloucester transept

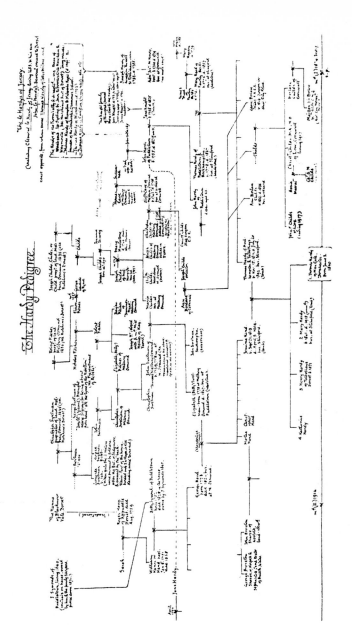

4 Hardy's family pedigree in his handwriting

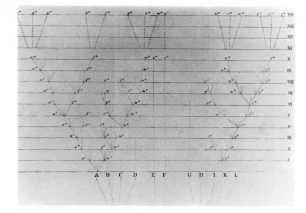

5 *Left*: Darwin's diagram of the Pedigree of Species

6 *Below*: Gérôme: 'Golgotha: "It is Finished"'

7 Hobbema's 'The Avenue' and Hardy's drawing for 'Her Death and After'

8 Boldini's 'Morning Stroll' and Hardy's drawing for 'The Burghers'

W. STRANG
1910

Thomas Hardy.

9 Strang's 1910 Order of Merit portrait of Hardy

10 *Facing page*: Strang's 'The End'

12 *Above*: Cathedral Façade at Salisbury

13 *Below*: Hardy's drawing, following 'In a Eweleaze Near Weatherbury'

14 Pugin's *Contrasts*: (*above*) 'The Catholic Town in 1440 . . . (*below*) The Same Town in 1840'

THE SAME TOWN IN 1840

1. St Michael's Tower, rebuilt in 1750. 2. New Parsonage House & Pleasure Grounds. 3. The New Jail. 4. Gas Works. 5. Lunatic Asylum. 6. Iron Works & Ruins of St Marie's Abbey. 7. W.E.son Chapel. 8. Baptist Chapel. 9. Unitarian Chapel. 10. New Church. 11. New Town Hall & Concert Room. 12. Wesleyan Centenary Chapel. 13. New Christian Society. 14. Quakers Meeting. 15. Socialist Hall of Science.

15 'The Four Horsemen' from Dürer's *Apocalypse*

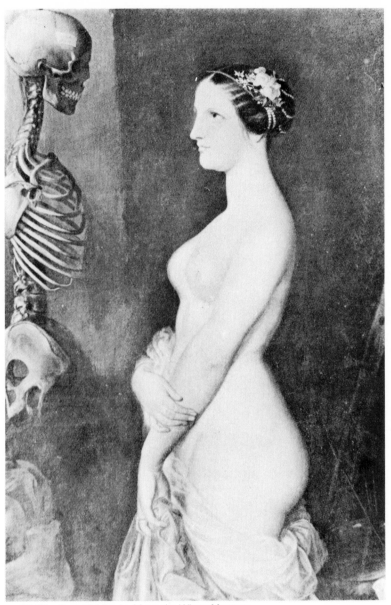

16 'The Beautiful Rosine' from the Wiertz Museum

17 Strang's 'Grotesque'

18 Strang's 'Danse Macabre'

19 *Above*: William Blake's 'Pity'

20 *Below*: Strang's 'War'

pattern in the 'shafts of sleet . . . a half-transparent blind / Riddled by rays from sun behind'. He hopes for summer only to find himself in winter again: 'Shadows of the October pine / Reach into this room of mine.' When did the 'happy suns' of summer occur? 'I, alas, perceived not when.' 'No prelude did I there perceive / To a drama at all,' Hardy writes in 'At the Word "Farewell"' (360), 'Or foreshadow what fortune might weave / From beginnings so small.' Hardy's most skilful example of literal foreshadowing is probably 'A Man Was Drawing Near to Me' (536):

> I'd no concern at anything,
> No sense of coming pull-heart play;
> Yet, under the silent outspreading
> > Of even's wing
> > Where Otterham lay,
> A man was riding up my way.
>
> . . . .
>
> There was no light at all inland,
> Only the seaward pharos-fire,
> Nothing to let me understand.
>
> . . . .
>
> And but a minute passed before,
> > With gaze that bore
> > My destiny,
> The man revealed himself to me.

We might apply to Hardy's poems John Livingston Lowes' suggestive remark about the novels: 'We move with Hardy at life's crucial moments through a taciturn, brooding, crepuscular world, in which dread things awaited come to pass, as if the waiting and the coming were, through some unconscious power that works through each, one thing.'[82] At least so it seems because of the terrible tricks reality plays on our minds.

'Lying Awake' as Synthesis

Hardy's most suggestive synthesis of the elements we have traced — branching patterns, engraved imprints, spectral illuminations, subtle shades — is perhaps 'Lying Awake' (844). It was first published the year before Hardy died.

> You, Morningtide Star, now are steady-eyed, over the east,
> > I know it as if I saw you;

You, Beeches, engrave on the sky your thin twigs, even the least;
   Had I paper and pencil I'd draw you.

You, Meadow, are white with your counterpane cover of dew,
   I see it as if I were there;
You, Churchyard, are lightening faint from the shade of the yew,
   The names creeping out everywhere.

The last line is surprising because it suddenly shifts the perspective from the speaker, presumably musing in his bed, to people underground, whose names creep out everywhere. The shift of perspective makes us wonder: who is lying awake? Are the living observer and the living dead in some sense the same? This eerie suggestion is supported by the change from the natural light of the star in the first stanza to the negative light cast by the shade of the yew in the last stanza.[83] Lying Awake seems to be an activity, partly conscious, partly organic, which includes everything – the 'steady-eyed' stars, the beeches which seem actively to engrave the sky, the meadow slumbering under *its* counterpane, and the speaker. The final 'lightening faint' emergence of the shadowy light is a fitting accompaniment to our shock at the life of those names. We glimpse that obscure depth where human awareness and nature meet and evolve into the consummate engravements of a white tombstone.

   John Betjeman's poem, 'The Heart of Thomas Hardy', may serve as a reading of 'Lying Awake'. His poem ends with an eerie cogency and suggests that unseen connection between the workings of the mind and the workings of nature. After Hardy's death, Tess, Jude, and the others

   Slowly started to turn in the light of their own Creator
   Died away in the night as frost will blacken a dahlia.

The play of light values comes right out of Hardy.[84]

Hardy's Theory of Poetry

Hardy's pattern represents an important response to nineteenth-century aesthetic theory. From Collins's 'Ode to Evening' through Keats and Shelley to Ruskin and the Pre-Raphaelites and finally to Hopkins, the pattern image represents the most widely shared view of the creative mind: the coalescence of mind and nature in an aesthetic harmony. Keats's image of the 'wreath'd trellis of a working brain' ('Ode to Psyche') captures this nicely. Hopkins's inscape most fully exploits the tradition. Hardy's development of the pattern image is at least as subtle as Hopkins's but has gone unrecognised. Hopkins indeed may owe one of his most famous pied patterns to a reading of Hardy.[85]

One reason Hardy proves so recalcitrant to many readers like Blackmur is that he represents an aesthetic that radically modifies the mainstream tradition. Hopkins's patterns, as in the fragment on 'Asboughs', represent 'old earth's groping towards the steep / Heaven whom she childs us by'. Hardy's patterns represent mind and earth, gripped by each other and growing out of touch as time passes. The pattern is 'a going to Nature' and 'yet the result is . . . purely the product of the writer's own mind'. Synchronically, this is a contradiction. Diachronically, it is tragically true. The linking term between the two phrases (from Hardy's statement which we quoted at the outset) is 'idiosyncrasy' which Nature gives the artist so that he observes one 'pattern among general things'. This pattern is developed by 'the writer's own mind' but remains within the larger pattern of reality, two patterns which will jar when consummation comes. 'At Moonrise and Onwards' is a good expression of Hardy's aesthetic which must be sharply distinguished from the kind of mainstream aesthetic expressed, for example, in Archibald Macleish's *Ars Poetica*:

> A poem should be motionless in time
> As the moon climbs,
>
> Leaving, as the moon releases
> Twig by twig the night-entangled trees,
>
> Leaving, as the moon behind the winter leaves,
> Memory by memory the mind –

Hardy re-conceives entirely the poem's relation to reality. It is not a Keatsian urn which transcends the time-bound pattern it expresses.

'What the imagination seizes as Beauty must be truth,' Keats said, and Hardy was fascinated by the kind of romantic image which expresses this harmony. In *Endymion* he made a notation against Keats's description of Peona's bower: 'an arbour, overwove / By many a summer's silent fingering.'[86] Shelley's 'The Woodman and the Nightingale' is a lush exploration of this kind of imagery, and from it Hardy copied in his notebook: 'Traceries [of trees] in which there is . . . the mute persuasion of unkindled melodies.' Hardy added that Shelley's passage shows 'the future in the present'.[87] He may have remembered Keats's classic statement: 'The Imagination may be compared to Adam's dream – he awoke and found it truth.'

But for Hardy the imagination 'comes true' in a way that exposes the dream. In the winter of 1887 Hardy wrote: 'Nature is played out as a Beauty, but not as a Mystery. . . . I want to see the deeper reality underlying the scenic, the expression of what are sometimes called abstract imaginings. . . . The 'simply natural' is interesting no longer. . . . [I]t is a student's style – the style of a period when the mind is serene and unawakened to the tragical mysteries of life; when it does not bring anything to the object that coalesces with and translates the qualities that are already there, – half hidden, it may be – and the two united are depicted as the All' (*Life*, 185). The difference between this notion of coalescence and the romantic notion lies in the phrase, 'the tragical mysteries of life'. I hardly mean to imply that Hardy's predecessors were not awakened to the tragical mysteries or that their poems are not profound responses to these mysteries. But I do wish to suggest that the design of Hardy's poetry, its meditative structure, its images, its language, and its rhythms, dramatise the tragic mysteries in a unique and consistent way.

Indeed, there is one more image in the mainstream tradition which may have keyed Hardy's new understanding of the tragic dimension of an aesthetic pattern. Shelley influenced Hardy more than any other poet. The image is from Shelley's 'Alastor'. Alastor is caught up in a visionary 'web / Of many-coloured woof' produced by the music of 'woven sounds of streams of breezes'. But the vision fades and Alastor journeys to a well which '[i]mages all the woven boughs above' and 'some inconstant star, / Between one foliaged lattice twinkling far'. In the well he sees his eyes' 'own wan light through the reflected line / Of his thin hair'.

From 'Alastor' to 'A Light Snow-Fall after Frost' is a complex pilgrimage. And the road goes through a forest of Gothic architecture.

The theory of artistic creation associated with Gothic architecture is perhaps the closest equivalent to Hardy's theory of the creative mind. The theory that Gothic architecture originated by an unconscious growth out of plant and arboreal forms or else by a conscious imitation of these forms lingered long in popular consciousness. Hardy knew well Scott's description in 'The Lay of the Last Minstrel' of the moon shining through 'slender shafts of shapely stone, / By foliaged tracery combined':

> Thou would'st have thought some fairy's hand
> 'Twixt poplars straight the osier wand,
>   In many a freakish knot, had twined;
> Then framed a spell, when the work was done,
> And changed the willow-wreaths to stone.

(Canto Second, XI)

Hardy's description in *The Mayor of Casterbridge* of 'the dark dense old avenues, or rather vaults of living woodwork' (17, p. 125) typifies the nature-architecture parallel which he often noted and cited in his novels.

The theory of the connection, however, was widely attacked by informed commentators.[88] Ruskin, for example, said that Gothic was not derived 'from vegetation, – the symmetry of avenues, and the interlacing of branches' but rather 'developed itself into, a resemblance to vegetation'. But he then added:

> It was no chance suggestion of the form of an arch from the bending of a bough, but a gradual and continual discovery of a beauty in natural forms which could be more and more perfectly transferred into those of stone, that influenced at once the heart of the people, and the form of the edifice.

Ruskin does not say how early this discovery began to occur, nor does he make clear whether the influence worked by conscious imitation or by unconscious association. Thus he could be cited as a support for the theory of origins which he attacked. But this parallel between forms of stone and forms of nature, and the rich ambiguity of this parallel, expresses well the aesthetic underlying Hardy's poems.

Hardy's aesthetic pattern is in the world and in the mind. It is something seen and it is that by which we see. It originates in ourselves and in a world that works through us. It works in the present and binds us to the past. It is the conscious object of the artist and it is his unconscious inspiration. It is his art and his life. It is beautiful and tragic.

Hardy's final drawing in the main section of *Wessex Poems* is a good expression of this aesthetic (see Illustration 13). A pair of eyeglasses is juxtaposed on the natural landscape. It is unclear whether we are looking through them at the scene, or the scene is looking through them at us. In either case, the pattern in the scene is brought to a focus through man's aging crippled eyes.[89]

Might it still be said that Hardy's concern with tragic patterns is obsessive and restrictive? For myself, I experience exhilaration in following Hardy's patterns. They are complex and beautiful and economical in themselves. And they intimate the world outside the glasses, a world whose variety exceeds any monopolisation of it for literary purposes. The typical Hardy poem is a model of a binding and a collision between these two hemispheres, but each poem also leaves us a little freer, 'less deceived', more able to see in time, but never fully able. 'If way to the Better there be, it exacts a full look at the Worst.'

THE DEVELOPMENT OF HARDY'S PATTERNS:
THE NOVELS

One of the specific ways of seeing Hardy's development as a poet is by tracing the way he evolved a deeper understanding of the pattern image.

Of the eighty-eight examples we have given in all connections, only sixteen come from the period before Emma's death in 1912. Of these, three are from the 1860s, nine were written about the turn of the century, four are from the period shortly preceding Emma's death.[90] Five of these were cited as examples of Hardy using a Gothic setting in a novelistic way as the background of his poem. After Emma's death in 1912, we see a pronounced trend on Hardy's part to internalise the Gothic pattern. Seventy-two of the examples were written or published after Emma's death. The most elaborate and intricate examples of the *gestalt* pattern seem to occur late: 'The Pedigree' (1916), the second stanza of 'A Light Snow-Fall after Frost' (pub. 1925), 'In Sherborne Abbey' (pub. 1925), 'A Hurried Meeting' (pub. 1925), and 'Lying Awake' (pub. 1927).

In his important essay on Hardy's novels, John Holloway has explored Hardy's interest in Nature as a complex system modifying and controlling the immense variety of life. 'Nothing can be seen in isolation. Hardy's view always quickly expands until it depicts something of a whole landscape, of the varied integration of a region.'[91] Holloway does not cite many images of a pattern; nor can I hope to treat the subject adequately here. But a few suggestions can be made.

Hardy's first sentence in his first published novel begins with the phrase: 'In the long and intricately inwrought chain of circumstance.' Knowledge of the pattern is the beginning of 'Taking Thought', as Cytherea discovers at her father's death and she steps into a 'labyrinth . . . to continue a perplexed course along its mazes. . . .' (*Desperate Remedies* I, 3, p. 9). Toward the end of the novel Hardy writes: 'Each and all were alike in this one respect, that they followed a solitary trail like the inwoven threads which form a banner, and all were equally unconscious of the significant whole which they collectively showed forth' (XVI, 4, p. 354). What we will see in Hardy's novels is a deepening sense of life-patterns which takes the form of a philosophical statement or an image. The most common images in the early novels are interlaced branches (through which starlight or firelight penetrates) and silhouetted outlines against the sky. Examples of these and others occur in *Under the Greenwood Tree* (1872), where the image stands for the pastoral network of the novel; in *A Pair of Blue Eyes* (1873), where the image is also associated with a process of discovery; and in *Far from the Madding Crowd* (1874), where the pied patterns at the beginning climax in the dance of death patterns of the lightning storm. *A Laodicean* and *Two on a Tower* begin with interesting pattern images but the early potential of these novels is perhaps not fulfilled. *The Return of the Native* (1878) and *The Mayor of Casterbridge* (1885) are periodically enriched by the image. The latter also associates the image with a Gothic context. Lucetta's residence, though a Paladian structure, is built around a Gothic door with a chipped gargoyle: 'At night the forms of passengers were patterned by the lamps in black shadows upon the pale walls'.[92]

Hardy's climactic use of pattern imagery occurs in *The Woodlanders* (1887) and *Tess of the d'Urbervilles* (1891). *The Woodlanders* contains almost as many pattern images as all the earlier novels put together.[93] The novel repeats the *Desperate Remedies* type of statement: 'their lonely courses formed no detached design at all, but were part of the pattern in the great web of human beings then weaving in both hemispheres' (3, p. 21). But in the later novel such general statements are extraordinarily enriched by the multitude of images associated with the woodland tracks of Little Hintock.[94] Such an exploration of his favourite image is also consistent with what George Fayen points out about this novel, that it represents an important stage in Hardy's growing self-consciousness about his art. This is also the novel in which Hardy seems most interested in the meditative reveries of his characters: their 'reasoning proceeds on narrow premises, and results in inferences wildly imaginative' (I, p. 4). Pattern images are often associated with a character's reverie and they symbolise both external world patterns and internal mental patterns bound in a complicated mesh. The novel bears several resemblances to *Middlemarch* (discussed above), but where Eliot's pattern metaphors tend to remain abstract, Hardy's are rooted in Hintock vegetation. This is also the novel in which, as Fayen points out, Hardy is most interested in his own point of view as narrator for whom the novel is an act of memory. In order to make the transition from novel to poem, Hardy must lift himself into the novel, cease to be the detached observer, and find the patterns within his own reveries.

Perhaps Hardy sensed the poetic potential of the novel when he reread it in 1912. He said he liked it '*as a story*, the best of all. Perhaps that is owing to the locality and scenery of the action, a part I am very fond of' (*Life*, 358, also see 185). The comment asserts the vital connection of the story and the scenery. He also told Frank Hedgcock: 'He liked *The Woodlanders*, too, more for its trees than its actors.' ('Reminiscences of Thomas Hardy', p. 225.)

The last nature network image which I have been able to find in the novels is, for me, the most interesting of all. It is the crystallised cobweb image which occurs late in *Tess of the d'Urbervilles* after a series of earlier images.[95] It will later be used in one of Hardy's most interesting stanzas, the second stanza of 'A Light Snow-Fall after Frost' which was discussed in the Introduction.

In the last chapter of *Tess* Hardy also makes an interesting discovery about the Gothic sources of his pattern imagery. It should be connected with an earlier passage in *The Woodlanders*, where Giles Winterborne has followed the woodland track into Sherton Abbas:

> . . . the churches, the abbey, and other mediaeval buildings on this clear bright morning having the linear distinctness of architectural drawings, as if the original dream and vision of the conceiving master-mason were for a brief hour flashed down through the centuries to an unappreciative age. Giles saw their eloquent look on this day of transparency, but could not construe it. (5, p. 39)

Hardy would construe the image for the rest of his life. The last chapter of *Tess* includes another architectural picture:

> The prospect from this summit was almost unlimited. In the valley beneath lay the city they had just left, its more prominent buildings showing as in an isometric drawing – among them the broad cathedral tower, with its Norman windows and immense length of aisle and nave, the spires of St Thomas's, the pinnacled tower of the College, and, more to the right, the tower and gables of the ancient hospice, where to this day the pilgrim may receive his dole of bread and ale. Behind the city swept the rotund upland of St Catherine's Hill; further off, landscape beyond landscape, till the horizon was lost in the radiance of the sun hanging above it.
>
> Against these far stretches of country rose, in front of the other city edifices, a large red-brick building, with level grey roofs, and rows of short barred windows bespeaking captivity, the whole contrasting greatly by its formalism with the quaint irregularities of the Gothic erections. It was somewhat disguised from the road in passing it by yews and evergreen oaks, but it was visible enough up here. The wicket from which the pair had lately emerged was in the wall of this structure. From the middle of the building an ugly flat-topped octagonal tower ascended against the east horizon, and viewed from this spot, on its shady side and against the light, it seemed the one blot on the city's beauty.

I have quoted this passage at length because it may draw upon what is perhaps the most famous picture of Gothic architecture in the nineteenth century, namely that which Pugin used to illustrate the second edition of his *Contrasts: or, a Parallel between the Noble Edifices of the Middle Ages, and Corresponding Buildings of the Present Day; Shewing the Present Decay of Taste.* Pugin includes juxtaposed pictures of an English town as seen in 1440 and in 1840. (See Illustration 14.) Readers will enjoy comparing Hardy's details with Pugin's. Of course, Hardy's town 'Wintoncester' is also modelled on Winchester, the Saxon Wintanceaster. Of such parallels, Hardy said that 'the portraiture of fictitiously named towns . . . was only suggested by certain real places, and wantonly wanders from 'inventorial descriptions of them' (*Writings*, 47). While many details correspond, Hardy's imaginative rendering was probably influenced by Pugin's panorama, with its sense of prospect, its clarities, its sharp outlines, its sense of tradition, and, above all, its contrasts between the old and the new (with a prison dominating the new). Hardy's first paragraph gives the 'old' Wintoncester, his second paragraph gives the 'new'. What he has done – or what Winchester like many English towns has done – is juxtapose the two views and re-arrange many of the characteristic details. And he has placed the image at the final point of the novel. The old order is giving place to the new, and Tess is symbolically the victim of this change.[96]

In *Jude the Obscure*, Gothic Christminster is the central setting of the novel. Returning to the image Giles could not construe in *The Woodlanders*, Hardy has Jude contemplate the ancient setting, 'the lines of the buildings being as distinct in the morning air as in an architectural drawing' (III, 9, p. 223). The Wessex Edition of *Jude* has a beautiful frontispiece photograph illustrating this prospect. Indeed, although Jude is the victim of Christminster's obsolete medievalism, he cannot help marvelling at the poetry of the old forms:

> The City of learning wore an estranged look, and he had lost all feeling for its associations. Yet as the sun made vivid lights and shades of the mullioned architecture of the façades, and drew patterns of the crinkled battlements on the young turf of the quadrangles, Jude thought he had never seen the place look more beautiful. (III, 8, p. 213)

While he was writing *Jude*, Hardy said he regretted the social system 'under which all temperaments are bound to shape themselves to a single pattern of living'.[97]

THE DEVELOPMENT OF HARDY'S PATTERNS: *THE DYNASTS* AND THE POEMS

The change to poetry, Hardy said, 'was not so great as it seemed. . . .

He had mostly aimed at keeping his narratives close to natural life and as near to poetry in their subject as the conditions would allow' (*Life*, 291). In 1897, the year before *Wessex Poems* appeared, he said that he 'meant to make a poem of the strange feeling implanted by this black silhouette of the mountain [the Matterhorn] on the pattern of the constellation; but never did, so far as is known' (*Life*, 294). Many of the cosmological poems, written about this time and published in 1901, rely on the pattern image. The natural pattern becomes the 'world-webs' (80) woven by the blind 'World-weaver' (82) which results in the coils of 'right enmeshed with wrong' which Mother Nature has 'wrought unwittingly' (85). *The Dynasts* (1904 – 8) is a vast expansion of such imagery. Hardy had said in 1886 that he hoped to show the 'human race . . . as one great network or tissue . . . like a spider's web' (*Life*, 177). The Immanent Will is a cosmic artist who 'works unconsciously, as heretofore, / Eternal artistries in Circumstance . . . patterns, wrought by rapt aesthetic rote'. The 'sum' of the 'fibrils, veins, / Will-tissues, nerves, and pulses of the Cause, / that heave throughout the Earth's compositure' is 'like the lobule of a Brain / Evolving always that it wots not of' (Fore Scene). The patterns of the Will, whose 'willing was . . . immediately the aim and immediately the attainment of the aim',[98] conditions each human mind in *The Dynasts*. Wellington, for example, is seen 'acting while discovering his intention to act' (III, 7, vii, p. 230).

This coalescence of the internal and external dimensions of pattern is very promising. But Hardy does not yet see in himself what he sees in the Will. In the novels and the epic, he remains the omniscient narrator or dramatist paring his fingernails behind the scenes. Only when the scales drop in 1912 will he be able to show, in the mature poetry, how the patterns of the scene shape himself.

One of the important differences, however, between the novels and the epic is that in the latter Hardy is more intrigued by the point of view of the onlooker. Looking at the planet earth, we see the Will's 'brain-like network . . . interpenetrating, entangling, and thrusting hither and thither the human forms' (I, 6, iii, p. 150). When our cinematographic point of view focuses more closely ('The point of view then sinks downward through space'), the cosmic pattern gives way to concrete scenes of 'the peoples, distressed by events which they did not cause . . . writhing, crawling, heaving, and vibrating in their various cities' (Fore Scene). Beholding these scenes we forget the pattern which becomes evident again only when our lens 'zooms' away. The effect owes much, I suspect, to passages in Ruskin and Schopenhauer, as well as to paintings like those by Sallaert and Van Alsloot which Hardy noted in the Victoria and Albert Museum.[99] Another surprising source, from a fictional treatment of the Napoleonic material, is Hugo's 'The Intestine of Leviathan' with its elaborate 'bird's-eye view of the subterranean network of the sewers' of Paris in *Les Misérables* which Hardy may have read twice in the late 1880s. In *Notre Dame* Hugo gives aerial views of the streets of Paris, which in turn may have influenced Ainsworth's panoramas of London in *Old Saint Paul's*. It is fascinating to see Hardy draw on these patterns and then translate them into the private world of his lyrics where he internalises the image. The paradox of the Immanent Will, evolving what it wots not of, becomes the paradox of Hardy's awareness caught within the patterns of its own making.

In 1911 Hardy composed 'The Abbey Mason', his 'personal aesthetic' of '[p]etrified lace-work – lightly lined / On ancient massiveness behind'. A few months later, Hardy wrote 'The Convergence of the Twain' (248). The Immanent Will has welded together the 'paths coincident' of the iceberg and the Titanic which now '[c]old currents thrid, and turn to rhythmic tidal lyres'. Does Hardy yet see the connection between the aesthetic patterns of 'The Abbey Mason' and the patterns of fate in 'The Convergence of the Twain'?

After 1912 he discovers the connection and dramatises the 'intimate welding' of aesthetic pattern and world pattern. And this welded pattern begins to be felt very clearly not only in actual images of moon and branch, but in patterns of language and patterns of rhythm. The 'chiselled shapes' Hardy cited in 'Rome: The Vatican: Sala delle Muse' begin to combine. What happens in miniature in the individual mature poems seems to characterise the entire lifetime's work as its patterns become increasingly clear.

3 Hardy's Apocalypse

In 1917 Hardy defined his central aesthetic principle, that of the exhumed emotion:

> I believe it would be said by people who knew me well that I have a faculty (possibly not uncommon) for burying an emotion in my heart or brain for forty years, and exhuming it at the end of that time as fresh as when interred. For instance, the poem entitled 'The Breaking of Nations' contains a feeling that moved me in 1870, during the Franco – Prussian war, when I chanced to be looking at such an agricultural incident in Cornwall. But I did not write the verses till during the war with Germany of 1914, and onwards. Query: where was that sentiment hiding itself during more than forty years? (*Life*, 378)

This well-known passage is often assumed to show that Hardy's poetry does not change, that a poem of 1914 is a simple reflection of an 1870 event, and that neither the memory nor the poetic sensibility has changed much in forty-four years. In fact, the memory of an experience goes through several stages, both literary and personal. A review of 1915 in Hardy's collection noted that 'mere memories in Mr. Hardy put to shame the actualities of most poets' (*Nation*, 4 February). Hardy underlined the sentence. The actuality of Hardy's memories is not, however, the actuality of an instant impression or instant photograph. Rather their actuality comes from long cultivation in the mind, from being, in Middleton Murry's phrase, 'the culmination of an experience'. Hardy's career is deceptively static because his advance in awareness coincides with a regression into memories which are eventually seen in their final form and matured significance. Hardy's central interest is in what happens to an old emotion which lies hidden for years and is then exhumed in all its paradoxical freshness.

The exhumed emotion passage is particularly complex because it links something very public, a great war poem of 1915, with something very private, an incident in Cornwall in 1870. Cornwall in 1870 was the most important setting of Hardy's emotional life. It was there and then that he courted Emma. 1914 is not only the date of the beginning of the First World War; it is also the date of the publication of 'Poems of 1912–13' in *Satires of Circumstance*, which draw on other impressions of the Cornwall scene and all that had happened in between. Hardy's early happiness with Emma can be felt as the background of the cited poem's last stanza:

I
Only a man harrowing clods
    In a slow silent walk
With an old horse that stumbles and nods
    Half asleep as they stalk.

II
Only thin smoke without flame
    From the heaps of couch grass:
Yet this will go onward the same
    Though Dynasties pass.

III
Yonder a maid and her wight
    Come whispering by;
War's annals will fade into night
    Ere their story die.   (500)

Much more has gone into this poem than a simple feeling produced by seeing 'an agricultural incident' in 1870. Presumably this feeling was the contrast between the ordinariness of life which endures and the false glamour of Dynasties which die. Yet the poem itself, written forty-four years later, contains elements which are difficult to explain:

(1) the harrowing of clods which, in the context of Jeremiah quoted in the title, suggests a biblical harrowing of souls and the popular notion of the harrowing of hell;

(2) the word 'stalk' with its dreamlike urgency. In the poem immediately preceding (and in 'The Five Students') the word stalk is used with its normal connotations of tension and stiffness and perhaps pursuit. When the choice of the word was attacked in two reviews in Hardy's collection,[1] Hardy replied: 'his motion is precisely a "stalk"'. But the word, like other elements in the poem, interferes with the pastoral peace supposedly intended by the imagery;

(3) the heaps of couch grass, produced by the harrowing of clods and then burned – which suggests a further biblical dimension, the separation of the tares and the wheat. In *Desperate Remedies* (x, 2, p. 193) Hardy notes the 'volcano-like smoke' of the smouldering couch grass which untended can be extremely dangerous and indeed bursts forth and consumes the neighbouring buildings;

(4) the maid and her wight becoming an immortal story. The same two reviews in Hardy's collection attacked his choice of the word wight, to which he replied: 'What's the matter?' The matter is that the archaic word may suit the high romanticism of the image, and the image may contrast with war's fading annals, but it also contrasts with the ordinariness of daily life; [2]

(5) the title's reference to Jeremiah 51 : 20 and God's harrowing of Babylon (cf. Jeremiah 51 : 33, 'it is time to thresh her'), which may either parallel the frenzy of dynasties or be their condemnation. Indeed the full title of the poem – 'In Time of "The Breaking of Nations" ' – is somewhat ambiguous. Like the title of the preceding poem, 'In Time of Wars and Tumults', it probably means that the poem's setting is that of wartime. But there is another possibility, that the poem is written in the 'time' or tempo of a hymn, of which 'The Breaking of Nations' is the typically abbreviated title.

Moreover, when Hardy wrote the poem, he knew very well what had happened to one maid and her wight. How did his personal tragedy contribute to the urgency of the poem? How did it affect this final expression of this exhumed emotion of Cornwall?

My point is that the above oddities and ambiguities reflect many other strands in Hardy's experience during the forty-four year interval between the time he first saw the agricultural incident and the time he wrote the poem. We can understand the rationale behind these anomalies only if we understand the long development. Hardy revisited Cornwall several times between 1871 and 1873, and again in 1913. He had also used the Cornwall setting for literary purposes in *A Pair of Blue Eyes* (1872) and again in many poems, most notably those of 1912–13. The imagery in 'In Time of "The Breaking of Nations" ' is thus not an isolated reflex of an early single incident. The imagery is related to many other images which were mulled over, made into literature, the literature reviewed, the initial scene revisited, the memory redefined again and again. At a key point in the ongoing memory of the 1870 scene a critical shock occurs: the death of Emma and the First World War. With these the poem is written (rather quickly, within about two weeks of an editor's request). Three years later, still thinking about the poem, Hardy defines his principle of the exhumed emotion.

But the story of this exhumed emotion does not end here. Sometime after 1917 Hardy began work on his *Early Life* and reviewed the entire sequence which had led to the poem and the principle. He now pointedly connects the poem with incidents of his early courtship of Emma. He also makes connections with other themes. The passage is a long one, but it enables us to begin to trace the complex of strands in Hardy's development of the principle of memory. We can slowly begin to see how Hardy's interest in memory and the poet's creative process contributes to something which seems far removed from such private concerns, namely his vision of the tragedy of men in war. (Though the following passage comes early in the *Life* it was written after the notebook passage on the exhumed emotion, which Hardy is merely quoting in the *Later Years*.)

His hosts drove him to various picturesque points on the wild and rugged coast near the Rectory, among others to King Arthur's Castle, Tintagel, which he now saw for the first time; and where, owing to their lingering too long among the ruins, they found themselves locked in, only narrowly escaping being imprisoned there for the night by much signalling with their handkerchiefs to cottagers in the valley. The lingering might have been considered prophetic, seeing that, after it had been smouldering in his mind for between forty and fifty years, he constructed *The Famous Tragedy of the Queen of Cornwall* from the legends connected with that romantic spot. Why he did not do it sooner, while she was still living who knew the scene so well, and had frequently painted it, it is impossible to say.

H. M. Moule, who by this date knew of the vague understanding between the pair, sent them from time to time such of the daily and weekly papers as contained his leading articles on the war. Concerning such wars Hardy entered in his notebook: 'Quicquid delirant reges, plectuntur Achivi!' On the day that the bloody battle of Gravelotte was fought they were reading Tennyson in the grounds of the rectory. It was at this time and spot that Hardy was struck by the incident of the old horse harrowing the arable field in the valley below, which, when in far later years it was recalled to him by a still bloodier war, he made into the little poem of three verses entitled 'In Time of "the Breaking of Nations"'. Several of the pieces – as is obvious – grouped as 'Poems of 1912 – 13' in the same volume with *Satires of Circumstance* and three in *Moments of Vision*, namely 'The Figure in the Scene', 'Why did I sketch', and 'It never looks like Summer now', with doubtless many others, are known to be also memories of the present and later sojourns here in this vague romantic land of 'Lyonnesse'. (*Life*, 78–9)

The context of the exhumed emotion is thus much larger than the earlier 1917 entry would make us suspect. The context includes not only two wars and the Cornwall agricultural incident, but also the 'picturesque . . . wild and rugged coast', the Arthurian ruins at Tintagel, the 'Gothic' plot of being locked in the castle, the later *Queen of Cornwall*,[3] the sense that the latter was written too late for Emma to see, the news and articles on the war, Horace, Tennyson, 'Poems of 1912 – 13', and three poems in *Moments of Vision*. Four of Tennyson's *Idylls of the King* had been published in 1869 – including 'The Coming of Arthur', which would become the first book in the completed series. It ends triumphantly: 'And Arthur and his knighthood . . . in twelve great battles overcame / The heathen hordes, and made a realm and reign'd.' The Horatian quote, 'Quicquid delirant reges, plectuntur Achivi', from Epistle I, ii, 14, seems to be in ironic juxtaposition with Tennyson: 'When rulers rave, their subjects pay.'[4]

I am intrigued then by the connections being set up in Hardy's memory: picturesque ruins, the death of Arthur, the weeping of the Achaeans, the romance of great battles, the tragedy of war. And again, picturesque ruins, Emma and Hardy, Emma's death, Hardy's belated poetry, the romance of love, the tragedy of love. Admittedly a hodgepodge brought together by biographical circumstance. But I am interested in how these themes, associated in the romance of Lyonnesse, interpenetrate and become mutually illuminating over a forty-four year period and beyond. I am also intrigued by another connection:

> Only thin smoke without flame
> From the heaps of couch grass. . . .

The lingering might have been considered prophetic, seeing that, after it had been smouldering in his mind for between forty and fifty years, he constructed . . . *the Queen of Cornwall.*

Is this parallel a coincidence? Or, in looking back, does Hardy see something else smouldering in that idyllic scene, some hidden conclusion ready to burst forth in flame in the gathering years?[5] This ominous possibility seems to lurk in the pastoral details of the poem of 1915. And then when Hardy reassesses, again, the context of 1870, does he discover something about his own mind, its lingerings, its reveries, its blindnesses? And might he finally have discovered, to his horror, that there was a deep connection between the way his mind worked and the way the minds of his countrymen worked – until both he and they reached parallel, and terrible, conclusions in the second decade of the twentieth century?

Much of this remains to be seen. My intention in this chapter is to see how Hardy gradually draws connections between the various elements in the 1870 context, and then how he fully develops their implications in his last fifteen years of poetry. I will be treating a series of subjects which generally parallel those given in the long passage quoted above: memories and legends, prophetic visions and literary myths, Gothic contexts and their ghosts and grotesques, war myths and war. As Hardy goes from one subject to another, he does so in pursuit of his central theme, more deeply exploring its possibilities in another vein. He rarely abandons any single subject, but at a given stage his interest in a particular subject brings on a new discovery about the implications of exhumed memory. We will be following a string of changes which turns memory into vision, vision into something ghastly and grotesque – the grotesque connotation of 'exhumed' emotion is no accident. The epiphany of 1870 evolves into a kind of grotesque apocalypse experienced by the individual visionary and by a whole society. The final image of this apocalypse is war. Under individual subjects, I will be connecting Hardy's work with the various traditions he draws upon. But I hope the string on which these beads are strung will remain visible. The procedure is somewhat cumbersome, but it corresponds to the manifold diversity, and striking unity, of Hardy's poetic career.

BALLAD MEMORY, 1866–1912

As he begins to write poetry, Hardy is obviously intrigued by the way in which memories control the lives of his characters. His favourite dramatic speaker is one who appears

> Numb as a vane that cankers on its point,
> True to the wind that kissed ere canker came;
> Despised by souls of Now, who would disjoint
> The mind from memory, and make Life all aim. . . .   (16)

Such speakers are compelled like the ancient mariner to live over the scenes of their past and tell them to all who will listen. The past is so over-whelming a reality that it sometimes blinds Hardy's characters to the realities of the present or else maddens them with remorse. Memories are often associated with music, the music which drives Jenny out to the Christmas dance, or leads soldiers back to the marches of old, or guides Christmas choirs over the fields. Consistent with his interest in music and memory, Hardy's most common literary form is the ballad. His ballads include (a) narrative ballads which draw on ancient traditions and broadside traditions, and on the complex strands of the 'Victorian Popular Ballad', (b) short lyrical ballads spoken by Wessex characters, and (c) short lyrical ballads spoken by Hardy himself.[6] In Hardy's development from the 1870s through *Time's Laughingstocks* (1909), narrative ballads generally dominate the early period. Then around the turn of the century Hardy composes a series of short lyric monologues by Wessex characters who are memory-driven: 'Bereft' (1901), 'Autumn in King's Hintock Park' (1901), 'A Daughter Returns' (1901), 'The Inquiry' (1902), 'The Farm-Woman's Winter', and 'She Hears the Storm', these last undated and published in *Time's Laughingstocks*. 'In a Eweleaze near Weatherbury' (1890) is an earlier example. These economical lyrics[7] eliminate much of the quaint machinery of some of the earlier ballads.

This tendency to personalise the ballad form contributes to another set of lyrics composed about the same time which are Hardy's own memories: 'The Ballad-Singer' (1901–2), 'Former Beauties' (1902), 'Shut Out That Moon' (1904), 'Last Words to a Dumb Friend' (1904), 'I Look Into My Glass', 'The Self-Unseeing', and 'The House of Hospitalities', these last published in his first three volumes respectively. 'Reminiscences of a Dancing Man' and 'Wessex Heights' seem to be from 1895–6.[8] In a sense, Hardy is beginning to lift himself into his ballad, becoming one of its characters, and exploring its implications in the form of his own life. He is now memory-driven and time makes its ironic comment on the form of his consciousness:

> Yet at midnight if here walking,
> When the moon sheets wall and tree,
> I see forms of old time talking,
> Who smile on me.   (156)

Hardy's ultimate achievement in this early form of personal ballad will be 'The Ghost of the Past'. Remembering is hardly distinguishable from awareness itself. When memory begins to die, the mind begins to die – an irony caught beautifully in the skeletal formality of the verse, 'We two kept house, the Past and I. . . .'

> It looms a far-off skeleton
> And not a comrade nigh,
> A fitful far-off skeleton
> Dimming as days draw by.   (249)

In the 1900s, therefore, Hardy grew increasingly interested in the way memories lived on in himself. Back in 1875, when he was writing or beginning the series of long narrative ballads, he had described an old war veteran who may have inspired 'Valenciennes': 'The wet eve of the battle, when they slept in the rain with nothing over them, he spoke of as "last night"', as if he were speaking on the actual day' (*Life*, 106). In June, 1899, Hardy found himself no longer the onlooker of such an experience but its subject. While hearing a lady friend recite Gray's 'Elegy' – 'With startling suddenness . . . he seemed to have lived through the experience before.' Then he realised that the lady friend reminded him of a dairymaid who used to recite to him over forty years before (*Life*, 303 – 4). In 1901, Hardy gave his first definition of the exhumed emotion principle. Asked if he remembered the contents of love letters he used to write for the village girls, he replied: 'Possibly, in a sub-conscious way. The human mind is a sort of palimpsest, I suppose; and it's hard to say what records may not lurk in it.' In this same conversation, Hardy describes himself as 'morbidly imaginative', by which he means: 'I should think I am cut out by nature for a ghost-seer.'[9] What ghosts are these? Hardy explains in 'Night in the Old Home' in *Time's Laughingstocks*: 'My perished people who housed them here come back to me' (222). In 1902, Hardy applies to himself the experience he had applied to Old Norbert in the earlier poem, 'Leipzig': 'And whenever those notes in the street begin, / I recall her, and that far scene, / And her acting of how the Allies marched in, / And her tap of the tambourine' (24). In his 1902 poem, 'One We Knew', Norbert's mother has become Hardy's grandmother whose story catches both teller and hearer in a common spell: 'Past things retold were to her as things existent, / Things present but as a tale' (227). In 1905, Hardy wrote thanking Herbert Pentin for the collection of rural rhymes he had sent: 'They interest me because they . . . are those I remember from my own childhood *now*, though many had escaped me during all the intervening years.'[10]

In 1907, Hardy discovers, after finishing *The Dynasts*, that aesthetic creation begins to get confused with the workings of memory: 'I have been living in Wellington's campaigns so much lately that, like George IV, I am almost positive that I took part in the battle of Waterloo, and have written of it from memory' (*Life*, 453). In his later years such an impression practically became an illusion. T. E. Lawrence reported in 1923: 'Napoleon is a real man to him, and the country of Dorsetshire echoes that name everywhere in Hardy's ears. He lives in his period, and thinks of it as the great war.'[11] Hardy had first become fascinated with the Napoleonic period when he was eight years old (*Life*, 16–17). When he was thirty-five he intended to use it for 'A Ballad of the Hundred Days' (*Life*, 106). Then, 'on a belated day', as Hardy said, *The Dynasts* was outlined, *c.* 1896–8.[12] In 1923, when Hardy was eighty-three, this often exhumed emotion seemed to engulf his consciousness.

Hardy, as we saw, began writing narrative ballads in the 1870s and was to continue to write them throughout his career. In them we can see an interesting development which reflects his deepening realisation of the power of memory. He increasingly highlights certain traditional ballad characteristics: the refrain which seems 'irrelevant', the sharp primitive scenes which focus the action and are like spare memory images,[13] the cut-off effect of those endings which return us to the present many years after the time of the story, the ballad associations with music and memory and melancholy. Increasingly, the aesthetic characteristics of the ballad contribute to the psychological profile of the narrator.[14] As Hardy writes more narrative ballads, the narrator becomes caught up in the spell of the past scenes, he becomes mesmerised by the rhythms of old tunes and dances, he is fixated on old irrelevant details which persist in his consciousness, he is surprised by sharp returns to the present. We might begin by noting the ending of 'The Dance at the Phoenix', one of the earliest ballads (28). Jenny's tragedy is completed, and the narrator concludes about the soldiers: 'And truly they were martial men, / The King's-Own Cavalry. / And when they went from Casterbridge . . . 'Twas saddest morn to see.' This is a near irrelevance which is perhaps traditional enough here. But Hardy will later emphasise the ironic possibilities of this kind of closure: as in the jarring last stanza, repeating an earlier one, of 'The Satin Shoes',[15] or the strang irrelevance of the last line of 'The Rash Bride'.[16] In the latter poem, the narrator is one of the participant onlookers of the tragedy. In 'The Trampwoman's Tragedy', the narrator is the central character. The difference between her and the tellers of the 1870s tales is her sharper sense of scene, her greater self-consciousness about the mysterious spells of those scenes, her final assessment that she is still haunted.[17] A similar narrator can be found in 'The Sacrilege' but here we see yet another development. One narrator-participant is replaced, somewhat surprisingly, by another who in turn is replaced, more surprisingly, by the traditional third person narrator in the last stanza: 'he will hear that scream / Until his judgement-time' (we expect 'I will hear that scream . . .).[18] This conflation serves to unite the tragic character, haunted by his past, with Hardy the narrator who is analogously haunted. In other words, Hardy is discovering deep connections between the character's tragedy and the narrator's aesthetic experience. In his unpublished notebooks, Hardy makes an interesting entry from an article by Andrew Lang: '*A traditional ballad*. "All the more because it is so *dreamlike and confused*. I am inclined to think that this is really a traditional version." ' [19] The comment is interesting because it finds the element of dream not only in the plot but in the form.

Hardy's ballads represent his most numerous and varied production, and this account is hardly adequate. But I hope the reader can sense the process by which Hardy, using the principle of exhumed memory, increasingly makes the aesthetic experience consistent with the tragic experience of his character. He also plays on the reader's identification with the past scene and makes the reader's aesthetic experience parallel the character's tragic experience. This increasing interest in the shape of the reader's experience can be seen in 'The Dead Quire' (1897), which leaves the 'listener' entranced: 'The sad man spoke his phantasies / He seems to speak them still. . . . The sad man ceased; and ceased to heed / His listener.' 'The Paphian Ball' makes the effect much more startling. The narrator tells his tale and then turns out to be dead when a second narrator intrudes: 'The man who used to tell this tale / Was the tenor-viol, old Michael Mail; / Yes; Mail the tenor, now but earth! – / I give it for what it may be worth.' The last stanza of 'The Inscription' (1907), repeating an earlier one, pointedly makes the association between the script-haunted wife of the story and the script-haunted reader: 'And hence, as indited above, you may read even now / The quaint church-text.' Finally, the most striking example, published in 1917, is 'The Choirmaster's Burial' with its clipped dimeter lines (like those in 'The Phantom Horsewoman'), its apparent narrator looking back ('But 'twas said . . .), and its final surprise in the manner of 'The Paphian Ball': 'Such the tenor man told / When he had grown old.' At this the reader feels, in Browning's phrase, 'chilly and grown old'. [20]

By means of ballad narratives, Hardy might have seen how a bridge could be made between the novel and the poem which includes the narrator in its drama and organises the reader's experience more tightly. The teller begins to enter the tale and Hardy begins, in a sense, to enter his memories.

VISIONARY MEMORY, 1913–27

Summary. In the years 1913–17, Hardy's most interesting explorations of memory take place. After developing the exhumed emotions of 'Poems of 1912–13', Hardy begins to wonder whether memory, and the aesthetic form it inspires, may in some sense be more real than time. He explores the possibility to its limit. The limit he finds reveals itself in an intriguing way. Committed to a memory-vision which seems eternal, and losing himself in it, the poet discovers that such visions turn grotesque. Hardy is the most important lyric explorer of what we might call the 'apocalyptic grotesque', an imaginative vision internally deformed by reality's hidden changes. This is Hardy's version of the 'return of the repressed'. We shall then see that Hardy's apocalyptic grotesque takes one more interesting turn. It becomes imaged in warfare, and the social implications of grotesque vision become most evident. Whole societies abandon themselves to static myths which are like memories forestalling adjustment to changed circumstances. The grotesque unreality of these myths is revealed in the fact that they lead to war.

In 'Poems of 1912–13', the power of memory and the power of time are generally held in equal balance. However in some of the later poems of 1913 we notice a tendency for memory to take on an increasingly intense power and dominate reality. Past and present begin to fuse. In 'A Dream or No' (February 1913), the past is 'some necromancy' (revised in 1919 to 'some strange necromancy') charming the poet with its dreams. While he wonders if it ever existed, we feel it present, interfering with the rational structuring of the verse. In 'On a Discovered Curl of Hair' (February 1913) a conventional memory takes on a surreal intensity. Even now, Hardy says, it seems he could place the curl back on 'the living brow / By bearing down the western road / Till I had reached your old abode'. In March Hardy revisits Cornwall and he is led on by a vivid living ghost: 'Facing round about me everywhere, / With your nut-coloured hair, / And gray eyes, and rose flush coming and going. . . . I am just the same as when / Our days were a joy. . . .' While the past is maturely 'placed' in 'After a Journey', we also see a tendency for it to usurp the present in these months: 'I am laughing by the brook with her . . . And then it is a blankness looms' ('The Dream Is – Which?', March 1913). In March Hardy began 'The West-Of-Wessex Girl' and when he finished it (it was published in 1922) he had added a stanza which records an apocalyptic hallucination: Emma's 'phantom draws me by the hand', not in the ironic contexts of waked birds and flopping seals in 'After a Journey', but '[w]hen midnight hammers slow'. Similarly, 'The Shadow on the Stone', begun in 1913 and finished in 1916, conjures up a memory image in the first stanza and in the last defends it: ' "Nay, I'll not unvision / A shape which, somehow, there may be." . . . So I went on softly . . . My head unturned lest my dream should fade.' [21]

Oddly intense confusions of inner and outer realities begin to occur. Like the ghost of Catherine Earnshaw, Emma taps at the window in 'Something Tapped' (August 1913), but the tapping is only a 'pallid moth'. In a similar poem, 'A Night in November', published in 1922, the plot works in reverse: 'Dead leaves blew into my room. . . . One leaf of them touched my hand, / And I thought that it was you.' Indeed, in many poems published after 1916, 'The Background and the Figure', 'The Figure in the Scene' (cited in the exhumed emotion passage), 'The Curtains Now are Drawn', 'On Stinsford Hill at Midnight', the vision takes on a power which dominates the present scene which, in earlier poems like 'The Voice' and 'At Castle Boterel', had dominated the vision.[22]

We also notice a curious psychological phenomenon in Hardy in these 'later years', especially in the 1920s. I have counted twelve different instances in which people noticed in Hardy about this time a curious susceptibility to spells of reverie, dreaminess, trances. The following comments by T. E. Lawrence in 1925 and Leonard Woolf in 1927 are typical: 'a film seems to slip over his mind at times now: and the present is then obscured by events of his childhood.' 'Through his talk of plain local and diurnal business, there came the feeling that he was also attending to some quite different, distant, unspoken, incommunicable world of consciousness.' This sensation of losing the thread of where he is can be felt even in the grammar of such poems as 'If It's Ever Spring Again' and 'As 'Twere To-Night', both published in 1922.[23]

Florence Hardy blamed these 'absences' on old age, but Hardy remained to the end an extraordinarily acute observer of the current scene. Many things contributed to his deepened contemplation of the past. There is a 'sense of an ending' about his life at this time. He is putting together his first *Collected Poems* in 1919 and his second in 1923. For them, he reviews all his past poems, reliving them and revising them. He is also preparing the new Mellstock Edition (1919–20) of his works and rereading them yet again. In preparing *Late Lyrics and Earlier* for publication in 1922, he discovers an unusal number of early discarded poems. The volume represents every decade between 1866 and 1921 except for the 1880s. Hardy is also putting together his *Early Life* and *Later Years*, with the help of Florence Emily. The work occupies his last decade and involves reviewing an enormous number of personal papers. Of these he says, 'they raise ghosts'. Where he had never taken much 'interest in himself', he now records at the end of 1917, about the time he started the *Early Life*: 'Hardy's mind seems to have been running on himself at this time to a degree quite unusual with him.' Back in 1899 he had said: 'No man's poetry can be truly judged till its last line is written.' Now in 1920 he says of those 'who are late to develop' that the value of old age 'just enables them to complete their job'.[24]

In a psychological sense Hardy's life seems to him to be harmonising into a perfect round. All things of the past, he begins to speculate in 1922, 'are framed to be / Eternally'. Perhaps, 'events always were, are, and will be (e.g. Emma, Mother and Father are living still in the past)'. Lost ones abide in 'dateless dure . . . Afar, yet close to us'; 'Time is toothless, seen all through.' Not only the real dead but the fictional dead seemed to exist in these years: 'He talked of Tess as if she was someone real whom he had known and liked tremendously.'[25]

Immortal Visions

Growing more engulfed by his reveries, Hardy began to find intersections of the finite and the infinite, instants 'made eternity', Abt Voglerian harmonies. Indeed it is interesting that only at this late date (1913–28, especially 1915–23) did Hardy begin to yield wholeheartedly to the visionary imagination he had admired in the poets of his youth.[26] The phantom horsewoman, in a poem published in 1922, is launched 'Towards some radiant star.' A kiss travels 'aethereal rounds / Far from earth's bounds / In the infinite'. Did an old joy, Hardy speculates, continue 'its lustrous roll / In upper air' and did his 'late irradiate soul / Live on somewhere'? Did a young man's visionary light 'travel on, to be a new young dreamer's freight, / And thence on infinitely'? Other experiences – the song of a bird, the voice of a contralto – may be blending 'Mid visionless wilds of space . . . In the full-fugued song of the universe unending'; 'Such a dream is Time.' In 'Apostrophe to an Old Psalm Tune' (1916) the tune, lately wakened, lives 'still on – and onward, maybe, / Till Doom's great day be!' Thus in this period Hardy's 'ecstatic temperament, extraordinarily sensitive to music' responds to the powerful notes of an old love song, the 'wild wavering tune' of the phantom horsewoman. Perhaps an ecstatic reverie can last and last, until it is fixed in an eternity.[27]

Hardy's vision of some cosmic awakening is also strikingly enthusiastic in these years. Back in 1867, he had speculated: 'Had the teachings of experience grown cumulatively with the age of the world we should have been ere now as great as God.' 'When wilt thou wake, O Mother?' he had asked of nature in 'The Sleep-Worker', published in 1901. In this same year he had speculated: 'there may be a consciousness, infinitely far off, at the other end of the chain of phenomena, always striving to express itself, and always baffled and blundering'. Aside from what Hardy called the 'childish thought' of 'God-Forgotten' and 'Agnosto Theo' (p. 1901), the only serious indulgence in apocalyptic hope before 1912 is the ending of *The Dynasts*: 'a stirring thrills the air' and there is a hint of deliverance, 'Consciousness the will informing, till It fashion all things fair'. Hardy soon recanted this ending which, among other things, is strikingly contradictory to the Schopenhauerian assumptions of the epic work. Now, however, in the last fifteen years of his life, Hardy's apocalyptic speculations take on a new intensity. God may reach consciousness '[b]y some still close-cowled mystery'. The Immanent Doer may 'lift Its blinding incubus'. The cosmos may break its '*spell*' in 'Xenophanes', written in 1921. Near this poem in the 1925 volume is placed 'There Seemed a Strangeness' where a great light shines and a Voice announces: 'The Great Adjustment is taking place!' In two poems written in 1922, the 'Absolute' explains that the 'Present, that men but see, / Is phasmal. . . . With me, "Past", "Future", ever abide' – and all is then revealed.[28]

From memory to apocalypse – this is an important plot in Hardy's poetry. And in these last years, the claim of memory mingles with striking claims Hardy now makes for literary experience. Browning's literary epiphanies condition, as we have seen, some of Hardy's late reveries. Literary myths mingle with the memory of Emma. In 1916 Hardy said, 'I visited the place [Cornwall] 44 years ago with an Iseult of my own, and of course she was mixed in the vision of the other.' He visits Cornwall again, 'and thence to Tintagel'. In the same year he begins *The Queen of Cornwall* and finishes it in 1923: '53 years in contemplation, 800 lines in result.' The play is full of both Shelleyan and Wagnerian echoes. Tristram and Iseult, Hardy and Emma, celebrate the eternal hour of their 'form of fantasie'. With their death, 'sea and sky darken, and the wind rises, distant thunder murmuring'. The play, Merlin says, raises an 'antique spell' for its audience and one cannot help but think of Tennyson's Arthurian epic.[29]

The wryly qualified celebration of writers in 'Poems of Pilgrimage' published in 1901, now becomes a radiant tribute to a Shakespeare whose 'harmonies . . . cow Oblivion' in a poem written in 1916. In 'The House of Silence', published in 1917, dance and music flood the poet's brain as he captures an 'aion in an hour' and represents the 'visioning powers of souls who dare / To pierce the material screen'. Hardy is also reading Proust (or about Proust) in these years and may be impressed by Proust's aesthetic of an involuntary memory which triumphs over time and decay. I also detect in Hardy's 1917 and 1922 volumes the influence of Blake, despite the fact that Florence Hardy said her husband was repelled by Blake's 'insanity'. Nevertheless, Hardy compared his poem, 'A New Year's Eve in War Time', composed 1915–16, to Blake's print of 'Pity'. 'The Robin' strongly resembles the rhythms and paradoxes of Blake's 'The Fly'.

'The Chosen', especially its last stanzas, recalls Blake's 'The Crystal Cabinet'. 'The Wanderer' recalls Blake's 'Mad Song'. 'Weathers' recalls the scene and peculiar pastoral quality of 'The Echoing Green'. And 'On a Midsummer Eve' may recall Blake's Introduction to *Songs of Innocence*. Blake was evidently on Hardy's mind – he talked about the great visionary with Vere Collins in 1922 – and may have influenced the stark, almost violent, way in which Hardy presents the visionary imagination at this time. The 'vision-seeing mind' of St Paul renders the surrounding scene 'Charmless, blank in every kind'. Against the claims of a fallen reality (where 'trees fret fitfully' and 'Slime is the dust of yestereve') Hardy sharply opposes the vision of lovers for whom the 'fog is sweet / And the wind a lyre'. In 'After a Romantic Day', 'poetry of place' is no longer fallaciously pathetic, it sears the landscape:

> The bald steep cutting, rigid, rough,
>   And moon-lit, was enough
> For poetry of place: its weathered face
> Formed a convenient sheet whereon
> The visions of his mind were drawn.[30]

Hardy's visionary enthusiasm of these years may also account for the strange intensity of the pastoral images in 'In Time of "The Breaking of Nations"'. The poem may indeed reflect the prophetic enthusiasm of Shelley's 'On Life'. 'What are changes of empires, the wreck of dynasties,' Shelley says, 'compared with life?' The more Shelley thinks about life in this essay the more apocalyptic 'life' seems to become. In man 'there is a spirit . . . at enmity with nothingness and dissolution. This is the character of all life.' Then, Shelley notes that those who are most in tune with this 'life' are 'subject to the state called reverie' and 'feel as if their nature were dissolved into the surrounding universe, or as if the surrounding universe were absorbed into their being'. They realise the unity of 'ideas and of external objects'.

HARDY AND THE GROTESQUE

The last two lines of 'After a Romantic Day' presumably mean that the mind's visions triumph over reality, apparelling it with celestial light. But the drawing of a sheet over a face also suggests a death, and the connotations of 'drawn' are harsh. There seems to be a subsidiary echo, if we consider the context of the bald 'cutting', that vision is drawn and quartered by reality. In an essay of 1878, 'Dreams and Realities', Leslie

Stephen had written: 'The underlying emotion deserves our respect, although the images which it generated become grotesque and horrible when we have learnt to put more bluntly the decisive dilemma of fact or fiction.'[31] The possibility of this kind of reversal, of visionary emotion into grotesque imagery, leads us to Hardy's remarkable experiments in the art of the grotesque. The enthusiasm which leads Shelley from the celebration of 'life' to the celebration of 'unity' and its realisation in 'the state called reverie' – leads Hardy in a different direction. For Hardy such reverie eventually becomes a last, terrible confusion.

In order to see the full significance of Hardy's mature lyric grotesques, we need to see where Hardy stands in the tradition of the grotesque.

Hardy began to write at an interesting moment in English discussion of the grotesque. The word itself seems to have originated 'as a term descriptive of the fanciful murals, in which human and animal motifs were combined with foliage and floral decoration, found in the chambers ('grotte') of Roman buildings excavated about 1500'.[32] Thus in *Desperate Remedies* Hardy refers to Miss Aldclyffe's 'washing-stand . . . carved with grotesque Renaissance ornament' (v, 2, p. 74). After being used as a specific historical term, the word in seventeenth-century England broadened into an aesthetic description of painting or sculpture which imitated such forms. The word was also applied to forms in general, 'characterized by distortion or unnatural combinations' (*OED*). Thus Giles's lantern 'marked grotesque shapes upon the shadier parts of the walls and ceiling' (*Woodlanders*, 3, p. 21). In *Two on a Tower*, the wind accomplishes 'its grotesque purpose' (16, p. 120). (In the seventeenth century John Hall applied the term to 'Grotesco Maximes . . . that doe so disfigure and misguide the life of man'. Thus Hardy in *Tess* cites 'the hideous defacement' in the signpost maxims, 'the last grotesque phase of a creed which had served mankind well in its time' [12, p. 101].) It then became customary to speak of natural phenomena and landscapes as grotesque. The word also became associated with gargoyles (Walpole, 1762–5), then presumably with Gothic architecture in general. Thus in *A Pair of Blue Eyes* Hardy says that the gables of Endelstow House 'were surmounted by grotesque figures in rampant, passant, and couchant variety' (5, p. 39). And in *Jude*, Sue speaks of 'the grotesque childishness' of Gothic architects who try to imitate the vanished Roman forms (v, 6, p. 369). How the two traditions of the 'Gothic' and the 'grotesque' relate, how the latter became associated with Gothic architecture and, presumably, with the Gothic novel, has not, to my knowledge, been satisfactorily explored.[33] In the nineteenth century the word could be used in any of the above ways, and Hardy's usage ranges up and down the scale. Poe's *Tales of the Grotesque and Arabesque* is a title which captures both the origin and later development of the term.

The connotation of the word grotesque tended to change between the eighteenth and nineteenth centuries. Hardy's use of the word draws on the traditions of both centuries. In the eighteenth century the word, when used as a general descriptive term, usually had a negative connotation, of ludicrous distortion. As a specific aesthetic term, it was usually applied to the art of caricature. The Romantic reaction against the Age of Reason tended to exalt the grotesque and associated it in various complex ways with the sublime (Burke had contrasted sublime seriousness with 'odd, wild grotesques' – *OED*). The Gothic novel, Gothic revivals, 'picturesque' ruins like those at Tintagel, also helped promote the new attitude toward the grotesque.

While evidence of the serious or fearful or sublime grotesque is widespread in English Romantic art and literature, critical discussion of the notion was rare: only passing statements by Coleridge and Hazlitt, and Scott's 1827 essay, 'On the Supernatural in Fictitious Composition, and particularly on the Work of . . . Hoffmann.' Scott preferred the term 'fantastic' to 'grotesque' and defined it as a mode of writing 'in which the most wild and unbounded license is given to an irregular fancy, and all species of combination, however ludicrous, or however shocking, are attempted and executed without scruple'. Of Hoffmann Scott said: 'Thus was the inventor, or at least first distinguished artist who exhibited the fantastic or supernatural grotesque, so nearly on the verge of actual insanity, as to be afraid of the beings his own fancy created.' Scott obviously deplores this mode. But he is also fascinated with it and respectful of it because of its connection with man's hunger for the supernatural which 'our corporeal organs' are 'too coarse and gross to perceive'. Scott, therefore, seems to straddle eighteenth-century rationalistic disapproval of the grotesque and Romantic exaltation of it. This ambivalence may be felt in some Gothic novels.

In the period when Hardy came to literary consciousness, the term came into its own as a major aesthetic category. Thus in *Far from the Madding Crowd* Hardy noted: 'It has been sometimes argued that there is no truer criterion of the vitality of any given art-period than the power of the master-spirits of that time in grotesque; and certainly in the instance of Gothic art there is no disputing the proposition' (46, p. 360). In making this statement, Hardy may be thinking of any of a number of important treatments of the grotesque in his time – by Thomas Wright, or Ruskin, or Bagehot. After these followed discussions by Pater (in 'Romanticism'), Stephen, and Symonds. Wright's A History of Caricature and Grotesque (London, Virtue Bros.) was published in 1865 and was the only book-length history of the grotesque in the English language before the

translation of Wolfgang Kayser's *The Grotesque in Art and Literature* in 1963.
Wright, however, used the word in its eighteenth-century sense. A much
more significant treatment, which Hardy knew, was Ruskin's discussion in
The Stones of Venice. Ruskin's treatment is quite complex but, generally, he
defined the grotesque as a mixture of caricature and seriousness, the
ludicrous and the fearful. The more fearful and serious the grotesque, the
more noble it was – as in the 'true Gothic grotesque'.[34]

The treatments of the grotesque which most influenced Hardy's later
poetry were, I suspect, Bagehot's and Stephen's. Hardy greatly admired
Bagehot's *Estimates* (*Life*, 33) and probably knew Bagehot's 1864 essay,
'Wordsworth, Tennyson, and Browning; or, Pure, Ornate, and Grotesque
Art in English Poetry'. At one point in his essay, Bagehot associated the
grotesque with the medieval Gothic period, an age trying to maintain its
spiritual principles in the face of a barbaric world. Browning's 'Caliban'
reflects this tradition and depicts '*mind in difficulties* – mind set to make out
the universe under the worst and hardest circumstances'.[35] Hardy also
probably knew Stephen's use of the word in his fine essay, 'Dreams and
Realities': 'if you choose to dream, you must have your nightmares as well
as your visions of undying bliss. Dreams must be at least distorted and
grotesque shadows of realities.'

Hardy's novels[36] reflect both eighteenth-century and nineteenth-
century traditions of the grotesque. The earlier tradition is reflected in the
comic caricature of the rustics in *Under the Greenwood Tree*, *Far from the
Madding Crowd*, and *The Mayor of Casterbridge*. The later tradition is reflec-
ted in the landscapes of *Two on a Tower*, *The Woodlanders*, and *The Return of
the Native*, and in the more sinister character grotesques of this latter novel.
Ruskin said that Dürer's grotesque, because of its 'nobler terribleness',
'passes into perfect sublime'. He cited Dürer's 'Apocalypse' (see Illus-
tration 15) and 'Knight and Death'.[37] Ruskin's remarks, and Hardy's own
admiration for Dürer, influenced the famous hill fire scenes in *The Return of
the Native* which, Hardy says, are 'drawn with Dureresque vigour and
dash'. The fires represent man's 'Promethean rebelliousness' against the
black chaos. In the firelight, '[a]ll was unstable. . . . shadowy eye-sockets,
deep as those of a death's head, suddenly turned into pits of lustre. . . .
Nostrils were dark wells; sinews in old necks were gilt mouldings. . . .
Those whom Nature had depicted as merely quaint became grotesque, the
grotesque became preternatural; for all was in extremity' (i, 3, p. 18).

Hardy's poetry also reflects both eighteenth- and nineteenth-century
traditions of the grotesque. He is famous, of course, for his satiric
grotesques, 'satires of circumstance', though we should add that the
circumstances are 'grotesque' in a rather general sense: 'All tragedy is

grotesque – if you allow yourself to see it as such' (*Life*, 296). But what I
am interested in is his serious lyric grotesque which he explores after 1913,
when he begins to apply the grotesque more intimately to his own
impressions. When Hardy in 1920 claimed again that his poetry rested on
'mere impressions', he now saw the grotesque element: 'only a confused
heap of impressions, like those of a bewildered child at a conjuring show'
(*Life*, 410). Hardy's mature lyric grotesque constitutes a major develop-
ment out of nineteenth-century theory. It is no accident, of course, that
Hardy developed his lyric grotesque in the decades of the First World War,
Kafka, and the surrealists. It is at this time also that the 'scales fell' in
Hardy's personal life and he found working within himself the satire of
circumstance he had formerly found in the outer world.

Ghosts

Discussion of Hardy's lyric grotesques property begins perhaps with his
use of a venerable Gothic stage property – ghosts. Hardy's sensibility, we
know, was influenced by late versions of the Gothic novel, in Scott,
Dumas, Ainsworth, Grant and others.[38] In later years Hardy became in-
creasingly interested in the reality of ghosts, in their grotesque properties,
and in what they revealed about the visionary mind.

Hardy explicitly connected his ghosts with two themes discussed above:
romantic visions and apocalyptic awakenings. The possibility of ghosts,
Hardy said, provides 'another domain for the imagination to expatiate in',
in a material world which is otherwise 'so miserably bounded, circum-
scribed, cabin'd, cribb'd, confined'. Also, Hardy said, the incompleteness
of ghosts is like the incompleteness of the universe where a cosmic
consciousness is 'always striving to express itself, and always baffled and
blundering, just as the spirits'. At the same time, Hardy said, 'I quite
admit the pitiful ineffectualness, even grotesqueness, of all the alleged
manifestations of the spirit world, and the eeriness of spirits, to our
seeming'. The grotesqueness of ghosts may have suggested to Hardy an
application to visionary experience in general.[39]

As early as 'A Sign-Seeker' in *Wessex Poems* Hardy said he wanted to see
'a phantom parent, friend' or lover as a sign offered those who are 'rapt to
heights of trancéd trust'. Like Shelley's Alastor, he would force 'some lone
ghost . . . to render up the tale / Of what we are'. 'When I was a younger
man', Hardy told a friend in 1901, 'I would cheerfully have given ten years
of my life to see a ghost – an authentic, indubitable spectre. . . . I should
think I am cut out by nature for a ghost-seer. My nerves vibrate very
readily; people say I am almost morbidly imaginative; my will to believe is

perfect.' Hardy repeated this to Hermann Lea: 'I have always wanted to see a ghost: I am receptive and by no means sceptical. I would willingly concede ten years of my life if I could see any supernatural thing that could be proved to me to exist by any means within my capacity.' On 24 December 1919, one of the oddest incidents of Hardy's life occurred. Florence Emily writes: 'He saw a ghost in Stinsford Churchyard on Christmas Eve, and his sister Kate says it must have been their grandfather upon whose grave T. H. had just placed a sprig of holly – the first time he had ever done so. The ghost said: "A green Christmas" – T. H. replied "I like a green Christmas". Then the ghost went into the church, and, being full of curiosity. T. followed . . . and found no-one. That is quite true.' The supernatural anecdotes which Hardy delighted to hear and relate in his early years seemed to start happening to him in his later years. He even began to look like a ghost, according to Florence Emily.[40]

The possibility of a true ghost vision may account for several curious poems Hardy published between 1917 and 1922. The ghosts in Hardy's earlier poems had been more or less conventional ghosts, like those in *revenant* ballads and traditional lyrics, where we are more interested in the ghosts' function than in their being. They reproach their pessimistic descendant in 'Night in the Old Home'; they haunt old lovers in 'Her Immortality' and 'A Trampwoman's Tragedy' and 'Wessex Heights'; they preach against war in 'The Souls of the Slain'; they proclaim their ironic detachment in 'Friends Beyond'. In 'Poems of 1912–13', most of the poems like 'The Haunter' and 'His Visitor' do not present Emma as a physical – spiritual curiosity. We do perhaps experience some shock in 'After a Journey', 'Something Tapped' and 'A Night in November' when the ghost of Emma, with her 'nut-coloured hair . . . and rose-flush coming and going', wastes away to a thin ghost or is replaced by a dead leaf or pallid moth. But the ghost of Emma is not much more than a memory image.[41]

Now, however, in the post-1913 years and inspired perhaps by the power of that memory image, Hardy seems to be wondering: what sort of a thing is a ghost? Can it sit on a bench? Does it have a material consistency? Does it have nerves? As we lie in our graves and grow into trees and plants, do we feel the sun and rain? As Hardy's ghosts become more real they take on a grotesque phenomenality. They move upon furniture with 'tentative touches that lift and linger / In the wont of a moth'. 'As light as upper air', they sit upon benches which will soon 'break down unaware'. They are invulnerable to cold and yet they are like the breath of decay undermining the bench: 'Quite a row of them sitting there.' There is a certain comic awkwardness in this scene, and the 'upper air' is an odd amalgam of material and spiritual essence. Ghosts like these '[o]bsess . . . rooms'. Their 'dead fingers' film the clavier, like 'tapering flames – wan, cold – / Or the nebulous light that lingers / In charnel mould'. Past handlers seem to clutch the old viols whose harmonies linger on like the soul in the old materialist analogy. In 'Voices from Things Growing in a Churchyard', the ghosts are carefully – and grotesquely – specified. They are syntheses of human personality and graveyard objects. The promiscuity of Eve Greensleaves becomes the promiscuity of 'innocent withwind' kissed 'now by glowworms and by bees'. Fanny Hurd's flightiness enters the fluttering 'daisy shapes'. Lady Gertrude's superfine satins change to shiny leaves. The immortality of ghosts is ambiguously triumphant, comic, and painful. Can ghosts feel their exposed veins? Do they live their deaths?

> So, they are not underground,
> But as nerves and veins abound
> In the growths of upper air,
> And they feel the sun and rain,
> And the energy again
> That made them what they were!

Indeed, the ghostly condition seems to invade Hardy himself: 'their murmurous accents seem to come / thence hitheraround in a radiant hum, / All day cheerily, / All night eerily.'[42]

Hardy's mature ghosts are grotesque because they are here and not here; they are immortal and they are only decaying bits of nature; they are the living past that has ceased to exist – and yet they are part of us. Present reality, wrought into visionary material by the ghosts and the fervid ghost-seer, threatens to 'return' in the form of the grotesque.

THE VISIONARY GROTESQUE

Ghosts who are past their time are analogous, in Hardy, to romantic visions and apocalyptic moments that are past their time. To be caught in an 'instant made eternity' is soon, for Hardy, to be caught in a misplaced past. The grotesque in Hardy is the mental distortion of reality produced by the juxtaposition of two time zones – the one we think we are in, the one we are actually in. For example, Hardy says of the hero (who exhibits 'the artistic nature') of his last published novel: 'His record moved on with the years, his sentiments stood still'; his 'inability to ossify with the rest of his generation threw him out of proportion with the time'; his life was a 'ghost story'. According to Hardy, this novel, *The Well-Beloved*, was tragic – comic rather than frivolous (somewhat like Ruskin's distinction between the noble and ignoble grotesque): 'There is, of course, underlying the fantasy followed by the visionary artist the truth that all men are pursuing a shadow, the Unattainable, and I venture to hope that this may redeem the tragi-comedy from the charge of frivolity.' When Pierston finally sees, in the novel's original conclusion, the temporal disproportion of his life in its full intensity, it 'brought into his brain a sudden sense of the grotesqueness of things'.[43]

Similarly, after Tess makes her confession, Clare says: 'You were one person; now you are another. My God – how can forgiveness meet such a grotesque – prestidigitation as that' (35, p. 292). A few chapters later, 'humanity stood before him no longer in the pensive sweetness of Italian art, but in the staring and ghastly attitudes of a Wiertz Museum, and with the leer of a study by Van Beers' (39, p. 331). Illustration 16 reproduces one of the most striking examples from the Wiertz Museum. Hardy also probably knew William Strang's 1897 etching, entitled 'Grotesque', which juxtaposes images of a skull and an elegant lady.[44]

'I Rose Up as My Custom Is' (311) clearly connected Hardy's ghosts, Hardy's grotesques, and his theme of the well-beloved. The ghost returns to see if he is still valued by his 'former love'. But she has moved far beyond him and scorns his interest in 'one's Love of long ago':

> Her words benumbed my fond frail ghost;
> The nightmares neighed from their stalls,
> The vampires screeched, the harpies flew,
> And under the dim dawn I withdrew
> To Death's inviolate halls.

This is probably a poem of 1910–11. It is a humorous poem but its imagery will deepen in the coming years.

In the years following 1913, Hardy yields both to apocalyptic fantasies and the serious grotesque. The more Hardy identified with his visionary experience the more grotesque it became. For Ruskin, the fearful grotesque can be a result of an ungovernable imagination not yet able to rise to the sublime. For Hardy, the grotesque is the ultimate conclusion of the sublime from which men cannot free their imaginations. We can see this development if we place 'Could I But Will' (595) next to 'A Merrymaking in Question' (398).

In 'Could I But Will', Hardy desires apocalyptic power to raise the
dead, make the 'frozen scene' flower, and rejoin old friends walking
'[w]ith weightless feet and magic talk / Uncounted Eves': 'I'd have afar
one near me still, / And music of rare ravishment, / In strains that move
the toes and heels!'[45] In 'A Merrymaking in Question', the apocalyptic
wish is more frenzied: 'I will . . . call to the neighbours to come.' Nature
then answers the visionary:

> From the night came the oddest of answers:
>   A hollow wind, like a bassoon,
> And headstones all ranged up as dancers,
>   And cypresses droning a croon,
>   And gurgoyles that mouthed to the tune.

The rhythm of the second stanza mimics that of the first. Only now the
record is stalled at a slower speed, the film keeps skipping back to earlier
frames. The apocalyptic vision keeps stuttering into time. In writing 'A
Merrymaking in Question', Hardy may have remembered William
Strang's etching, 'Danse Macabre'. (See Illustration 18.) In his notebook
Hardy pasted a clipping describing the etching: 'the ballet of skeleton
monks on stilts has no intruders to upset its fantastic logic and *macabre*
sportiveness. Bones prances by Bones, and Deadhead whispers Deadhead in
a natural nightmare way.'[46]

   The grotesque, then, is Hardy's way of showing what happens to
romantic vision and apocalyptic fantasy in a changing world. The
imagination begins to expatiate and the material world subtly begins to
spring its cribbed and confining distortions (cf. above, page 106). The
fusion of imagination and material world, like the fusion of ghostly spirit
and material medium, results in the ominous distortion of each.

   In 1890 Hardy made a remark which is in the tradition of Blake's
celebration of the 'Ancient Poets' in *The Marriage of Heaven and Hell*: 'This
"barbaric idea which confuses persons and things"', Hardy said, 'is, by
the way, also common to the highest imaginative genius – that of the
poet' (*Life*, 230). The apocalyptic visionary transforms the world into
imaginative shapes, so that, in Coleridge's words, he makes 'nature
thought, and thought nature' ('On Poesy or Art'). But for Hardy these
imaginative shapes eventually turn on the visionary and seem to threaten
him. Underneath the imaginative fusion of mind and nature, there is an
ominous hidden diffusion, which results in a grotesque confusion. The
visionary has been made one with nature, and when it begins to come apart
he begins to come apart: 'I know the happenings from their sound. . . .

The tree-trunks rock to their roots, which wrench and lift / The loam where they run onward underground. . . . The westward fronts of towers are saturate, / Church-timbers crack, and witches ride abroad' (699). Because he can no longer see the boundaries of mind and nature, he cannot control their relationship. His visionary power seems to lay him open, dispersing his identity. His images begin to strain and separate, as death approaches: 'the flag-rope gibbers hoarse' (439).

In such 'grotesque' poems, the imagery goes haywire. Nature is over-personalised: 'Curious crude details seem installed, / And show themselves . . . As they were personalities.' At the same time man is de-personalised: 'Three clammy casuals wend their way. . . . Six laughing mouths, six rows of teeth . . . beneath / Six yellow hats' (851). They do not see what the lyric poet sees: 'a gray nightmare / Astride the day, or anywhere.' One of Hardy's many skills is his ability to convey the terrific helplessness of the visionary who can no longer sort out his world. 'There is some hid dread afoot / That we cannot trace' – perhaps a 'spirit astray' – which makes the speaker's images seem to turn on him: 'The rain smites more and more, / The east wind snarls. . . . The tip of each ivy-shoot / Writhes on its neighbour's face' (400). In 'The Ageing House' (435), the romantic pastoral vision of the first stanza receives its due consummation in the second: 'slow effacement / Is rife throughout, / While fiercely girds the wind at the long-limbed sycamore tree!' 'The Wind's Prophecy' (440) is a long debate between nature and the lover who wishes to be loyal to his old well-beloved, though he is about to meet his new. As his visionary personifications of nature grow in intensity, nature responds with increasing violence so that the personifications seem to explode from within.[47] Yet the lover holds on to his old vision and the poem ends with a grotesque image out of Norse mythology:

> Yonder the headland, vulturine,
> Snores like old Skrymer in his sleep,
> And every chasm and every steep
> Blackens as wakes each pharos-shine.

Hardy thought about this poem for many years and rewrote it from an old copy. He added the name of the Norse god in 1919. The extraordinarily ominous imagery suggests, I think, the time to come when, after 1913, the well-beloveds are dead, the speaker stands alone, and nature reveals that it has nothing to do with the attributions we give her.

Living out the confusion of vision and reality in his later years, Hardy experienced its terrifying elements. Part of us is inside and part of us is outside. Our subjective conscious identities are also physical objects within a scene. The grammatical ending of 'Nobody Comes' (715) gives us the feel of this dispersion. At the beginning of the poem, 'Tree-leaves labour up and down, / And through them the fainting light / Succumbs to the crawl of night'. This obscure inner and outer disturbance symbolises the slow hidden processes of nature which will leave each of us, like a passing car, 'in a world of its own'. We end in 'a blacker air; / And mute by the gate I stand again alone, / And nobody pulls up *there*', (my italics). This is Hardy's 'Skunk Hour' when, as in Robert Lowell,[48] the nonhuman world which helps make up our identity turns against it, so that we seem to be in mortal conflict with ourselves.

'A New Year's Eve in War Time' (507) was written in 1915 – 16 and, like most of the other examples of lyric grotesque, was published in 1917 or thereafter. The poem elaborates the fearful mingling of inner and outer weather:

I

Phantasmal Fears,
And the flap of the flame,
And the throb of the clock,
And a loosened slate,
And the blind night's drone,
Which tiredly the spectral pines intone!

II

And the blood in my ears
Strumming always the same,
And the gable-cock
With its fitful grate,
And myself, alone.

The falling of the slate seems almost to occur within the speaker's own mind. Time throbs both inside the self and in the scene around the self. Both share a blind community of inner haemorrhage and decay. When Hardy then looks for an apocalyptic revelation, a pale horse and pale rider, he finds: 'No call of my name, / No sound but "Tic-toc" / Without check.'

Interestingly, Hardy said of the poem that the Blake print, 'Pity', 'in some respects almost matches the verses'.[49] Hardy may later have thought of the print when he wrote of the 'gray nightmare / Astride the day' (851). The print may also have reminded him of the phantom horsewoman. The soul of the sleeper is caught up in an apocalyptic embrace, while the body of the sleeper remains stretched out in the grotesque tautness of death. (See Illustration 19.)

What makes Hardy's apocalypses horrible is, I think, temporal reality whose spring is hidden and belated. The visionary cannot find out where he is in the temporal stream; his record may have moved on and yet his sentiments may be locking him in the past. As in 'Who's in the Next Room' (450), he may be about to die. The ecstasy of Hardy's dreamlike moments where time is a 'dream' or a 'fiction, past and present one' thus tends to become a nightmare from which he wishes to awake but cannot – since the nightmare is characterised by the 'trancelike trust', 'rare ravishment', and 'rapt thought' of the original moment of vision.

On a number of occasions in these later years, Hardy refers to his dreams. He tells Sydney Cockerell in 1919: 'My dreams are not so coherent as yours. They are more like cubist paintings and generally end by my falling down the turret stairs of an old church owing to steps being missing.' He told Elliott Felkin in 1918 that 'he dreamt so much and it was all stupid and unrelated, and that it must be a great strain on one, as one woke up so excited'.[50] In his conversation with Felkin, Hardy seemed uninterested in the psychology of Jung. Nor, to my knowledge, did Hardy ever mention Freud. (The first English translation of *The Interpretation of Dreams* had appeared in 1913.) Yet in 1919 Freud published one of the most significant studies in the psychology of the grotesque, 'The Uncanny', an essay curiously overlooked in most histories of the grotesque. Like Scott, Freud uses Hoffmann as his major example. For both Freud and Hardy – despite their important differences[51] – the grotesque results from the confusion between present reality and the mind's past dreams of omnipotence and wish-fulfilment. The phenomenological result of this confusion for Hardy is that the present natural scene and the mind seem to share a common nightmare. One of Hardy's most interesting images now linking man and nature is that of the thrashing of the sleeping body unable to awake from its dream.

Thus, in 'A Procession of Dead Days', the speaker calls upon 'the ghost of a perished day. . . . but come again: yes, come anon!' The days remembered are days of increasing joy peaking in meteor-like triumph. But the idyll ends in a conclusion which now paralyses the mind: 'I close my eyes; yet still is he / In front there, looking mastery.' The final day is a day of nightmare still confounding past and present, just as it had destroyed the idyll:

> Yes; trees were turning in their sleep
> Upon their windy pillow of gray
> When he stole in.

In 'The Whitewashed Wall', a mother performs a 'raptured rite' of memory which continues into the night: 'And when she yearns / For him, deep in the labouring night, / She sees him as close at hand, and turns / To him under his sheet of white.' The combination of strong rhyme and run-over line in 'yearns / For him' and 'turns / To him' gives us a vivid sensation of the woman dreaming. In 'How She Went to Ireland', Hardy uncannily projects the nightmarish motion into a corpse, as though one could be dead and still dream one was alive. Dora dreams of going to Ireland but goes only in death, 'Through the drift and darkness / Onward labouring'. At the heart of many of these dreams is the common night-marish paradox of trying to advance and being unable to move as in 'Memory and I'. (Pierston also describes the sensation in *The Well-Beloved*.) In 'He Follows Himself', the rational self is caught by the dreaming 'Heart' who cultivates the memory of a dead friend: 'And I seemed to go; yet still was there, / And am, and there haunt we / Thus bootlessly.' The self seems to advance with the years and yet is drawn back into the past. The result is a stasis during which the self is '[d]imming his hours to gray'. In 'The Five Students', a man's whole life seems like a nightmare in which he walks fast while the track he is on moves back-wards. Struggle as he might, he cannot escape the embrace of time and nature which has taken away all his friends. We might call this a grotesque version of the tortoise and the hare, the hare of mental activity seeming to advance and yet being overtaken by the tortoise of temporal change.[52]

In 'A Nightmare, and the Next Thing' (851), what is the 'next thing' which follows the nightmarish confusion of human and natural realities? Hardy does not say in this poem, but in another poem he suggests that the 'next thing' is an experience of absolute contradiction, dissolving stasis, life in death, going and staying. 'Going and Staying' (528) first proposes that moments of happiness 'were going' but that seasons of woe 'were staying'. Hardy added a third stanza after the poem's first publication in 1919 and suggested something more ghastly:

> Then we looked closelier at Time,
> And saw his ghostly arms revolving
> To sweep off woeful things with prime,
> Things sinister with things sublime
> Alike dissolving.[53]

Such is the grotesque apocalypse of the *eternal moment* of the romantic vision.

WAR

What happens to the individual visionary can be a model for what happens to an entire society:

> Thou, whose whole existence hitherto was a chimera and scenic show, at length becomest a reality: sumptuous Versailles bursts asunder, like a Dream, into void Immensity; Time is done, and all the scaffolding of Time falls wrecked with hideous clangour round thy soul. (Carlyle, *The French Revolution*, I, 1, iv)

'The old order changeth, yielding place to new,' Arthur proclaimed triumphantly in 'The Coming of Arthur' (Hardy quoted this passage in *Tess*, 52, p. 465). With 'The Passing of Arthur', also published in 1870, the phrase is repeated but the triumph has turned to tragedy, the Arthurian image of the mighty world 'now . . . dissolved'. Hardy knew better than most that old images persist in a changed world, plunge the mind into grotesque confusions of dream and reality, and lead to the nightmare of war waged in the name of some apocalyptic fantasy. This connection Hardy makes between the art of the grotesque, apocalyptic vision, and war was suggested to him by a number of writers he read.

In his notebooks Hardy copied down excerpts from James Thomson's 'The Lady of Sorrow'. The following passage, from which Hardy copied the first sentence, links an experience like Pierston's ('His record moved on with the years, his sentiments stood still'), with a vision of confused humanity pursuing shadows:

> Still the earth's time passed over me, unperceived, unregarded: but the true time, which is change, wrought within me. Besieging persistently the gateways of my senses, gradually the whole outer world – the innumerable armies of woes, sins, fears, despairs – the dreadful legions of all the realities – poured in upon and overwhelmed my spirit. The earth was become massy, substantial, intolerably oppressive, a waking Nightmare; its inhabitants were no shadows; their lives were woven into no fantastic mime, but into a vast tragedy ruthlessly real.[54]

As in other passages from the Victorian period, the war imagery is strangely proleptic of what is to come. In two 1878 essays by Leslie Stephen, Hardy might have noticed a specific connection between visionary dreaminess and the phenomenology of war. In his 'Dreams and Realities' essay, Stephen had described men misled by obsolescent beliefs in supernatural realities: 'Strange spectacles meet us everywhere in a period of speculative fermentation, when men's thoughts are heaving and working they know not why, and their minds, like those of half-aroused sleepers, are unable to distinguish between dreams and perceived realities.' In his essay on 'War', Stephen had applied similar imagery to the state of war: 'We . . . shuddered as we thought of the ominous forms which might be hidden in the gathering twilight. . . . Yet we can talk and read as quietly as though the whole affair were a grotesque nightmare which had vanished with sleep.'[55] With Thomson and Stephen, another major inspiration for Hardy was Tolstoy's letter on war in *The Times* in 1904. Hardy praised the letter for its 'masterly general indictment of war as a modern principle, with all its senseless and illogical crimes' (*Life*, 322). 'Again war . . . again the universal stupefaction and brutalization of men,' Tolstoy wrote. 'One longs to believe that it is a dream and to awake from it. . . . But no, it is not a dream but a dreadful reality!'[56] We shall see that Hardy drew other specific details from these sources for his greatest war poem, ' ''And There Was a Great Calm'' '.

'It must be remembered that in 1914 our conception of war was completely unreal. We had vague childish memories of the Boer War, and from these and from a general diffusion of Kiplingesque sentiments, we managed to infuse into war a decided element of adventurous romance. War still appealed to the imagination.'[57] Indeed, 'the actual outbreak of war was greeted with a surge of enthusiasm which transcended all bounds of class and party and was unlike anything in previous English history'.[58] As Paul Fussell has recently demonstrated, 'The war . . . proceeded in an atmosphere of euphemism as rigorous and impenetrable as language and literature skillfully used could make it'.[59] This was the romantic dream whose progress Hardy watched over the next years. Like Henry James, he knew what the war meant for the whole Victorian period. In a letter of 4 August 1914 James called the war 'this unspeakable giveaway of the whole fool's paradise of our past. It throws back so vivid a light – *this* was what we were so fondly working for!'

> The plunge of civilization into this abyss of blood and darkness by the wanton feat of those two infamous autocrats is a thing that so gives away the whole long age during which we have supposed the world to be, with whatever abatement, gradually bettering, that to have to take it all now for what the treacherous years were all the while making for and *meaning* is too tragic for any words.

The whole long age, to which James refers, was not merely an idyll of course. It had been haunted, especially since the Franco – Prussian war of 1870, by an uneasy apprehensiveness.[60] When the Great War came it was both a terrible surprise and something expected. The sinking of the *Titanic* in 1912 was the penultimate catastrophe. Leslie Stephen's essay on 'War' is remarkably prophetic of both events: 'We are like a steamship running at full speed, through a fog, towards an unknown shore.' An even earlier, more strangely prophetic, passage had occurred in *The French Revolution* where Carlyle describes the death of Mirabeau, the great representative of the old order: 'His death is Titanic, as his life has been! Lit up, for the last time, in the glare of coming dissolution, the mind of the man is glowing and burning. . . . He is as a ship suddenly shivered on sunk rocks.'[61]

Hardy found himself in an unusually key position to understand and represent what his countrymen were experiencing in the growing nightmare of the Great War. Indeed, his experience of half a century, from the idyll of 1870 to the disasters of 1912, and 1914, matched the experience his countrymen were having: 'All agree that the prewar summer was the most idyllic for many years.'[62] The summer of 1914 became, in retrospect, a metonymy for the whole, long, late-Victorian and Georgian idyll. Hardy was singularly positioned to express the shock of awakening, and connect his personal tragedy with the world's tragedy. 'The year 1912, which was to advance and end in such gloom for Hardy, began serenely. . . . But in February he learnt of the death of his friend General Henniker and in April occurred the disaster to the *Titanic*' (*Life*, 357). Then followed Emma's death in November: 'Why, then, latterly did we not speak? . . .' Then, 'August 4, 11 P.M. War declared with Germany. . . . But the full dimensions of what the English declaration meant were not quite realized at once. The whole news and what it meant burst upon Hardy's mind next morning. . . . He had been completely at fault . . . on the coming so soon of such a convulsion as the war' (*Life*, 365). Like James, he had dreamed the world was bettering. 'We have awakened from an opium-dream of comfort', Edmund Gosse wrote in 1915.[63] The act of awakening from a reverie, of knowing too late the shape of one's dreams, is the central plot which Hardy finds in himself and in England.

Thus we find the central most important image Hardy associates with war, that of a troubled reverie. As his thinking on war develops, his tendency to dramatise war as such a reverie increases. Finally, in his climactic war poem, ' "And There Was a Great Calm" ', he brings together the experiments he has been conducting in lyrics of memory, visions, apocalypses, ghosts, and grotesques. Here the apocalyptic vision of the poet becomes the model for the apocalyptic vision of an entire nation, a collective reverie troubled by its grotesque conclusion. Each age perhaps 'redefines the grotesque in terms of what threatens its sense of essential humanity'.[64] Hardy's definition of the grotesque as temporal dislocation and paralysed vision responds to the long 'treacherous' idyll of decades which contained within it an ultimate threat to essential humanity.

The Stages of Hardy's War Poetry

Harold Orel, in *The Final Years of Thomas Hardy*, has discussed Hardy's growing despair over war and the future of humanity. He also noted Hardy's ambivalences about war, his internationalism and his patriotism, his exposure of the horror of all wars and his occasional puzzling self-deception 'about the honourableness of wars fought in the past'.[65] In concluding this chapter, I wish to trace the process by which Hardy connected the cause of war with the romance of war, and grew increasingly pessimistic about its cure because he saw its roots in his own mind. This growing understanding enabled him to dramatise with increasing profundity what we might call the phenomenology of war, the way it is experienced by the mind, the way it represents the grotesque conclusion of the mind's own tendencies.

This development can be roughly divided into five stages: (1) Poems associated with the Napoleonic wars and published in *Wessex Poems* (1898); (2) the Boer War poems of 1899–1901; (3) *The Dynasts* (1904–1908); (4) the First World War poems; and (5) ' "And There Was a Great Calm" '.

1. In the war narratives of *Wessex Poems*, Hardy is basically interested in the battles as good stories. He is intrigued by the way old veterans are haunted by their memories, though this phenomenon has little bearing on the causes of war. He shares the awe felt by the speaker of 'Leipzig': 'My mother saw these things!' As a child, Hardy had been fascinated by the romance of the Napoleonic wars. Fascination, mingled with elegaic regret, motivates *The Trumpet-Major* (1880): 'it was a period when romance had not so greatly faded out of military life as it has done in these days of short service . . . and transient campaigns' (41, p. 372). In 1887 he visited the battle scene of Lodi, and enjoyed recapturing the romance of the battle as it had been rendered in 'an old French tune of his father's' (*Life*, 195). 'Some time after the excursion', he wrote 'The Bridge of Lodi', published in 1902:

> In the battle-breathing jingle
> Of its forward-footing tune

> I could see the armies mingle,
>   And the columns cleft and hewn. . . .   (74)

But the irony of the poem is not the irony learned by Owen and Sassoon after the first months of the First World War. Rather the irony is that the townspeople have forgotten the battle and only Hardy remembers: 'the whole romance to see here / Is the dream I bring with me.' Hardy is like the lover who holds to his dream in 'My Cicely': ' 'Tis better / To dream than to own the debasement. . . .' Hardy's ultimate evaluation of these speakers is unclear: he partly identifies with them and partly laughs at them.

2. On 11 October 1899 Hardy noted in himself a mixed reaction to the Boer War. Deploring this 'old and barbarous' method of settling disputes, he nevertheless admitted, 'few persons are more martial than I, or like better to write of war in prose and rhyme'. Four months later he noted: 'I take a keen pleasure in war strategy and tactics, following it as if it were a game of chess; but all the while I am obliged to blind myself to the human side of the matter: directly I think of that, the romance looks somewhat tawdry, and worse.' At the end of 1900, he concluded: 'War resembles a snow storm in one respect: it is grand and romantic at the first, but dreary and tedious in its disappearance.' The Boer War poems are muted impressions of war, particularly 'as perceived by its victims'. And Hardy could congratulate himself that 'not a single one is Jingo or Imperial — a fatal defect according to the judgement of the British majority at present'. M. van Wyk Smith has recently shown how the Boer War marked a new stage in war mythology. 'As England's real imperial supremacy declined in the 1890s, so did public school myth-making increase.' In the Boer War, more soldiers came from the educated classes, more war poems were produced, and more newspapers created more 'vicarious excitement' then ever before. Ironically, war mythology grew in intensity as war conditions became more horrible. W. T. Stead was the main anti-war spokesman of this period, and Hardy associated himself with Stead's efforts by reprinting 'A Christmas Ghost-Story' in Stead's *War Against War in South Africa*. But the last poem in Hardy's series, 'The Sick Battle-God' (1901), shows some ambivalence. It describes the 'days when men had joy of war' and the Battle-God was invoked 'in rune and rhyme': 'His haloes rayed the very gore, / And corpses wore his glory-gleam.' The sarcasm seems clear, and yet Hardy sounds like the regretful speaker of 'The Impercipient' when he says: 'souls have grown seers, and thought outbrings / the mournful many-sidedness of things. . . . He scarce impassions champions now.' One

of the champions Hardy mentions is Nelson. When the poem concludes, 'Let men rejoice, let men deplore', what we should rejoice at is clear, but what we should deplore is not.[66]

Nevertheless, 1901 is an important year because Hardy begins to define more clearly for himself the various elements which contribute to the war frenzy. 'This Imperial idea is, I fear, leading us into strange waters.' In his 1899 poem, 'A Christmas Ghost-Story', Hardy had made the conventional contrast between Christianity and war. Now, in 1901, he notes how Christianity can be made into a war principle. Asked his opinion of the effect of the war on English literature, he cited 'the issue of large quantities of warlike and patriotic poetry' and 'the disguise under Christian terminology of principles . . . obviously anti-Christian, because inexorable and masterful'. At the same time, he hopes that war is 'doomed by the gradual growth of the introspective faculty in mankind. . . . In another aspect, this may be called the growth of a sense of humour. . . . in the fullness of time, war will come to an end . . . because of its absurdity.' He will read a similar expression of hope in Tolstoy's 1904 letter: 'The hypnotism by which people have been stupefied and by which Governments still endeavour to stupefy them soon passes off, and its effect is becoming weaker and weaker.' What Hardy will progressively realise, with the coming of the First World War, is how deep and fundamental the hypnotism is.[67]

3. *The Dynasts* is an important step forward in Hardy's understanding of war. He makes the 'Spirit Sinister' represent the romantic literary approach to war: 'we've rare dramas going'; 'begin small, and so lead up to the greater. It is a sound dramatic principle. I always aim to follow it in my pestilences, fires, famines, and other comedies'. 'War makes rattling good history; but Peace is poor reading.' Hardy then uses the Spirit of Irony to stress the grotesque contrast between the sinister romance and the human actuality: 'Quaint poesy, and real romance of war!'[68]

The Dynasts is also important because Hardy senses that some central spell drives the peoples to war and he develops a consistent strain of imagery to describe it. In the Boer War poems there had been few such images – only a brief mention of 'wroth reasonings' and 'puppets' in 'Departure'. But in *The Dynasts* the spell binds men's minds and determines all actions, and war is one of the patterns 'It' weaves. 'It', of course, is the Immanent Will, a sort of cosmic reverie, 'listless', 'in-brooding', 'drowsed', working by 'rapt aesthetic rote, . . . [e]volving always that it wots not of'. What it wots not of is what Hardy calls the 'grotesque shape' of war:

So doth the Will objectify itself
In likeness of a sturdy people's wrath,
Which takes no count of the new trends of time,
Trusting ebbed glory in a present need.

Towards the end of the drama, the Spirit of Pities pictures the Will in an image which unites all the important elements: reverie, frenzied crowds, apocalypse, the grotesque:

I see an unnatural Monster, loosely jointed,
With an Apocalyptic Being's shape,
And limbs and eyes a hundred thousand strong,
And fifty thousand heads; which coils itself
About the buildings there.

But how strange the whole conception is, even if we are asked, as Hardy says, 'to look through the insistent, and often grotesque, substance at the thing signified'.[69]

My feeling about *The Dynasts* is that Hardy discovered that 'It' drove people to war, but he did not yet know what 'It' was. He thought it was something out of Schopenhauer. Thus the analysis of the 'grotesque' in *The Dynasts* is not clearly focused. The grotesque defines a kind of relationship between mind and reality, but the Will is not related to anything else, because it includes all things. As Fitzpiers says in *The Woodlanders*, 'strangeness is not in the nature of a thing, but in its relation to something extrinsic – in this case an unessential observer' (18, p. 153). To an outside observer, the Will may be grotesque but only on the contradictory premise that the observer can be outside the Will. This is one of the troubling inconsistencies at the heart of the drama.[70]

Nevertheless, *The Dynasts* plays an important part in Hardy's growing understanding of war, just as it does in his understanding of patterns and metrical possibilities. For the Will acts very much, not like reality, but like an apocalyptic vision of reality, submitting all things to its form. Hardy's insistence on its grotesqueness is potentially a critique of its claims. But Hardy is here misled by Schopenhauer's visionary identification of the world as Will. *The Dynasts* is an example of Hardy's visionary appetite before he had formed his mature critique of vision. In the end, Hardy's norm will remain the Darwinian world which is always larger than the visions and species which evolve within it. In Hardy's mature conception of war, the apocalyptic dreamer and villain of the Napoleonic war is Napoleon, and all the people who joined in the frenzy. Hardy might well have remembered Hugo's description of Napoleon after Waterloo: 'It was Napoleon endeavouring to advance again, mighty somnambulist of a vanished dream' (*Les Misérables*, II, i, 13). Later Hardy will read William Inge's *Outspoken Essays* which note that Rousseau's ideal of a General Will has become a stuffed idol and turned into an evil spirit'. 'There is no General Will. All we have a right to say is that individuals are occasionally guided by reason, crowds never' ('Our Present Discontents', cf. below p. 135).

What we see in the years following *The Dynasts* is that Hardy retains the imagery but not the abstraction. He demythologises war by seeing its cause, paradoxically, in myths and madness, not in a cosmic Will. In a poem he began during the end of *The Dynasts* years but did not finish till years after, he states: 'Mankind, you dismay me / When shadows waylay me, ... by your madnesses . . . Acting like puppets / Under Time's buffets; / In superstitions / And ambitions . . . Led by . . . prescience-lessness / Into unreason / And hideous self-treason' (817). Asked in 1909 for his view of 'the culture and thought of the time', Hardy cited the 'incubus of armaments, territorial ambitions smugly disguised as patriotism, superstitions, conventions of every sort' (*Life*, 347).

4. 'Channel Firing', written in April 1914, was, Hardy said, singularly 'prophetic' of the First World War (*Life*, 365). It is a new kind of apocalyptic war poem. It shows Hardy re-assessing the runes and rhymes of his youth, namely the popular English ballad of war and heroism. (One of the early motives behind *The Dynasts* was Hardy's desire to write a ballad on English participation in the Napoleonic wars – a patriotic motive which, Harold Orel points out, can still be felt in the epic drama.) The *Life* shows that in 1912 Hardy quoted a sentence from a 1911 *Edinburgh Review* article (*Life*, 359).[71] The article, entitled 'Modern Developments in Ballad Art', discussed the English ballad and cited, among others, ' "The Burial of Sir John Moore", killed while covering the embarcation of his troops'. Hardy had read this poem, about a famous hero of the Napoleonic era, long before in Palgrave. The *Edinburgh* writer praised the ballad's 'joint appeal to personal enthusiasm – devotion to a dead leader, and to impersonal sentiment, – the glory of a soldier's honourable dying'. The article quotes the stanza beginning, 'We buried him darkly at dead of night, / The sods with our bayonets turning.' It then praises the poem's 'dignity' which is produced by 'the descriptive literalism telling how, uncoffined, un-shrouded, the fallen hero was laid to rest while the random guns of the enemy broke the stillness'. The setting, the situation, and the final detail of 'Channel Firing' are quite similar to elements in the poem and the article's

account. But Hardy's emphasis is on the grotesque contrast between the graveyard setting and the war passion.

'Channel Firing' is also a grotesque parody of an apocalypse. (It may recall the apocalypse John Donne calls off in 'At the Round Earth's Imagined Corners'.) The risen dead are only buried corpses disturbed by the guns. The Judgement consists in a few cynical remarks by a God who threatens to 'blow the trumpet'. God is mad because men are mad – 'Mad as hatters' – and they play God, plying a vengeance which wakes the dead: 'Again the guns disturbed the hour, / Roaring their readiness to avenge.' But temporal reality remains what it always has been and looms grotesquely through man's apocalyptic desires: 'The glebe cow drooled.' Robert Lowell, coming from a different tradition and responding to another war, had an analogous insight into war's apocalyptic violence, when he described the whaleboats trying to sound the drowned bodies:

> To Cape Cod
> Guns, cradled on the tide,
> Blast the eelgrass about a waterclock
> Of bilge and backwash, roil the salt and sand
> Lashing earth's scaffold, rock
> Our warships in the hand
> Of the great God, where time's contrition blues
> Whatever it was these Quaker sailors lost
> In the mad scramble of their lives. . . .
>
> ('The Quaker Graveyard in Nantucket')

What we see during the First World War is that Hardy brings together the various elements he has seen contributing to war: romance, music, drama, ballads, the imperial idea, and the idea of a holy war. His ultimate understanding of war is that it is caused by a kind of apocalyptic madness in which people allow themselves to be caught up. Nietzsche helped Hardy come to the conclusion.

Hardy was apparently one of the early readers of Nietzsche in English translations,[72] which began to appear in 1895: 'with many of his sayings I have always heartily agreed'.[73] Between 1895 and 1903, Nietzsche was widely reviewed and also widely attacked in England – though defended by some of Hardy's friends like Arthur Symons and Havelock Ellis. Hardy refers to Nietzsche in the *Life* for 1902, and he read various articles on Nietzsche about this time.[74] In 1903 a serious vogue began to develop for Nietzsche, and between 1909 (when a translation of his *Complete Works* began to appear) and 1912, he became 'the philosopher *à la mode* in England'.[75]

In the face of Nietzsche's growing reputation, and in the light of his own attraction for parts of the philosophy, Hardy made a series of reflections about Nietzsche in 1914 – just before the war began and in its opening months: 'He used to seem to me . . . to be an incoherent rhapsodist.' He and his school 'insanely regard life as a thing improvable by force to immaculate gloriousness, when all the time life's inseparable conditions allow only clumsy opportunities for amelioration by plodding compromises and contrivances'. 'What puzzles one is to understand how the profounder thinkers in Germany and to some extent, elsewhere, can have been so dazzled by this writer's bombastic poetry. . . . His postulates as to what life is on this earth have no resemblance to reality.' What Nietzsche assumes is what Hardy himself had hoped for in his own apocalyptic speculations about a cosmic consciousness: 'A continuity of consciousness through the human race would be the only justification of his proposed measures.'

I am less interested in how fair Hardy is to Nietzsche,[76] than in how his remarks reflect his maturing understanding of the cause of war. For Hardy, apocalyptic versions of personal fulfilment come to bear too dangerous a likeness to apocalyptic versions of political solutions. He is less interested in the personal self-enhancing dimensions of Nietzsche's thought than in its potential debasement into naive and dangerous utopian thinking. He worries about Nietzsche's influence not only on Germany but on England. Like Tolstoy in his 1904 letter, Hardy is amazed at what Tolstoy named 'so-called enlightened men', 'who but yesterday were proving the cruelty, futility, the senselessness of war'. They 'now think, speak, and write only about killing as many men as possible'. Bagehot, in his 1864 essay on the grotesque, discussed above, gave an example of modern grotesques: 'The most earnest truth-seeking men fall into the worst delusions; they will not let their mind alone; they force it towards some ugly thing, which a crotchet of argument, a conceit of intellect recommends, and nature punishes their disregard of her warning by subjection to the ugly one, by belief in it' (p. 359). Hardy's poem, 'Tolerance' (272), written sometime after his wife's death, may have been written with the superman in mind:

> But now the only happiness
> In looking back that I possess –
> Whose lack would leave me comfortless –
>
> Is to remember I refrained
> From masteries I might have gained,
> And for my tolerance was disdained;

> For see, a tomb. And if it were
> I had bent and broke, I should not dare
> To linger in the shadows there.

In 1915 Hardy refers to the war lords as the 'masterful of Europe'.

There is a striking difference between 'Poems of War and Patriotism', on the First World War, and 'War Poems', on the Boer War. In the later grouping, the moral indignation, whether directed against war or against England's enemies, is much more intense. The power of this indignation, and its confused object, will teach Hardy a crucial lesson about mind and war.

The very title, 'Poems of War and Patriotism', with its typically askew phrasing, reflects the confusion of the 1914–15 poems in the series. Some, like the first poem, 'Men Who March Away', praise the 'faith and fire' of patriotism, while others, like the second poem, 'His Country', denounce such patriotism: 'Whom have I to fight' since 'My country' is every-where?[77] Quoting one of Hardy's anti-war poems in the series, Siegfried Sassoon saw himself carrying on Hardy's attempt 'to unmask the ugly face of Mars and – in the words of Thomas Hardy – "war's apology wholly stultify"'. At the same time Sassoon notes about himself: 'Yet, in spite of my hatred of war and "Empery's insatiate lust of power", there was an awful attraction in its hold over my mind.'[78] In the poems he wrote in 1916 and later, Hardy seemed to realise the full implications of the awful attraction. One unrealised irony in the earlier 1914 – 15 poems is that Hardy's anger at the senselessness of war becomes a war-serving anger against thy German perpetrators: 'May . . . thy children beg their bread' (501). 'May . . . their brood perish everlastingly' (498). But the sad consequences of such indignation are not yet clear. Hardy was somewhat embarrassed by 'Men Who March Away'. He said in 1914: 'I fear they were not free from some banalities which it is difficult to keep out of lines which are meant to appeal to the man in the street.'[79] But Hardy is still not immune to what he calls the 'blatant mood' (495) and as late as 1917 wrote the patriotic 'A Call to National Service' (505). 'Then and Now' (504), written in 1915, celebrates ancient wars when men were chivalrous and knightly. Harold Orel poses the question: 'Why did Hardy, on occasions, deceive himself about the honourableness of wars fought in the past?' One answer is that the awful attraction could still cast its un-conscious spell. Writers called upon to aid the war effort were particularly vulnerable. In 1915 Hardy could still take a utopian view of the war and entertain the fancy that it would have a good effect on literature, 'by removing (from literature) those things that are shaken, as things that are made, that those things that cannot be shaken may remain'. Not yet had the last days of the war taken away Wilfred Owen, Isaac Rosenberg, Edward Thomas, and other unknown talents rendered mute and less glorious than they might have been. In 1925 Hardy would be far beyond this blatant mood: 'No one is justified in trying to make out that war has had a beneficial effect upon things aesthetic. . . . there are no lessons of war. War is a fatality. It has nothing to do with either reason or intelligence. War is something irresistible. It seems to obey some kind of devilish determinism.' [80]

This 'devilish determinism' is no longer exactly the Immanent Will. The later war poems borrow many of their images from *The Dynasts* but also represent an important development. They refer to 'throes of artifical rage', 'Foes of mad mood', and 'Nations . . . mad, aswoon'. But no longer are these images connected with Schopenhauer's abstraction. War's waking nightmare, wherein '[b]rown martial brows in dying throes have wanned', is the achievement of men alone who have 'nursed . . . dreams to shed your blood'. Men do not wage war 'warely, or from taste, / But tickled mad by some demonic force'. Like 'some kind of devilish determinism', the image is obviously intended as a metaphor for something else: how a supposedly free mentality can become enslaved to its own conceptions. No longer does the vehicle, 'demonic force', etc, usurp the tenor, human responsibility. Such 'usurpation' Hardy later sees in '"And There Was a Great Calm"' as the fatal sophistry of the Sinister Spirit who sneers: 'It had to be!' That wars need not be is the more terrible lesson of the Spirit of Pity who 'whispered, "Why?"' In a poem he published in 1925, Hardy would conclude that men

> Set them with dark-drawn breaths
> To knave their neighbours' deaths
> In periodic spasms!
> Yea, fooled by foul phantasms,
> In a strange cyclic throe
> Backward to type they go. . . .

Perhaps Hardy had been influenced by Freud's classic statement of this point in 'Thoughts for the Times on War and Death'. [81]

In the later First World War poems we see Hardy realising the full force and nature of the foul phantasm as an apocalyptic passion. In one of the earlier poems he had described his Utopian dream. 'On the Belgian Expatriation' (496), written in 1914 and included with some revisions in *Moments of Vision*, opens with a Tennysonian dream vision of bells and peace. 'Then I awoke,' Hardy says, and we may remember Tennyson's confirmation of the dream in 'The Epic' and 'Morte d'Arthur': 'At this a hundred bells began to peal, / That with the sound I woke, and heard indeed / The clear church-bells ring in the Christmas-morn.' But Hardy's dream is replaced by a nightmare vision: 'lo, before me stood / The visioned ones, but pale and full of fear. . . . Foes of mad mood / Had shattered these [carillons] to shards. . . .' In a few years, this process of awakening from a Utopian dream will be clearly seen by Hardy as the process of awakening to a grotesque enslavement in a dream of mastery. To make this connection, Hardy must first connect the 'mad mood' of the foes with the awful attraction he himself is capable of feeling.

This development we can see taking place in the last three poems of 'Poems of War and Patriotism', the first written in 1915–16, the second written in 1916, the last undated. This triad of related poems serves as an approach to Hardy's climactic synthesis in ' "And There Was a Great Calm" '.

'A New Year's Eve in War Time' (507) is the first of these. We have already seen how the speaker waits for an apocalyptic announcement from a spectral horseman but hears only the sound of the clock. He then surmises that the horseman may be announcing: 'More Famine and Flame! – / More Severance and Shock!'

'A New Year's Eve in War Time' is remarkably like the opening passage of Wallace Stevens's 'The Pure Good of Theory':

> It is time that beats in the breast and it is time
> That batters against the mind, silent and proud,
> The mind that knows it is destroyed by time.
>
> Time is a horse that runs in the heart, a horse
> Without a rider on a road at night.
> The mind sits listening and hears it pass.
>
>   . . . .
>
> Even breathing is the beating of time, in kind:
> A retardation of its battering,
> A horse grotesquely taut. . . .

Against time, Stevens pits a 'platonic person': 'A capable being may replace / Dark horse' with, what Stevens calls later in the poem, the 'universal flare' of imaginative vision. This capable being seems to be that 'noble rider' whose 'violence from within' protects him 'from a violence

without. It is the imagination pressing back against the pressure of reality'
('The Noble Rider and the Sound of Words'). In such imaginative
violence, however, Hardy sees another kind of violence, the flare of
exploding bombs, as in Joyce's logic: 'A phrase, then, of impatience, thud
of Blake's wings of excess. I hear the ruin of all space, shattered glass and
toppling masonry, and time one livid final flame' (*Ulysses*, Nester episode).
The violence from within *leads*, in Hardy's view, to a violence from
without, and time is abused as in his image of 'the crazed household-clock'
in 'Before Marching and After.'

We can use the Stevens and Joyce passages as a way of explicating 'A·
New Year's Eve in War Time'. We have already quoted the first two
stanzas with their eerie confusion of inner phantasms and outer world. The
poem concludes:

III

The twelfth hour nears,
Hand-hid, as in shame;
I undo the lock
And listen and wait
For the Young Unknown.

IV

In the dark there careers –
As if Death astride came
To numb all with his knock –
A horse, at mad rate
Over rut and stone
While tiredly the spectral spines intone.

V

No figure appears,
No call of our name,
No sound but 'Tic-toc'
Without check. Past the gate
It clatters – is gone.

VI

What rider it bears
There is none to proclaim;
And the Old Year has struck,
And, scarce animate,
The New makes moan.

VII
Maybe that 'More Tears! –
More Famine and Flame! –
More Severance and Shock!'
Is the order from Fate
That the Rider bears on
To pale Europe; and tiredly the pines intone.

The Stevens and Joyce passages help explain the nightmarish power of
these images. Temporal reality is 'retarded' by the visionary who waits
expectantly for 'the Young Unknown'. So retarded or repressed, temporal
reality turns into a 'horse grotesquely taut' which then seems to approach
with spectral speed. Once arrived, the horseman's only announcement is
the ruin of all space and time, the ruin both of the visionary split asunder as
in Blake's print discussed earlier, and the ruin of an entire nation subject to
flame and severance. Hardy surely remembered Carlyle's image of the
French National Convention as a kind of 'Apocalyptic Convention, or
black *Dream become real* . . . how it covered France with woe, delusion and
delirium; and from its bosom there went forth Death on the pale Horse'
(III, 2, i).

The next poem in the triad which concludes 'Poems of War and
Patriotism' is 'I Met a Man' (508), written in 1916. The poem repeats a
theme of 'Channel Firing' but more clearly connects the wrath of God
with the wrath of men. The poem is also the first connection Hardy makes
between modern war rage and Old Testament holy war prophecy. God
threatens to

. . . mend that old mistake of mine
I made with Saul, and ever consign
All Lords of war whose sanctuaries enshrine
Liberticide, to sleep. . . .

'It repenteth me,' God continues, 'I bred / Chartered armipotents lust-led
/ To feuds. . . .' Ironically in this poem God's 'utterance grew, and
flapped like flame' as though he now meant to impose a new apocalyptic
solution. In 1918 Hardy will write 'Jezreel' (521) and note how the
English attack on Jezreel by Allenby was a repetition of the raid on Jezreel
by Jehu in II Kings, Chapter 9. Elisha the prophet had commissioned Jehu
to fight a holy war against Ahab. 'On war-men at this end of time . . .
Flashed he who drove furiously?' Such are the 'hauntings of men of to-
day'.

In reading Stephen and Tolstoy on the troubled dream of war, in seeing the dangers of the Nietzschean apocalypse, in seeing the war passion as a kind of perverted prophetic passion, and in noting his own proneness to patriotic passion, Hardy approached nearer to the realisation that there was an intimate connection between the way the imagination works and the way war is created. We may be able to see the last poem in the triad as beginning to make this final connection.

I Looked Up from My Writing' (509) gives us one of Hardy's most traditional situations, an interrupted reverie:

> I looked up from my writing,
>   And gave a start to see,
> As if rapt in my inditing,
>   The moon's full gaze on me.

The poem does not explain what Hardy's 'blinkered mind' is composing. The possible pun in 'inditing' (indict and indite come from the same root) may suggest the war poems which this poem concludes. The moon reveals a father sorrowing for his slain son, and the sorrow makes literary endeavour look like a superfluous activity indeed. Here, as always, Hardy continues to awake from illusion, and as he does so he better understands the illusion that has trapped his countrymen.

5. '"And There Was a Great Calm"' (545), written in 1920 and published with some revisions in *Late Lyrics and Earlier*, is Hardy's greatest war poem and the great synthesising poem of his series of war poems. 'In the middle of the night . . . an idea seized him, and he was heard moving about the house looking things up' (*Life*, 407). The first three lines capture beautifully the sense of confusion which characterises the collective social mind during wartime:

> There had been years of Passion – scorching, cold,
> And much Despair, and Anger heaving high,
> Care whitely watching, Sorrows manifold. . . .

Reality has been transformed into abstract shapes which are now troubled by the conclusion to which they have led. Hardy's style imitates well how these shapes come back to haunt the mind, like grotesque lumbering figures in some nightmarish allegory. In the same year Hardy wrote '"And There Was a Great Calm"', Yeats wrote 'The Second Coming': 'The best lack all conviction, while the worst / Are full of passionate intensity.' Now the 'best', the 'so-called enlightened men' of Tolstoy's letter, are caught up in the same eerie surreality.

Hardy's second and third stanzas seem to synthesise material from Stephen and Tolstoy which Hardy was perhaps 'looking . . . up'. 'Newspaper correspondents', Stephen said, 'vied with each other in the vivid description of ghastly suffering.' These descriptions horrify and yet excite the mind. Now 'we can talk and read as quietly as though the whole affair were a grotesque nightmare which had vanished with sleep'. Tolstoy denounced 'all this dreadful, desperate, newspaper mendacity, which, being universal, does not fear exposure [of its] misty patroitic phrases'.

> Stupefied by prayers, sermons, exhortations, by processions, pictures, and newspapers, the cannon's flesh, hundreds of thousands of men, uniformly dressed, carrying diverse deadly weapons, leaving their parents, wives, children, with hearts of agony, but with artificial sprightliness, go where they, risking their lives, will commit the most dreadful act of killing men whom they do not know and who have done them no harm. . . . Those who remain at home are gladdened by news of the murder of men, and when they learn that many Japanese have been killed they thank some one whom they called God.

Tolstoy's last sentence may remind English readers of Coleridge's 'Fears in Solitude', ll. 86 – 129.

Thus Hardy writes:

II

Men had not paused to answer. Foes distraught
Pierced the thinned peoples in a brute-like blindness,
Philosophies that sages long had taught,
And Selflessness, were as an unknown thought,
And 'Hell!' and 'Shell!' were yapped at Lovingkindness.

III

The feeble folk at home had grown full-used
To 'dug-outs', 'snipers', 'Huns', from the war-adept
In the mornings heard, and at evetides perused;
To day-dreamt men in millions, when they mused –
To nightmare-men in millions when they slept.

Men become reduced to spectral phantasms which other men annihilate. Three years after Hardy wrote ' "And There Was a Great Calm" ', Yeats wrote 'Meditations in Time of Civil War': 'We had fed the heart on fantasies, / The heart's grown brutal from the fare';

> Frenzies bewilder, reveries perturb the mind;
> Monstrous familiar images swim to the mind's eye.
>
>   . . . .
>
>   In cloud-pale rags, or in lace,
> The rage-driven, rage-tormented, and rage-hungry troop,
> Trooper belabouring trooper, biting at arm or at face,
> Plunges towards nothing, arms and fingers spreading wide
> For the embrace of nothing; and I, my wits astray
> Because of all that senseless tumult, all but cried
> For vengeance. . . .

In 1888, Hardy had said: 'Apprehension is a great element in imagination. It is a semi-madness, which sees enemies, etc., in inanimate objects' (*Life*, 204). In 1916, knowing like Yeats what it was like to be led astray by all that senseless tumult, he connects the workings of the poetic imagination with the workings of the collective imagination: '*Apprehensiveness*', Hardy says, is a better term 'to express the cause of the present war' (*Life*, 373). Paul Fussell describes the British view of the 'Enemy' in the First World War: '"We" are individuals with names and personal identities; "he" is a mere collective entity. We are visible; he is invisible. We are normal; he is grotesque.'[82] In Hardy, these grotesque shapes, produced by an apprehensive imagination abusing the limits of imagination and reality, return as nightmare-men. (In 'Nineteen Hundred and Nineteen', Yeats had written: 'the nightmare / Rides upon sleep.') And the dreamers at home have themselves become ghostlike, enfeebled.

The article to which Hardy was responding when he discussed 'apprehensiveness' summarised many of the themes we have been tracing and was perhaps one of the items Hardy 'looked up' for ' "And There Was a Great Calm" '. 'What is Militarism', *TLS*, 27 July 1916, pp. 349–50, described the Prussian 'national hypochondria', a militarism rooted in the victory of 1870, which has come to see 'peace in terms of war . . . a perpetual effort to avoid defeat in war'. 'The officer is a priest to every Prussian', and militarism has become 'an obsession, so that they have become quite unable to distinguish between real and imaginary dangers'. For such a nation, 'there is only one romance, a sickroom romance of war and victory'. Recalling the English popularity of Frederick the Great, the article warned: 'there are people in England now who really do admire the Prussian state of mind.'

Hardy's fourth stanza contains perhaps the most interesting image of the poem:

> Waking to wish existence timeless, null,
> Sirius they watched above where armies fell;
> He seemed to check his flapping when, in the lull
> Of night a boom came thencewise, like the dull
> Plunge of a stone dropped into some deep well.

This image of an ambiguous lull surprised by the unforeseen event is an image Hardy may have borrowed from a favourite poem, Shelley's *Hellas*:

> In the brief trances of the artillery
> One cry from the destroyed and the destroyer
> Rose, and a cloud of desolation wrapped
> The unforeseen event. . . .   (ll. 493–6)

In Hardy's the lull seems to precede the boom and yet we do not notice the lull until the boom has occurred. So it is not clear whether the lull precedes or follows the boom, just as it is not clear whether we hear the dull plunge of a stone before or after it strikes the bottom of a deep well. (Interestingly, Hardy wrote 'Echo' rather than 'Plunge' in an earlier version of the poem.) Soldiers know well the kind of temporal tricks which apprehensive expectation can play on their minds. And this smaller confusion typifies the temporal confusion of the whole period of war, dissolved into 'years of Passion' when 'Men had not paused to answer'. The collective visionary wish to make reality 'timeless' has led to an ultimate weariness, a kind of death-wish to make reality 'dull'. But men cannot escape the terrible conclusions of their unreal phantasms.

Hardy's image of a stone plunging into a well is also important because he uses the same image in 'Where Three Roads Joined', the poem which precedes ' "And There Was a Great Calm" '. In so juxtaposing these images, he seems to underscore the connection between a collective fantasy and a personal fantasy, between the tragedy of war and the tragedy of love:

> I am sure those branchways are brooding now,
> With a wistful blankness upon their face,
> While the few mute passengers notice how
> Spectre-beridden is the place.
>
> Which nightly sighs like a laden soul,
> And grieves that a pair, in bliss for a spell

Not far from thence, should have let it roll
Away from them down a plumbless well

While the phasm of him who fared starts up,
And of her who was waiting him sobs from near
As they haunt there and drink the wormwood cup
They filled for themselves when their sky was clear.

The lovers caught up in that moment of bliss forgot the time until they
ended as phasms which haunt the place which is no longer what it once
was: it is 'now rutted and bare'. The pattern has come to its belated
spectral conclusion. The phasm seems to 'start up' like the sound of the
stone dropped into the well, and even then the wormwood cup was filling.
The lovers also had lost control of their lives but the consequences had not
come home until much later.

Such was the fate of the 'maid and her wight' who came 'whispering by'
in 'In Time of "The Breaking of Nations"'. Gradually, in Hardy's
development, the war annals and the lovers' annals begin to parallel.
Interestingly, Hardy bracketed '"And There Was a Great Calm"' and
'Where Three Roads Joined' with 'A Duettist to Her Pianoforte' (543)
and 'Haunting Fingers' (546). Both describe the spell-binding rhythms of
war songs. These are associated in the first poem with a romantic moment
whose consequences were unseen. In the second poem they are made into a
spectral rhythm which seems to outlive life itself. Hardy probably knew
Strang's remarkable etching, 'War', in which Death the drummer makes
music over the ruined town. (See Illustration 20.)

'"And There Was a Great Calm"' also ends with song: 'the aimed-at
moved away in trance-lipped song.' The war is over and men find
themselves in another lull: 'Breathless they paused . . . all was hushed.'
People raise anxious queries ('Strange, this! How?'), the Spirit of Irony
smirks, the Sinister Spirit sneers, while from 'Heaven distilled a clemency'.
But this mild millennial moment, like the poem's title, is deceptive. Years
before, Hardy had put double lines next to Dryden's line: 'And peace itself
is war in masquerade.' Indeed it was only in the peace following the war,
like the lull following the boom, that Hardy, like Yeats, realised the nature
of the lull preceding the war and the trance which led to war. As in
'According to the Mighty Working', 'Peace' is 'hid riot', hidden war.
The title, '"And There Was a Great Calm"', like the title 'In Time of the
"The Breaking of Nations"', may either contrast or parallel the biblical
passage to the war frenzy and its aftermath. The peace of Christ may
oppose the peace imposed by men. Or, men have played God and taken His

power unto themselves: 'Then he arose, and rebuked the winds and the sea; and there was a great calm' (Matthew 8 : 26). In the last stanza, Hardy takes Luke 2 : 14 and rewrites it: 'There was peace on earth, and silence in the sky.' (In the first edition, the comma was a semi-colon to make the caesura more pronounced.) The great effort to impose world order ('Peace is war') has ended in the most terrible of all grotesques, an apocalyptic silence.[83]

Conclusion: Hardy and the Witch of Endor

Another item Hardy may have looked up before writing ' "And There Was a Great Calm" ' was Dean William Inge's *Outspoken Essays*. He had read and admired the essays the year before when they had first appeared (*Friends of a Lifetime*, p. 306). The similarities between Inge's first essay, 'Our Present Discontents', and Hardy's 'Apology' to *Late Lyrics and Earlier* are striking. 'The possibility of another dark age', Inge wrote, 'is not remote.' He hoped that 'science and humanism can work together'. He regretted that superstition and complacency prevented the national Church from being a credible guardian 'of our intellectual and spiritual birthright'. But he hoped that 'the epochs of apparent decline may be those in which the race is recuperating after an exhausting effort'. Defining the root cause of the present discontent, Inge said: 'we have been led astray by a will-of-the-wisp akin to the apocalyptic dreams of the Jews in the last two centuries before Christ. . . . The myth of progress is our form of apocalyptism.' Inge found apocalyptism in the current theory 'that though the Deity is not omnipotent yet, He is on His way to become so'. Quoting Richard Trench on the power of words (from *On the Study of Words*), Inge said: 'The democracy is a ready victim to shibboleths and catchwords.' In the second essay, Inge dissected the shibboleth of patriotism, cited its 'atavistic and pathological' motives, and concluded, 'it is certain to become an immoral obsession if it is isolated and made absolute. We have seen the appalling perversion – the methodical diabolism – which this obsession has produced in Germany.'[84]

Hardy's 'Apology' to *Late Lyrics and Earlier* gives us his 1922 assessment of the state of England. He cites 'the barbarizing of taste in the younger minds by the dark madness of the late war'. He also notes: 'we seem threatened with a new Dark Age.' He discusses the alliance of religion and humanism, the role of the national Church, the looped orbit of progress. He finds distressing signs of atavism and superstition in poetry and religion. And he points to the danger of apocalyptism:

... these, I say, the visible signs of mental and emotional life, must like all other things keep moving, becoming; even though at present, when belief in witches of Endor is displacing the Darwinian theory and 'the truth that shall make you free', men's minds appear, as above noted, to be moving backwards rather than on.

Hardy's reference to the Witch of Endor can be seen to represent his mature understanding of the relation between imagination and war. The image had been used in various contexts by Hardy, both personal and social contexts which now begin to parallel.

The story of the Witch of Endor in I Samuel 28 had always been one of Hardy's favourites. In *The Return of the Native* he associates the image with imaginative excitement. Eustacia tells Wildeve: 'I merely lit that fire because I was dull, and thought I would get a little excitement by calling you up and triumphing over you as the Witch of Endor called up Samuel' (I, 6, p. 73). In *the Mayor of Casterbridge* Henchard visits the weather-caster and feels 'like Saul at his reception by Samuel' (26, p. 214). The scene may owe something to that in *Lorna Doone* where John Ridd visits Mother Melldrum and remembers the parson's 'sermon about the Witch of Endor, and the perils of them that meddle wantonly with the unseen Powers' (XVII). Hardy associates Henchard's experience with submission to an obsolete superstition. In *The Well-Beloved*, the grotesque illusions of romance are exposed: 'The Juno of that day was the Witch of Endor of this' (*Illustrated London News*, 17 December 1892, p. 775). In 1893–4, two writers Hardy admired, Thomas Huxley and Andrew Lang, discussed the story as a signal instance of primitive mythology controlling the later development of religion.[85] In 1902 Hardy read Edward Clodd's *Thomas Henry Huxley* and wrote to Clodd: 'I have finished reading every word. . . . Part IV – "The Controversialist" – kept me up last night.'[86] In 'The Controversialist', Huxley's discussion of the Witch of Endor is the central topic. Huxley uses the story to illustrate the fact that the bible is 'an agglomeration of documents which certainly belong to very different ages. . . . In these we have the stratified deposits . . . left by the stream of the intellectual and moral life of Israel during many centuries' (Clodd quoting Huxley).

Hardy's next use of the story occurs in 1916, in 'Apostrophe to an Old Psalm Tune' (359): 'Now, a new stirrer of tones calls you up before me / And wakes your speech,

as she of Endor did
(When sought by Saul who, in disguises hid,

  Fell down on the earth to hear it)
   Samuel's spirit.

The enchantment of the old melody is so strong that it seems to point to some ultimate revelation which seems appropriate for the times:

  So, your quired oracles beat till they make me tremble
  As I discern your mien in the old attire,
  Here in these turmoiled years of belligerent fire
   Living still on – and onward, maybe,
    Till Doom's great day be!

In this same year, Hardy also wrote 'Quid Hic Agis?' (371), originally entitled 'In Time of Slaughter'. Here the reading of another biblical passage, a 'chapter from Kings', haunts Hardy's years 'as the Kalendar / Moved on, and Time / Devoured our prime'. The chapter is I Kings 19 in which Elisha is anointed and appoints Jehu who initiates the events which lead to the spectacle of 'Jezreel'. As Hardy listens to the chapter over the years, and as his relationship with Emma enters its tragic phase, the biblical prophecy grows more threatening. Now that it is too late, 'I feel the shake / Of wind and earthquake, / And consuming fire / Nigher and nigher'.

 The spectacle of men led by old enchantments, like Saul led by the Witch of Endor, frightened Hardy. When he used the image again in the 1922 'Apology', he may have remembered Carlyle's description, in 'Signs of the Times', of men misled by prophetic passion into war: 'the fratricidal fury spreads wider and wider, till at last even Saul must join in. . . . The casual deliration of a few becomes, by this mysterious reverberation, the frenzy of many.' The history of Europe was, for Hardy, a history of enchantments, the enchantments of words, music, poetry, religion, and he knew their power well in himself. And he feared their reduction to what Carlyle calls 'deliration' which brought with it such disastrous personal and social consequences. Against the power of such enchantments, the 1922 'Apology' opposes the Arnoldian and Joahnine principles: 'Not a having and a resting, but a growing and a becoming, is the character of perfection as culture conceives it; and here, too, it coincides with religion' (*Culture and Anarchy*, 1); 'And ye shall know the truth, and the truth shall make you free' (John 8 : 32).

 In the last year of his life, Hardy wrote two poems which he placed at the end of *Winter Words*. They conclude the *Collected Poems*. In the first poem, Hardy writes: 'We are getting to the end of visioning / The impossible within this universe. . . . Yes. We are getting to the end of dreams!' The dream of reason and brotherhood has failed, the nightmare and 'demonic force' of war may come again. The last poem draws on elements of previous poems and represents Hardy's challenge, not only to Ahasuerus of Shelley's *Hellas*, but to all apocalyptic dreamers:

> Let time roll backward if it will;
> (Magians who drive the midnight quill
>   With brain aglow
>   Can see it so,)
> What I have learnt no man shall know.
>
> And if my vision range beyond
> The blinkered sight of souls in bond,
>   – By truth made free –
>   I'll let all be,
> And show to no man what I see.

What does Hardy know? 'It is too like a sound of moan / When the charnel-eyed / Pale Horse has nighed.'

Thus we return to our initial claim, that as Hardy goes from subject to subject in his later years, his vision grows in depth and consistency. One of the last things he wrote was probably what is now chapter 32 in the *Life*. He records a notebook entry for 1914: '*August* onwards. War excitement. "Quicquid delirant reges, plectuntur Achivi!"' And he notes now: 'It was the quotation Hardy had made at the outbreak of the Franco – Prussian war forty-four years earlier' (*Life*, 365). Gradually, the exhumed emotion of half a century – with its unsorted elements of Arthurian romance, modern wars, ghosts of the past, and the romance of Emma – had assumed its final form. In his 1915 version of the exhumed emotion in 'In Time of "The Breaking of Nations"', he sketched an idyllic scene which yet contained portents of what was to come: the harrowing of men ('delirant' interestingly is the root of Carlyle's 'deliration' and comes from the root, *de lira*, 'to draw the furrow awry in ploughing'), the stalking of what would later be an apocalyptic horse, the smouldering of what would be explosive tinder, the deceptive security of a maid and her wight whose love would take on a spectral immortality. The full meaning of these images did not come clear until Hardy had explored the full implications of binding memory, visionary experience, the grotesque, and war delirium. Eventually Hardy realised the connection between his personal romance and the romance of war. The contrasts had become parallels. And his experience of half a century became his countrymen's experience. To borrow a figure from Auden, he had become his admirers.

Indian Summer: Hardy's Pastoral Poetry

Some time between 1922 and 1925, an interesting calm seems to settle over Hardy's career. It can be felt in several of the poems in *Human Shows*, published in 1925. Hardy is still reviewing early works, early notes, and memories, but the result now is that he experiments with a new kind of memory. This might be called *pastoral memory* to distinguish it from the *tragic memory* of 'Poems of 1912–13' and the *apocalyptic memory* of many poems written after 1913.

Some of the traditional paradoxes of pastoral are that Eden can only be known once it is lost, that pastoral happiness can only be hypothesised as something remembered, that the harmony of mind with nature can only be understood by a separated consciousness: 'those she has least use for see her best' (Larkin, 'Spring'). Also traditional in pastoral is the fancy that such paradoxes can be overcome, that harmony can be understood *and* experienced, that the mind can both *know* and *be* in a golden age. Thus William Empson says of one pastoral assumption that it combines 'the idea of the conscious mind, including everything because understanding it, and that of the unconscious animal nature, including everything because in harmony with it' ('Marvell's Garden'). Were such a condition attained, the memory of pastoral happiness would have to become identical with the living of it. What happened to pastoral with the coming of Wordsworth is still a subject of dispute. My impression is that with Wordsworth the pastoral hope became more than something entertained in fancy; it was to be something experienced by an imagination incorporated with nature. Against this romantic pastoral possibility, Hardy's meditative poetry poses its major challenge.

Nevertheless, in the 1920s, Hardy becomes a romantic pastoral poet in approximately a score of poems. His contribution to this genre has not been noted. Yet his skill at creating the pastoral illusion exceeds that of

many pastoral poets whose work is better known. At some point in the
1920s, Hardy begins to wonder: could the mind avoid the painful fixation
of old memories and the grotesque distortion of apocalyptic fancies? Could
the flow of impressions into memory become somehow identical with
present lived experience, so that, as in Auden's 'On This Island':

> the full view
> Indeed may enter
> And move in memory as now these clouds do,
> That pass the harbour mirror
> And all the summer through the water saunter.

Auden's phrasing contains the kind of grammatical finesse which seems
traditionally characteristic of the green language of 'Pastoral Poesy'. The
suggestion is made that not only will the clouds saunter through the water
all the summer, but so will the full view once it has entered into memory.
The phrasing suggests a harmony of physical and mental 'reflections'
which saunter together. The reflected and the reflector fuse. We will see
Hardy experiment with such tricks of phrasing in order to express the
fusion of that which logic divides.

The writer who might be considered the premier philosopher of such
pastoralism is Henri Bergson. It is significant for Hardy's later experi-
mentation that in 1915 he read Bergson's *Creative Evolution* and was deeply
impressed. Two long letters, and two versions of one of these, are given in
the *Life* (pp. 369–70, 450–2). 'His theories are certainly much more
delightful than those they contest,' i.e. the mechanist and finalist theories.
'Our conduct', Hardy quoted Bergson, 'extends between them, and slips
much further.'[1] According to Bergson, life is more than a mechanical
'association and addition of elements', and it cannot be explained in terms
of the finalist's 'preconceived plan with a view to a certain end'. Life, the
élan vital, is a vital unity, and its acting for an end is at once the achieving of
that end. Hardy is quoting from the paragraph in which Bergson writes:

> As soon as we go out of the encasings in which radical mechanism and
> radical finalism confine our thought, reality appears as a ceaseless
> upspringing of something new, which has no sooner arisen to make the
> present than it has already fallen back into the past; at this exact moment
> it falls under the glance of the intellect, whose eyes are ever turned to the
> rear.

The question Bergson pursues is how to turn the intellect around, how to
reconcile *intellect* and its belated abstractions with *instinct* which is blind but

is moulded on life. Could one achieve creative intuition, 'instinct that has become . . . self-conscious, capable of reflecting upon its object and of enlarging upon it indefinitely' until it knows 'life *in general*'. Creative intuition would thus know creative evolution.[2] Once achieved, such an intuition could be expressed only in a language which had overcome the static categories of '*adjective, substantive, and verb*'.[3]

Hardy was intrigued by Bergson, just as he was intrigued by some related ideas in Schopenhauer and Von Hartmann. But he could not buy the argument. 'His use of the word "creation" seems to me loose and vague. Then as to conduct: I fail to see how, if it is not mechanism, it can be other than caprice. . . .' Referring to Bergson's exaltation of the 'living' over the 'inert' object of the mechanists, Hardy said that he could not see 'why we should introduce an inconsistent rupture of Order into a uniform and consistent Law of the same'. Moreover, Hardy perceptively discerns the veiled transcendent impulse in Bergson, his hope for a life ('a sort of additional and spiritual force', Hardy calls it) and intuition which would be in time but also superior to time, not subject to its decay and obsolescence. Thus Hardy: 'I fear his theory is, in the bulk, only our old friend Dualism in a new suit of clothes – and ingenious fancy without real foundation.' He repeats the point in 1920 in his poem 'Our Old Friend Dualism' (881). Moreover when Hardy read Bergson in 1915, he had published *Satires of Circumstance* the year before and was in the midst of writing *Moments of Vision* with its World War poems. It is a time when he is experiencing more profoundly than ever, both in personal and public life, how the mind forces life into moulds of the past. Thus he sees little truth in Bergson's hopes. 'I cannot help feeling all the time that he is rather an imaginative and poetical writer than a reasoner.'

But the letters on Bergson also make some intersting admissions. 'You will see how much I want to have the pleasure of being a Bergsonian.' 'You must not think me a hard-headed rationalist for all this. Half my time – particularly when writing verse – I "believe" (in the modern sense of the word) not only in the things Bergson believes in, but in spectres, mysterious voices, intuitions, omens, dreams, haunted places, etc., etc. But I do not believe in them in the old sense of the word any more for that. . . .' We have seen how wholeheartedly in his later years Hardy explored the spells of spectres and dreams. Similarly Hardy remains impressed by Bergson and the romantic pastoral tradition which Bergson seems to epitomise. For a brief interlude some time after he published *Late Lyrics and Earlier* in 1922 Hardy will return to the 'ingenious fancy'.

Another influence to re-emerge in Hardy's consciousness after 1922 was that of William Barnes. In 1925 he reread Barnes's poetry. Back in 1879,

Hardy had written a review of Barnes in which he defined Barnes's pastoral serenity: 'His rustics are, as a rule, happy people, and very seldom feel the painful sting of the rest of modern mankind, the disproportion between the desire for serenity and the power of obtaining it.' The poetry of such a life is due to the peasant's 'absolute dependence on the moods of the air, earth, and sky'. It is obvious that Hardy thinks that Barnes's poetry has captured this serenity through this dependence:

> . . . The slow green river Stour, with its deep pools whence the trout leaps to the May-fly undisturbed by anglers, is found to be the dearest river of his memories, and inspirer of some of his happiest effusions. Its multitudinous patches of water-lilies yellow and white, its pollard willows, its heavy-handed bulrushes, are for ever haunting him.

The passage is interesting because according to Hardy, Barnes is not haunted by a past river, but by a present river; his remembering it is identical with his present experience of it. Such memory merges Barnes's mind with nature's rhythms, and leads to the poetic equivalent of the peasant's 'absolute dependence'. Such communion is characteristic, Hardy says, 'of the pervading instinct of the nineteenth century', an instinct with which Hardy will now briefly experiment in his own lyric poetry.[4]

Hardy's octogenarian turn to the possibilities of pastoral coincides with another vast rereading of his works and notes. The first had occurred in preparation for the 1895–6 Wessex Novels, and in the following period (1897–1913) Hardy uses those parts of the novels which most closely correspond to his interest in memory and reverie. He rereads his works again for the 1912–14 Wessex Edition in which later volumes of his poetry would be incorporated; and in the following period (c. 1913–22) he uses those parts which correspond to his interest in visions, apocalypses, and grotesques. He also rereads his novels for the Mellstock Edition (1919–20). In the next five years, Hardy continues to reread his works, notes, and letters, as he works on his *Life*. By 1926 he had nearly completed the *Early Life* for which he reviewed his works up to *Tess*. It is this last revisitation with which I am concerned in this chapter. *Human Shows* reveals that Hardy is intrigued by descriptions of pastoral harmony in the early works. He uses the novels' pastoral imagery again in these late poems, at a time when he is experiencing a 'full view', in Auden's phrase, of his life. He revisits the early novels in order to find his beginnings and link them with his endings, so that his whole life will seem a natural totality to be relived within the green vase of several poems in *Human Shows*.

The pastoral element in Hardy's novels has been widely noted.[5] In his early novels, especially, he indulges the reader's nostalgia for a greenwood world, though he is also aware that such novels could only be written after the world they record had begun to disappear. Indeed it is difficult to identify pastoral harmony with any specific rural life in Hardy. Pastoral exists rather as a possibility glimpsed in certain contexts by the narrator or his characters. The concluding section of *Under the Greenwood Tree* opens with imagery of spring and early summer,

> . . . when the landscape appears embarrassed with the sudden weight and brilliancy of its leaves . . . when the faces of the delicate flowers are darkened and their heads weighed down by the throng of honey-bees, which increase their humming till humming is too mild a term for the all-pervading sound; and when cuckoos, blackbirds, and sparrows . . . become noisy and persistent inmates. (v, 1, p. 193)

Such imagery connects with the mainstream literary tradition of Tennyson's 'Come Down, O Maid' where 'I, thy shepherd' calls his love to the valley where love goes 'hand in hand with Plenty in the maize, / O red with spirited purple of the vats . . . and sweet is every sound'. Tennyson's poem ends with the famous 'murmuring of innumerable bees'. Such images, and the following, we shall see again in Hardy's late poems.

In *A Pair of Blue Eyes*, Stephen walks through a lovely scene at 'a time when mere seeing is meditation, and meditation peace' (10, p. 101). But Stephen cannot 'avail himself of Nature's offer' because he belongs to an 'older' – i.e. modern – stage of civilisation. In *The Return of the Native*, Clym has a short happy life 'of a curious microscopic sort. . . . Bees hummed around his ears with an intimate air. . . . Tribes of emerald-green grass hoppers leaped over his feet' (IV, 2, p. 298). But the first serious disagreement with Eustacia immediately follows. In *The Trumpet-Major*, Hardy writes of the early festive scene: 'It was a cheerful, careless, unpremeditated half-hour, which returned like the scent of a flower to the memories of some of those who enjoyed it, even at a distance of many years after, when they lay wounded and weak in foreign lands.'[6] I suspect that Hardy deeply pondered that sentence as he prepared *Human Shows*. In *The Woodlanders*, Fitzpiers luxuriously contemplates Hintock happiness: 'these men's thoughts were coterminous with the margin of the Hintock woodlands' (19, p. 161). When later in the novel, Hardy describes Giles's and Marty's seeing the seasons 'from the conjuror's own point of view'

(44, pp. 399–400), he is not describing the lore of the Witch of Endor and the weather-maker, but rather a condition of being. It is as though finding 'tongues in trees, books in running brooks' were not just a luxury of courtly exile but an actual possibility of life. But such conditions prove fragile in Hardy and the pastoral marriages from *Under the Greenwood Tree* on are shadowed by increasing knowledge. The climactic pastoral image in *The Woodlanders* is that used to describe Fitzpiers's and Grace's reunion: 'Boughs . . . completely inclosed them, so that it was as if they were in a great green vase' (47, p. 433).

The 'agricultural and pastoral character' Hardy develops for Casterbridge is well known: 'Casterbridge was the complement of the rural life around; not its urban opposite. Bees and butterflies . . . flew straight down High street without any apparent consciousness that they were traversing strange latitudes . . . innumerable tawny and yellow leaves . . . stole through people's doorways . . . like the skirts of timid visitors' (4, p. 32; 9, p. 65). The middle chapters of *Tess*, set at Talbothays Dairy, contain the most elaborate of Hardy's pastoral images, at the same time that the pastoral world is more vulnerable than ever before. Seeing Tess in this setting carries Clare back 'into a joyous and unforeseeing past, before the necessity of taking thought had made the heavens gray' (18, p. 155). 'Another year's instalment of flowers, leaves, nightingales, thrushes, finches, and such ephemeral creatures, took up their positions where only a year ago others had stood in their place when these were nothing more than germs and inorganic particles' (20, p. 165). The sense of endless cycles seems to overcome the threat of death. It is also a time when conscious and unconscious seem fused, and separation is overcome: 'inanimate objects seemed endowed with two or three senses. . . . There was no distinction between the near and the far' (19, p. 157). As the chapters proceed, however, images of opium, swoon, and languor increase; and the sense of deception grows until the ideal photosphere breaks down with Tess's confession of a past. Many commentators have noted how the curse of thought reaches more and more deeply into Hardy's pastoral world as the novels proceed, until the possibility of pastoral happiness and wisdom has almost entirely disappeared by *Jude the Obscure*.

Some of the parallels between the poems of *Human Shows* and the above images are so striking that it may at first seem to the reader that the poems were written in the novel-writing years and held over for this volume. On the contrary, they are good examples of Hardy's later use and re-use of the materials of his past. We suggested earlier that in his transition from novel to poem, Hardy had, in a sense, to enter the world of his characters and explore his own proneness to their tragedies. In this late period, he re-enters the world of pastoral.

The Stages of Hardy's Pastoral Poetry

The story of Hardy's pastoral poetry before *Human Shows* is easy to tell because it is almost non-existent. His first known poem is a Words-worthian pastoral, 'Domicilium' (1), written between 1857 and 1860. It begins with a carefully modulated description of Hardy's home setting and proceeds to describe a memory within a memory – Hardy's grandmother describing *her* childhood. Then the poem stops. There is no concluding return to the present as in romantic pastoral mediation. It is as though Hardy's Wordsworthian career had barely begun before it was interrupted – perhaps by *The Origin of Species* (1859), perhaps by an unhappy love affair, perhaps by the need to leave home for London. In 1866 Hardy defines a pastoral ideal, but only as the hopeless yearning of a Poor Susan, here a city shopwoman:

> Our clock should be the closing flowers,
> Our sprinkle-bath the passing showers,
> Our church the alleyed willow bowers,
>   The truth our theme. . . .   (565)

In 'The Night of the Dance' (184), perhaps written now, Hardy plays with the pastoral illusion. But the more characteristic note is in 'From Her in the Country' (187), a frankly anti-pastoral poem of this year. 'Misconception' (185) was also probably written about now. 'The Bride-Night Fire' (48), also written in 1866 and 'The Alarm' (26), written perhaps in the 1870s, reflect the humorous, if doomed, pastoral worlds of *Under the Greenwood Tree* and *The Trumpet-Major* respectively.

Before 1901 Hardy made only one more significant attempt to express a Romantic pastoral consciousness: 'The Darkling Thrush', dated 'December 1900'. It contains specific echoes not only of Keats's 'Ode to a Nightingale' but also of Byron's description of Lake Leman (one of Hardy's favourite passages), Swinburne's 'To a Seamew', Wordsworth's 'To the Cuckoo', 'To a Skylark', and 'The Green Linnet', and Shelley's 'To a Skylark' – these last four grouped together with 'Ode to a Nightin-gale' in Palgrave's *Golden Treasury*. 'The Darkling Thrush', Hardy said, was a 'poem on the Century's End' (*Life*, 307) and it expressed, for him, the bankruptcy of the Romantic pastoral lyric. On the surface, the poem tries to recover the mind-nature continuity which Hardy associates with 'the pervading instinct of the nineteenth century'. But the poem's style, with its stage-managed images, its abstract rhetoric, and its severe qualifications, contradicts the hoped for experience. The last line lingers with the echo that Hardy is still as 'unaware' as ever. For Hardy, man is one who, '[w]atching shapes that reveries limn', seldom has 'eyes to see / The moment that encompassed him' (270). 'The Milkmaid' (126), published in the same volume as 'The Darkling Thrush', contains Hardy's more characteristic note. In 'The Two Rosalinds' (154), published in the following volume, the world of Arden is only a grotesque relic of Hardy's memory.

During 1900 – 22, the period of Hardy's great tragic reveries, there are certain rare exceptions to the prevailing tone, poems where Hardy begins to develop a pastoral consciousness. I am excluding from consideration 'A Singer Asleep' (265), which belongs to the pastoral elegy tradition, a tradition also reflected in the earlier 'Shelley's Skylark' (66). Under Milton and Shelley's influence 'A Singer Asleep' becomes a visionary poem which, like many pastoral elegies, stands quite far from the pastoral experience of natural harmonies explored in this chapter. A similar visionary mode, we saw, influences 'In Time of "The Breaking of Nations"' and changes it into something different from the pastoral manifesto it sets out to be. But a different kind of pastoral experience is represented in occasional examples before 1922, where Hardy, with humour and plays of language, tries to approach the condition where 'mere seeing is meditation, and meditation peace'.

The first clear examples are trivial but in the light of the later development perhaps worth noticing. In the two years before Emma's death, Hardy collaborated with Florence Dugdale on two children's books, *The Book of Baby Beasts* (1911) and *The Book of Baby Birds* (1912). His collaboration consisted in the composition or partial composition or correction of some and perhaps many of the poems which introduce the chapters. They seem to show Hardy's influence in some of the language ('when I muse thereon' from 'The Donkey') and in the extraordinary variety of metrical forms – fifteen such forms used for the nineteen poems in the *Birds* book. 'The Calf' (936), a known Hardy contribution to the first book (Purdy, 314), presents the calf speaking its pastoral hope: 'When grown up (if they let me live) / And in a dairy-home, / I may . . . get contemplative, / And never wish to roam, / And in some fair stream, taking sips, / May stand through summer noons . . . babbling pleasant tunes.' But the most interesting of Hardy's known contributions is 'The Yellow-Hammer' (938), which alternates rising and falling rhythms. It forecasts the autumn lavishness of the *Human Shows* poems and suggests the strange 'absence and presence' of the yellow-hammers which seize the corn: 'And are gone. . . . Thus you may / Often see us flit along, / Day by day.' A month after this poem was published, Emma died and the long, obscurely unhappy years were over. And the decade of unhappy realisation began. In 1915 Florence published another children's book, *The Book of Baby Pets*, which includes at least one Hardy poem, 'The Lizard' (942). It contains a nice anapestic imitation of the animal's 'quick trembling' and darting motions. At the end of *Moments of Vision* (1917) Hardy publishes his first great pastoral poem, 'Afterwards' (511). It is a surprising ending for a volume of tragic reveries.

Why did Hardy yield with increasing frequency to the pastoral impulse in his late years? Did his growing happiness with Florence Emily lead him to yield to the pastoral illusion as he had done lightheartedly in the child's verses he remembered writing for her? And might he have connected this last late happiness with his Bockhampton days, as described in 'Domicilium', when, the evidence seems to indicate, he was so happy that he did not wish to grow up? Or perhaps there is a more private poetic reason for the pastoral turn. In 1920 Florence Emily wryly noted that Hardy seemed to experience a great sense of 'well-being' while writing his most 'intensely dismal' poems.[7] As Hardy continued to dramatise reveries and fill out his grammar of illusion, might he not have felt himself getting closer to the great unformed life which is the elusive goal of much romantic meditation?

Whatever the cause, 'Afterwards' marks a new departure. As Merryn Williams says, it is 'a curiously optimistic poem'.[8]

When the Present has latched its postern behind my tremulous stay,
    And the May month flaps its glad green leaves like wings,
Delicate-filmed as new-spun silk, will the neighbours say,
    'He was a man who used to notice such things'?

Hardy's original first line, 'When night has closed its shutters on my dismantled day', was much less delightfully ambiguous, and also less consistent with the second line. His death may take place when the May month flaps its leaves, or when 'the dewfall-hawk comes crossing the shades to alight', or when 'the hedgehog travels furtively over the lawn'. But these are not so much sharply defined moments as ongoing processes, so that death seems a blending rather than a sharp leave-taking. Indeed Hardy's dying seems as light and 'tremulous' as his staying. As in many of Hardy's meditative reveries, the setting seems to change as the poem proceeds: the spring day of the first stanza becomes the dusk of the second, the nocturnal blackness of the third, and the wintry night of the fourth. But the fifth stanza seems to defeat this rigid progression. The funeral bells will sound, be interrupted by 'a crossing breeze', but then resound all the more like 'a new bell's boom'; so Hardy's loving perceptions may be interrupted by death, but death will not be the final interruption. As he is listening to the bells' 'outrollings' now, so his neighbours will listen then – and it is pretty much the same thing, a common seasonal consciousness which bridges individuals. The first line, then, is the last major addition Hardy made to the poem. C. Day Lewis notes that the line is 'an intolerably over-written variant of "When I am dead." Isolated thus, it is. And yet it does chime perfectly with the mood and diction of the poem as a whole: it is an example . . . of "the discords of individual tones" being "resolved in the complex . . . harmony of the whole group of lines".' [9] Indeed, the line expresses well the paradox of that contemplative consciousness which the poem as a whole explores. The 'Present' is Hardy's host who latches the postern behind Hardy's 'stay'. Presumably the Present is saying goodbye, but the grammar is such that the Present could be saying hello. Is Hardy going or staying? Where would he go? If he is staying, is he now 'staying' more than ever, merged with the organic present of May leaves and mothy blackness? We will see more striking examples of such grammatical play in later pastoral poems.

The period of *Late Lyrics and Earlier* (1922) is a period distinguished by Hardy's exploration of visionary moments which turn grotesque in time. But during this period he makes three more experiments with pastoral reverie. 'Weathers' (512) is, as John Crowe Ransom says, 'a deceptive beginning for the volume; it is refuted a hundred times'. [10] The poem recalls the playful spirit of Ariel's 'Where the bee sucks, there suck I' and achieves its curious effect by means of a refrain:

> This is the weather the cuckoo likes,
>   And so do I;
> When showers betumble the chestnut spikes,
>   And nestlings fly:
> And the little brown nightingale bills his best,
> And they sit outside at 'The Travellers' Rest',
> And maids come forth sprig-muslin drest,
> And citizens dream of the south and west,
>   And so do I.

Inside and outside, wet and dry, awake and dreaming, the observer abides in each of the scenes. In the second refrain, he loses himself in dream with the citizens. At the same time, because the second refrain echoes the first, it suggests that he stays with the day as it proceeds from morning to night. He enjoys an Ariel-like plasticity, of being in one place and in no place, and in one time and in no time. In the second stanza, the observer both shuns the weather like the shepherd and yet empathises with 'hill-hid tides'. 'And so do I' again echoes behind every line. The observer goes home with the rooks, and stays to hang on the gate-bars with the drops. Logical alternatives, 'whethers', merge in this pastoral weather. In the poem we are constantly poised between going and staying, as though each were at some point the same.

'Weathers' employs two techniques which Hardy had experimented with in earlier poems. The first is the use of a refrain whose pastoral timelessness cuts across the linear progress of the poem's plot. The second is a use of grammar which seems to circle back on itself in chiasmic fashion ending where it began. One or the other of these techniques can be noticed in 'The Night of the Dance', which may be a poem of the 1860s, 'Autumn in King Hintock's Park' (1901), 'Rain on a Grave' (1913), 'Joys of Memory' (published 1917), and 'I Worked No Wile to Meet You' (published 1922), which tends to echo the pattern of 'The Night of the Dance'. These hints culminate in the fully realised pastoral of 'Weathers' and one other poem of *Late Lyrics and Earlier*, 'If It's Ever Spring Again'. [11] This poem has been attacked, in an influential argument, for its 'multiple and awkward inversions' and the 'overworked and ineffective' repetition. But here again Hardy's evolving purpose has not been understood. The refrains, which open and close the stanzas, are curious in that the sequence of seasons is expressed as a series of hypotheses: 'If it's ever spring again. . . . If it's ever summer-time. . . .' These refrains suggest almost hypnotically a pastoral possibility which defeats time: once the possibility of reliving spring is achieved in imagination Hardy then goes on to the possibility of reliving summer. The pastoral spell is caught beautifully in the last line: 'If it's ever summer-time, / Summer-time, / With the hay, and bees achime.' We are left with a buzzing eternity, reminiscent of Tennyson's murmuring of innumerable bees. 'I shall go where went I then' is a chiasmus in which the first phrase ends where the second begins and the second ends where the first begins. If the phrase is awkward, it suggests that rounding of future experience upon past experience in an eternal pastoral round.

'The Fallow Deer at the Lonely House' (551) is the third example from *Late Lyrics and Earlier*. It is another masterpiece of delicate equilibrium between the observer's point of view and a nature which includes all points of view. In the first stanza, the speaker observes the distinction between the deer ('One without looks in') and the reverie-bound humans ('As we sit and think / By the fender-brink'). In a sense, the speaker is both inside being looked at and outside looking in. The second stanza develops this sense in an extremely curious manner:

> We do not discern those eyes
>   Watching in the snow;
> Lit by lamps of rosy dyes
> We do not discern those eyes
>   Wondering, aglow,
>   Fourfooted, tiptoe.

'We do not discern those eyes' tends to mean the opposite of what it says. The people who 'think' tend to merge with the deer who 'wonders'. 'Lit by lamps of rosy dyes' modifies both 'we' and 'eyes'. This compound of human and animal seeing seems to be symbolised in the poised body of the waiting deer, whose body merges with his eyes: 'those eyes / Wondering, aglow, / Fourfooted, tiptoe.' The effect of the last line is delightful. The whole poem leaves us 'tiptoe' between man and nature.

After the visionary intensities of *Late Lyrics and Earlier*, *Human Shows* (1925) represents an Indian summer in Hardy's life. The apocalypse has come and yet April's green endures. The light and humorous tone of 'Weathers' which was the exception in the 1922 volume now seems more common in the 1925 volume. The balance of the poems, of course, continues to demonstrate the 'tragedy' of blind reverie and hidden accident under this 'farce' of natural harmony:

> Freed the fret of thinking,
>   Light of lot were we,
> Song with service linking
>   Like to bird or bee.

But 'thought-endowment' has caught 'Creation's groan' (721). Nevertheless, the pastoral indulgence of *Human Shows* is very noticeable, in the imagery of ten poems and in the pastoral vision of another ten. In this small but significant group Hardy embarks on a last experiment. Hardy was perhaps thinking of this group when he wondered whether he had been 'rather too liberal in admitting flippant, not to say farcical, pieces into the collection' (*CP*, p. 834). In these poems, Hardy will take the nature imagery of his novels and transfer them to autumn contexts which reflect the autumn setting of his life. His purpose is much like Keats's in 'To Autumn', to create a nature-pastoral in which summer endings and winter beginnings subtly harmonise and in which the poet's contemplation is equal to the stillness in motion of nature.

In 'The Later Autumn', nature is ironically lavish, its decay being the excess of its ripeness: 'Toadsmeat is mangy, frosted, and sere; / Apples in grass / Crunch as we pass, / And rot ere the men who make cider appear.' Just past are the late summer 'bees, / Tangling themselves in your hair as they rush / On the line of your track, / Leg-laden', as in the heath scene with Clym. Here the entanglement continues into the grammar: it is unclear who is 'Leg-laden' with nature's abundance, the bees or the men. In 'Last Week in October', nature is flirtatious and extravagant in a manner which may remind us of Herrick: 'The trees are undressing, and fling in many places . . . Their radiant robes and ribbons and yellow laces.' The image recalls the one used in *The Mayor of Casterbridge*. In 'Shortening Days at the Homestead', 'Sparrows spurt' from hedges and the willows stand like 'shock-headed urchins, spiny-haired'. Out of such extravagance, Hardy's new muse – no longer a demonic fiddler – announces himself:

> Who is this coming with pondering pace,
> Black and ruddy, with white embossed,
> His eyes being black, and ruddy his face,
> And the marge of his hair like morning frost?
> > It's the cider-maker,
> > And appletree-shaker,
> And behind him on wheels, in readiness,
> His mill, and tubs, and vat, and press.

We are back in the world of Giles Winterbourne, 'Autumn's very brother', 'the fruit-god and wood-god' of *The Woodlanders*. And Hardy seems now to react like Grace Melbury reacted to Giles: 'Her heart rose from its late sadness like a released bough; her senses revelled in the sudden lapse back to Nature unadorned.' We are also back in the world of the Shaston fair and itinerant caravans whose existential gaiety momentarily brightens up *Jude the Obscure*. In *Human Shows* a companion muse to the cider-maker is the 'woman in red' at the shooting gallery. Despite her weariness, she lights up, 'Tosses her ear-rings, and talks ribaldry / To the young men around as natural gaiety'. Her gaiety matches that of nature which is restless and ribald: the breeze 'twitches the trees' and the 'fickle unresting earth' turns from 'its hot idol'. The gay spirited characters of *Human Shows* include the 'fair and wicked-eyed' Yeo-Lea who hands out butter at the Agricultural show; a woodsman 'Taking his life's stern stewardship / With blithe uncare, and hard at work / At four o'clock'; 'Seven buxom women' whose laughter is 'Loud . . . as they stagger and slide'; a thick-skinned vagrant who sings: 'O a hollow tree / Is as good for me / As a house where the back-brand glows.' Hardy makes the blithe woodsman contrast ironically with the visionary also up early to discover the 'cerule mystery' of Earth.[12]

In *Human Shows* poems which at first seem like Hardy's typical satires of circumstance are curiously light-hearted, cluttered, and burlesque. If sheep are doomed, the 'buyers' hat-brims fill like pails, / Which spill small cascades when they shift their stand / In the daylong rain'. The poor tinker swings his 'turk's-head brush (in a drum-major's way / When the bandsmen march and play)'. A curate 'stoops along abstractedly' in useless reverie but he is laughed at by the children as though he were a Dickensian caricature: 'Spectacled, pale, mustache straw-coloured, and with a long thin face.' Poems which are by no means light-hearted, 'Music in a Snowy Street' and 'Circus-Rider to Ringmaster', Hardy associates with light-hearted contexts in the *Early Life* (*Life*, 165–6): seeing itinerant musicians in High Street and going to circuses. Indeed Hardy is probably writing these pages in the *Early Life* and reviewing the scenes of 1884 at the same time that he is composing poems for *Human Shows*. The *Early Life* description of the itinerant musicians shows a potential for a pastoral transformation which is not present in the poem: 'I saw them again in the evening. . . . They were now sublimed to a wondrous charm. . . . *Now* they were what Nature made them, before the smear of "civilization" had sullied their existences.'[13]

Death loses its sting in these rich autumnal contexts of *Human Shows*. 'Gone are the lovers, under the bush / Stretched at their ease.' Stretched at their ease in death, or in love-making – the grammar leaves the possibilities pleasantly open. In 'Life and Death at Sunrise', a horseman carrying the news of the birth of baby Jack rides down the hill while a waggoner carrying the body of old John Thinn rides up the hill. These movements, and by extension all important human activities, emerge in the early morning hours along with the singing of 'woodlarks, finches, sparrows'. Just as the horseman is greeted by the waggoner, so the singing of the birds is answered by 'cocks and hens and cows and bulls' who 'take up the chime'. Over all this organic comedy the hills lazily look down: 'They are like awakened sleepers on one elbow lifted, / Who gaze around to learn if things during night have shifted.' In 'Winter Night in Woodland', another bunch of helter-skelter activities emerges out of the darkness: the barkings of a fox, the creeping of poachers, the labour of smugglers, the singing of a choir. As the choir finally goes home 'to their beds in the dawn', these activities seem to be folded back into the bed of nature. The names of the choir – Robert Penny, the Dewys, Mail, Voss, and the rest – seem to be organic objects on the same plane as 'woodlarks, finches, sparrows'.[14]

'Snow in the Suburbs' (701) is the central pastoral poem of *Human Shows*. It is like a Christmas scene inside a transparent ball decorated with frills of frosting. 'A Light Snow-Fall after Frost' (cf. Introduction) is the companion poem, and 'Snow in the Suburbs' represents its pastoral alternative. The frosty webs which bind the eye in the former poem are benevolently observed in the latter. The watcher, who failed 'defining quite' the changes in the scene until after they had occurred, is here fully attuned:

> Every branch big with it,
>   Bent every twig with it;
> Every fork like a white web-foot;
> Every street and pavement mute;
> Some flakes have lost their way, and grope back upward, when
> Meeting those meandering down they turn and descend again.
>   The palings are glued together like a wall,
>   And there is no waft of wind with the fleecy fall.
>
> A sparrow enters the tree,
>   Whereon immediately
> A snow-lump thrice his own slight size
> Descends on him and showers his head and eyes,
>   And overturns him,
>   And near inurns him,
> And lights on a nether twig, when its brush
> Starts off a volley of other lodging lumps with a rush.
>
> The steps are a blanched slope,
>   Up which, with feeble hope,
> A black cat comes, wide-eyed and thin;
>   And we take him in.

Here Hardy burlesques many of his tragic images: the concatenations of accident, the webbed pattern of fate, the losing of one's way in a changing nature, the whiteness of death. The sparrow is only near-inurned. The grammar dramatises how identities dissolve comically into a background: the line, 'And lights on a nether twig', could have for its subject either the sparrow or the snow-lump. The last stanza springs on us a double surprise. First, the empty scene has all along been 'seen' by a familial human consciousness. Secondly, the human act is merely one in a series of natural motions: the flakes rejoin the fleecy fall, the sparrow alights, and the cat is taken in. 'We take him in', and nature takes us in.

In *Human Shows* Hardy often becomes a bemused observer whose meditation seems as 'long' as that of nature. If a 'robin looks on' in 'The Later Autumn', so also does Hardy. He can wait and let time go by, like the stars in 'Waiting Both'. His contemplation seems to last a hundred years in 'A Bird-Scene at a Rural Dwelling': 'I know a domicile of brown and green, / Where for a hundred summers there have been / Just such enactments, just such daybreaks seen.'[15] Such poems may remind us of Barnes's 'Shepherd O' The Farm' who presides with timeless calm: 'An' wi' my crook a-thirt my eärm, / Here I do rove below the lark.'

In *Winter Words* we see remnants of this pastoral impulse but it seems to die away in this volume. The fourth poem in the volume is 'I am the One': 'I am the one whom ringdoves see / Through chinks in boughs.' Like the blackbirds in Arnold's 'The Scholar Gypsy' (l. 116), the ringdoves do not rouse at Hardy's step because 'He is one with us / Beginning and end'. The second poem is 'Proud Songsters'. It takes the passage we quoted from *Tess* and puts it in a form which evokes the haunting cycle of 'earth, and air, and rain', like Wordsworth's 'rocks, and stones, and trees'. But the sixth poem of *Winter Words* expresses the pastoral hope in an extremely forlorn form – as a 'Wish for Unconsciousness': 'If I could but abide / As . . . a hillock daisy-pied . . . I should . . . Have no evil dreams or wakings.' 'Christmastide' leaves us with a last pastoral figure: 'A sodden tramp . . . who, breaking / Into thin song, bore straight / Ahead, direction taking / Toward the Casuals' gate.'[16]

The remaining poems in *Winter Words* relevant to this pastoral grouping represent Hardy's final critique of the pastoral illusion. 'Lying Awake' lets the pastoral meditation become something more eerie and deathly, the meditation of names on a tombstone. In 'Childhood Among the Ferns', Hardy returns to a memory he said he remembered 'more distinctly than any' in his childhood time. He had used the experience briefly in *Jude*. He then refers to it briefly in the *Early Life*. In the poem, the third revisitation of the experience, he develops its pastoral associations and sees their close connection with his childhood happiness. The field in which he had lain now seems like the green vase enclosing Fitzpiers and Grace. And Hardy now queries, and perhaps also finds himself queried, 'in the green rays as I sate'. Adulthood lurks like a wolf at the door. In 'Dead "Wessex" the Dog to the Household' he again writes an animal poem and uses a metrical form he had quoted in *Under the Greenwood Tree*. The poem begins with a series of questions which hold out the possibility that Hardy's beloved dog has achieved what Hardy hoped to achieve in 'Afterwards'. But the poem ends with the sad announcement: 'I . . . Shall not come.' In 'The Boy's Dream', the Wordsworthian green linnet has become the frail cherished dream of a dying child. And in the penultimate poem of the *Collected Poems* the skylark, now caged, has become an image of man imprisoned 'in a latticed hearse'. 'We are getting to the end of visioning / The impossible within this universe'.[17]

Notes

1 'A Light Snow-Fall after Frost', *The Complete Poems of Thomas Hardy*, Variorum Edition, ed. James Gibson (London: Macmillan, 1979), number 702. Future references to the poem numbers in Gibson's edition appear in the text. The basic text of the Variorum is a very slightly revised form of the text of *The Complete Poems of Thomas Hardy*, ed. James Gibson (London: Macmillan, 1976).

2 *Tess of the d'Urbervilles*, 43, pp. 366–7. Future references to Hardy's novels and *The Dynasts* will be made in the text and are taken from *The Works of Thomas Hardy in Prose and Verse*, Wessex Edition (London: Macmillan, 1912–31). All chapter numbers and section numbers will be Arabic numerals. Part numbers will remain Roman numerals.

3 The poem is postcripted, 'Near Surbiton'. Hardy's postscripts, unlike his headnotes, indicate the time of composition. Hardy and Emma lived in Surbiton, Surrey, in 1874–5: cf. Richard Purdy, *Thomas Hardy: A Bibliographical Study* (London: Oxford University Press, 1954), pp. 237–8. The manuscript of *Human Shows* at Yale is a fair copy ready for the printer. The second stanza is inserted on this copy in heavier ink with 'pale presence' replacing 'existence'. Further corrections ('close' replacing 'just' and 'Pose' replacing 'Show') are made in the blue ink apparently used for final corrections throughout the manuscript. Thus, the stanza seems to have been added not long before the poem's publication, with two further corrections made just before. The second stanza also adds another unrepeated metrical stanza form to the poem. *Human Shows* is remarkable for its use of such forms.

4 In *The Past Recaptured*, Proust writes a passage which is an interesting parallel to Hardy's poem: 'The patches of snow-white beards, which had formerly been black, gave a melancholy air to the human landscape of this reception, like the first yellow leaves on the trees when one was thinking one could still count on a long summer and, before having made the most of it, one sees that autumn is already here. Then it was that I, who from my earliest childhood had lived along from day to day with an unchanging conception of myself and others, for the first time, from the metamorphoses which had taken place in all these people, became conscious of the time that had gone by for them – which greatly perturbed me through its revelation that the same time had gone by for me.' Cf. *Remembrance of Things Past*, vol. 2, trans. Moncrieff and Blossom (New York: Random House, 1932), p. 1035. 'Before and After Summer' (273) and other Hardy poems may have influenced this passage.

5 From a letter of 1895, in *The Letters of Thomas Hardy*, ed. Carl Weber (Waterville, Maine: Colby College Press, 1954), p. 41. Frank Hedgcock, 'Reminiscences of Thomas Hardy', *National and English Review*, 137 (1951), 220–8, 289–94, describes a visit to Hardy in 1910: 'He found nothing so boring as re-reading an early edition of a book in order to establish the definitive text. Still, after a lapse of years, one returned, at least in

thought, to some early creations with pleasure, birth-pangs having been forgotten' (p. 225).

6 James Gibson has summarised this publishing history in 'The Poetic Text', *Thomas Hardy and the Modern World*, ed. F. B. Pinion (Dorchester: Thomas Hardy Society, 1974).

7 Hardy is used by at least two writers to attack what Eliot called 'superficial notions of evolution' ('The Dry Salvages'). Cf. Lascelles Abercrombie, *Thomas Hardy* (London: Secker, 1912), pp. 60–1; also Larkin in *The Listener*, 17 August 1972, p. 209. Yet see *Poetry in the Making*, ed. Jenny Lewis (London: Turret, 1967), p. 15, for Larkin's desire for a chronological re-arrangement of Hardy's poems. Abercrombie adds: 'Who is to say how long an artist has been carrying the idea and the form of a work in his mind? Who can tell what unconscious characteristics of an earlier period will be precipitated when the work comes to be written down?' (pp. 60–1) Abercrombie's questions do not refute the possibility of a study of poetic development, but rather specify its conditions.

8 *New Statesman*, 4 November 1916; *Land and Water*, 13 December 1917; *TLS*, 13 December 1917; *Bookman*, January 1920 ('an ever completer comprehensiveness'); Middleton Murry, *Athenaeum*, 1919 ('There are restatements, enlargements of perspective'); *London Mercury*, July 1922. Also, the following not in Hardy's collection: *Saturday Review*, 19 December 1925 ('an increasing lyrical fluency'); *London Mercury*, December 1928 ('small but significant innovations, new moods, and new ways of dealing with the old'). Among many typical later statements are: 'A poet of almost perverse consistency', Hardy 'simply learned to use better what he already had' (Hynes, 130, 136); 'Practically all the Hardyan themes and obsessions of later years are there, but the proportions are rather different' (Marsden, 184); 'Hardy's poetry does not develop very much. Of course, he gained in technical expertness' (Stewart, 222). The evidence offered for these impressions are some revisions of phrases, some new stanza forms, some new subject matter, and a few new words. Cf. Bibliography.

9 *The Life of Thomas Hardy* (London: Macmillan, 1962), p. 292, originally published in two volumes, *The Early Life* and *The Later Years*.

10 *Original Manuscripts*, Reel 5. Cf. Bibliography.

11 Newbolt, *My World as in My Time* (London: Faber, 1932), p. 286. Earlier, an article entitled 'An Evening with Thomas Hardy', *Outlook* 49 (1894), 444–6, reported Hardy saying: 'I don't believe in that idea of man's imaginative powers becoming naturally exhausted; I believe that, if he liked, a man could go on writing till his physical strength gave out.' In his copy of this interview, Hardy wrote 'largely faked'. But if this particular quotation is accurate, it shows Hardy concerned with the romantic myth at widely separated periods of his life. In 1918, Hardy will again contrast the Romantics with 'those who accomplished late' (*Life*, 384).

12 *Life*, 405. The *Life* records that in 1899 Hardy said: 'No man's poetry can be truly judged till its last line is written' (*Life*, 302). The rough draft of the *Life* shows Hardy meant this statement to be phrased even more strongly: 'Hardy often said that a poet's writings could not be judged till the last line had been written. . . . the opinion was particularly true of his own poetry. . . .' (*Original Manuscripts*, Reel 7, 'T. H. Memoranda and Notes towards completing the remainder of vol. II': a scrap at the end of the notebooks.) An entry for 28 November 1927 reads: 'he had done all that he meant to do . . .' (*Life*, 444).

13 Cf. *Life*, 403, 409; *Thomas Hardy's Personal Writings*, ed. Harold Orel (Lawrence: University of Kansas Press, 1966), p. 49 (hereafter referred to as *Writings*); *Complete Poems*, 84, 558.

14 Thus Hardy will have the sense that he has grown beyond 'Satires of Circumstance': 'Some . . . do not precisely express my attitude to certain matters nowadays. . . .' (Cf. Chapter 1, p. 24.) Also cf. Hardy on 'A Young Man's Epigram on Existence' and 'The Bride-Night Fire', as instances of 'early cynicism' or youthful jest (*Life*, 409, 302). We may be able to see a development by which Hardy gradually comes to think of his poems less as dramatic monologues (as he defended them in the prefaces to his first three volumes) and more as expressions of a period of his mental life. In his Preface to Laurence Hope's poems (cited above, p. xv) he associates 'dramatic or personative' poems with the immature poems of youth which precede poems 'of larger scope and schooled feeling'. In a letter of 7 July 1914 Hardy says of *Satires of Circumstance*: 'the remainder of the book [i.e. following 'Poems of 1912–13'], and by far the greater part of it, will be poems mostly dramatic or personative' (Hardy and Pinion, *One Rare Fair Woman*, 163). Here the description Hardy once applied to his personal lyrics he now restricts to poems of a more satirical mode. In his 1922 'Apology' to *Late Lyrics and Earlier*, he speaks of his 'dramatic anecdotes of a satirical and humorous intention' and seems to distinguish them from the more serious lyrics which are ' "questionings" in the exploration of reality'. The evidence is far from clear but I suspect that Hardy is feeling his way toward a distinction between the quality of his poems and the dramatic irony of mask and *persona* which characterises the Browning tradition beloved of the new criticism.

15 *Literary Notes, II*, [95]: cf. below, note 20. These two persuasions seem to correspond to two of Harold Bloom's ratios of influence. Bloom's *A Map of Misreading* (New York: Oxford University Press, 1975) claims that the only 'strong' modern poets in English are Stevens and Hardy. On the subject of literary influence, Hardy also quoted Frederic Harrison: 'A style grows to perfection. Nothing more can be done in it. And no mere desire for change, no irreverence or impatience, but a necessity of artistic development pushes poets and artists into new channels of expression, new forms' (*Literary Notes II*, [247]). The quotation is from Harrison's 'Among My Books', *The Times* (10 October 1912). Hardy also quoted from a 1908 article in *TLS* a passage which may suggest the difference between his notion of creativity and Bloom's:

> The youthful poet, while he is learning his craft, is apt to be altogether literary, to live in a world imagined by his masters, and to hear nothing but their voices . . . and so he catches the emotions which other men have got from their experience. He may make good poetry out of these second-hand emotions. . . . But there comes a time when he must experience life itself as well as literature, if his inspiration is to last, and his enthusiasm not to grow forced and stale. (*Literary Notes II*, [208])

The 'anxiety of influence' approach to poetry is much debated now, and Hardy is a good test-case, since he is invoked by Bloom as a model instance and yet has traditionally been invoked as a poet of immediate experience. However the issue is resolved, Hardy certainly exemplifies the multiple interactions of literature and life, as this book hopes to show.

16 Kenneth Marsden gives a good summary statement of this point in *The Poems of Thomas Hardy* (New York: Oxford University Press, 1969), pp. 1–11.

17 'The best offer has been from a University Press which thought it might dispose of 500 copies. And yet some of the best critics of Hardy as a poet . . . have been American scholars. We cannot understand it.' (Letter received from James Gibson, 14 September 1976.)

18 The above-mentioned books by Wright, Millgate, Beatty, Gittings, Björk, Pinion,

Bailey, and Purdy are listed in the Bibliography. There is no comprehensive list of the books which Hardy owned and annotated. Those acquired by Colby College are noted in the *Colby Library Quarterly*. The Hodgson sales catalogue of 1938 is reprinted in the monograph, 'The Library of Thomas Hardy', ed. J. Stevens Cox (Guernsey: Toucan Press, 1969). There is no published list of Hardy books owned by the Dorset County Museum. Of the recent critical books, Tom Paulin's *Thomas Hardy: The Poetry of Perception* (London: Macmillan, 1975) explores Hardy's 'Mnemonic Silhouettes' and 'Eidetic Images' in a manner most relevant to the observations explored in this book's second chapter.

19 Purdy, pp. 265–6; Gittings, *Young Thomas Hardy*, pp. 1–2; also, *The Older Hardy*, p. 181.

20 *The Original Manuscripts and Papers of Thomas Hardy* (Wakefield, Yorkshire: EP Microform Ltd, 1975), Reel 9. This reel includes *Literary Notes I*, part of which has been published and annotated in Lennart Björk's *The Literary Notes of Thomas Hardy* (Göteborg: Acta Universitatis Gothoburgensis, 1974); *Literary Notes II*; *Literary Notes III*; *Literary Notes IV*, which is included in Björk and entitled 'The "1867" Notebook'; *Memoranda Book I*; *Memoranda Book II*; *Schools of Painting*; and *The Trumpet-Major Notebook*. These last four have been published in *The Personal Notebooks of Thomas Hardy*, ed. Richard Taylor (London: Macmillan, 1979). Another small notebook, entitled 'Studies, Specimens', dated 1865, is in Professor Purdy's private collection (Björk, p. xxix).

Reel 10 of the *Original Manuscripts* includes Hardy's various music books. Reel 6 contains the scrapbooks of Hardy's reviews. Reels 7 and 8 contain manuscripts of the *Life*; most of the variants are included in Richard Taylor's edition of the *Personal Notebooks*. Other reels contain manuscripts of some of the novels, *The Dynasts*, all of the poetry volumes except *Moments of Vision* (at Cambridge) and *Human Shows* (at Yale), and odds and ends from the Dorset County Museum. The richest sources of material are *Literary Notes I* with 112 unpublished pages and *Literary Notes II* with 263 unpublished pages. A bracketed page number in my references to these notebooks means that the page number is not supplied by Hardy but estimated by me (after allowing for inserts, etc.).

CHAPTER 1

1 Gross, *Sound and Form in Modern Poetry* (Ann Arbor: University of Michigan Press, 1964), p. 14.

2 'On Coleridge's philosophical premises, in this poem nature is made thought and thought nature, both by their sustained interaction and by their seamless metaphoric continuity,' according to Meyer Abrams; 'Structure and Style in the Greater Romantic Lyric', *From Sensibility to Romanticism*, ed. Hilles and Bloom (New York: Oxford University Press, 1965), p. 551. In 'Natural Supernaturalism's New Clothes', *Wordsworth Circle*, 5 (1974), 33–40, I discuss the kinds of dilemmas and finesse which Coleridge's premises lead to. This essay was written from a Hardyesque point of view.

3 Geoffrey Hartman, 'Wordsworth, Inscriptions, and Romantic Nature poetry', *From Sensibility to Romanticism*, p. 405. A topic worth considering is the history of reverie (as Shelley defines the term in 'On Life') from Cowper's *The Task*, Book IV, ll. 267–332, through 'Frost at Midnight' to 'Copying Architecture in an Old Minster'. Hardy seems drawn to the romantic premise of imagination as the fundamental constituent of mind

and then, following Jeremy Taylor or Samuel Johnson in 'The Luxury of Vain Imagination', pronounces it the cause of our tragedy. Another way to express Hardy's synthesis is that he takes an eighteenth-century notion of imagination, a faculty bound to past images and subordinate to other cognitive faculties, and combines it with a romantic notion of imagination, 'the living power and prime agent of all human perception'. The result is that in Hardy the prime agent of human perception binds the mind to its past. Hardy's use of the term 'reverie' is also worth considering. In Rousseau's 'The Reveries of a Solitary', reverie can denote two different experiences: a harmony of nature and mind, and an abstraction of the mind from nature. Wordsworth (if I can simplify Geoffrey Hartman's account in *Wordsworth's Poetry 1787–1814*) feared the process by which the former became the latter. In 'The Night of the Dance' Hardy describes a pastoral pause: 'The stars, like eyes in reverie, / Their westering as for a while forborne, / Quiz downward curiously' (184). In 'Self-Unconscious' he describes how the trance of reverie becomes ominous: 'Watching shapes that reveries limn . . . seldom he / Had eyes to see / The moment that encompassed him' (270). The ultimate trance and discontinuity which Wordsworth feared is described in 'My Cicely': 'she of the garth, who lay rapt in / Her long reverie' (31).

In a letter to Sir George Douglas, Hardy shows an interest in a meditative lyric which would combine eighteenth-century and nineteenth-century traditions. Douglas's 'Poems of a Country Gentleman', Hardy said, reminded him 'of a meditative man walking about his fields and hills, and writing down what is suggested by the natural objects before his eyes – their relations to mankind and the like: a sort of Thomson's Seasons with the added force of all the modern spirit we have acquired since Thomson's day.' Cf. Richard Purdy and Michael Millgate, eds., *The Collected Letters of Thomas Hardy* (Oxford: Clarendon Press, 1978), pp. 182–3.

4 *Desperate Remedies*, II, 3, p. 10: Just before his death, Cytherea sees her father on the church spire: 'I wish he would come down. . . . It is so dangerous to be absent-minded up there' (the incident may recall Ishmael's near fatal masthead reverie in *Moby Dick*). *Return of the Native*, II, 1, p. 127 and *Woodlanders*, 19, p. 165. *Mayor of Casterbridge* 39, p. 319: Lucetta's 'reverie' about her prospects 'was disturbed by a hubbub in the distance' which would eventually cause her death. *Mayor of Casterbridge* 41, p. 335: Henchard 'was developing the dream of a future. . . . He was disturbed by a knock at the door.' *Tess of the d'Urbervilles* 4, pp. 34–5: 'Tess fell more deeply into reverie than ever . . . examining the mesh of events in her own life . . . she no longer knew how time passed. A sudden jerk shook her in her seat.' *Jude the Obscure*, I, 6, p. 41; II, 1, p. 94; III, 4, p. 175. In *Jude* also see I, 2, p. 11, 3, p.22 and II, 5, p. 125.

On the subject of Hardy's characters 'transfixed by their own perceivings', cf. George Fayen, 'Hardy's *The Woodlanders*,' *Studies in English Literature 1500–1900*, I (1961): 'Coincidence and belatedness reveal the immobility of minds too obsessed or preoccupied to react in time' (pp. 99, 96). Also see Henry Christ, 'Semantics and Thomas Hardy', *English Journal*, 54 (1965), 738–40; Robert Kiely, 'Vision and Viewpoint in *The Mayor of Casterbridge*', *Nineteenth-Century Fiction*, 23 (1968), 189–200. Roy Morrell's *Thomas Hardy: The Will and the Way* (Singapore: University of Malaya Press, 1965) and J. Hillis Miller's *Thomas Hardy: Distance and Desire* (Cambridge: Harvard University Press, 1970) also bear on this issue.

5 In the novels there are certain interesting similarities between the characters, reveries and Hardy's narrative impressions. Like them he is spellbound by the past and haunted by old images: cf. *Woodlanders*, first paragraph, *Tess*, 34, p. 277 (the portraits at Wellbridge Inn 'haunt the beholder afterwards in his dreams'), *Trumpet-Major*, 5, p. 39: 'The

present writer . . . can never enter the old living-room of Overcombe Mill without beholding the genial scene through the mists of the seventy or eighty years that intervene between then and now'. Cf. discussion of ballads, Chapter 3, pp. 93–7.

6 Felkin, Elliott, 'Days with Thomas Hardy', *Encounter*, 18 (April 1962), pp. 30–1.

7 Since Hardy referred to Haeckel and copied from a review of *The Riddle of the Universe*, trans. Joseph McCabe (London: 1900), he probably knew Haeckel's famous statement: 'The great biogenetic law . . . reveals the intimate causal connection between the *ontogenesis* of the individual and the *phylogenesis* of its ancestors: the former seems to be a recapitulation of the latter' (p. 268). Whatever the statement's validity as a biogenetic law, as an imaginative insight it may have influenced Hardy. Cf. Wright, p. 53 and Hardy's 'The Pedigree'.

8 Tate, 'Hardy's Philosophic Metaphors', *Southern Review* 6 (1940), p. 107.

9 Hardy may have remembered a passage from *Far from the Madding Crowd* in which he described the sullen terror of the sheep and the ominous advance of the storm: 'Meanwhile the faint cloudlets had flown back into the south-east corner of the sky, as if in terror of the large cloud, like a young brood gazed in upon by some monster' (36, p. 282).

10 According to Rebekah Owen in Carl Weber's *Hardy and the Lady from Madison Square* (Waterville, Maine: Colby College Press, 1952), p. 135. However, in his letter to Hardy of 26 December 1898, Swinburne does not mention 'Friends Beyond' in the list of poems he admires in *Wessex Poems*. Cf. *The Swinburne Letters*, ed. Cecil Lang (New Haven: Yale University Press, 1959–62), Volume 6, p. 133. Either Rebekah Owen misremembered Hardy, or Hardy misremembered Swinburne (an interesting mistake), or Swinburne made the point somewhere else.

11 Hardy agrees with Gosse's estimate, as quoted in *The Works and Letters of Thomas Hardy: Catalogue of the Carroll Wilson Collection* (Libertyville, Illinois: Garryowen Press, 1949), p. 52A.

12 Hardy quotes this famous statement by Arnold in his *Literary Notes I*, 225. Other extended quotations from Arnold are in *Literary Notes I*, 110, 116–21, 134–6, 140–2, 146–57.

13 Hynes, Samuel, *The Pattern of Hardy's Poetry* (Chapel Hill: University of North Carolina Press, 1961), p. 22.

14 Abrams, 'The Correspondent Breeze', *English Romantic Poets*, ed. Abrams (New York: Oxford University Press, 1960), p. 44.

15 In 'The Widow Betrothed' (106), the 'sunset on her window-panes / Reflected our intent'. In 'Her Immortality' (32), 'she comes / Oft when her birth-moon climbs'.

16 Wordsworth's description of the gradual growth of a reverie until it engulfs the mind ('I gazed and gazed . . .') is one of the influences that became a natural part of Hardy's sensibility. In 'My Cicely' (31), 'a feeling stirred in me and strengthened'; in 'Her Immortality' (32), 'I lay, and thought and in a trance / She came'; in 'The Well-Beloved' (96) the speaker yields to a visionary mood as he 'quick and quicker walked'.

17 In a few poems written in the years just following Hardy's last published novel, he tries to blame such tragedy on a psychological foible alone. The speaker in 'The Well-Beloved' is seized by a 'Platonic idea' (*Life*, 286), a sort of Swinburnian vampire. Irresponsible idealism seems to be blamed in 'The Supplanter' (142) and 'The Tree' (133) which simplifies the more complex case of an Angel Clare.

18 Pound, *Confucius to Cummings: An Anthology* (New York: New Directions, 1964), Appendix I, p. 328.

19 Larkin, 'Lines on a Young Lady's Photograph Album', *The Less Deceived* (Marvell Press,

1955). I have touched on Hardy's influence on Larkin in 'The Riddle of Hardy's Poetry', *Victorian Poetry*, 11 (1973), pp. 265, 269–71.

20 Bailey, *The Poetry of Thomas Hardy*, p. 294; Evelyn Hardy and F. B. Pinion, *One Rare Fair Woman: Thomas Hardy's Letter to Florence Henniker 1893–1922* (London: Macmillan, 1972), p. 155.

21 Sir George Douglas, 'Thomas Hardy. Some Recollections and Reflections', *Hibbert Journal* 26 (1928), p. 391. In March 1913 Florence said: I have never before realized the depth of his affection and unselfishness as I have done these last three months' (Gittings, *The Older Hardy*, p. 151).

22 II, 6, p. 93; also see III, 1, p. 150 ('this inability to ossify with the rest of his generation threw him out of proportion with the time') and III, 4, p. 175 ('The person he appeared was too grievously far, chronologically, in advance of the person he felt himself to be'). Also see Chapter 3, pp. 108–9.

23 *Life*, 432; also cf. 286. The source of the second quotation from Proust has long been a mystery. Cf. Miller, *Thomas Hardy*, p. 177. Hardy's 'Note' is taken from his notebook, *Memoranda II*. After the second quotation and reference, Richard Taylor (*The Personal Notebooks*, p. 92) deciphers Hardy's handwriting to read: '&c. see "Marsyas." Juillet 1926.' A check of this obscure journal, published in Anvers, reveals an article by Denis Saurat, 'Proust IV. Les variations de la personnalité', *Marsyas* (Juillet, 1926), 329–30, reprinted in Saurat's *Tendances* (Paris: Les Éditions du Monde Moderne, 1928), pp. 204–11. Hardy is quoting both Proust passages from Saurat. The second quotation is Saurat's paraphrase of Proust's *Ombre*, II, 158, 159.

24 Sir Newman Flower, *Just As It Happened* (London: Cassell, 1950), p. 97. Flower's ellipses. Flower's account, like other recollections, may not be precise in its wording.

25 Thomas Wise, *The Ashley Library: A Catalogue of Printed Books, Manuscripts and Autograph Letters* (London: Dunedin, 1930), vol. X, p. 130.

26 Carl Weber, *Hardy of Wessex* (New York: Columbia University Press, 1965), revised edition, p. 256.

27 Johnson, *The Art of Thomas Hardy* (London: Mathews and Lane, 1894), pp. 207–8.

28 Weber, *Hardy and the Lady from Madison Square*, p. 187; Wilfrid Blunt, *Cockerell* (London: Hamish Hamilton, 1964), p. 223.

29 Purdy, p. 166; Lillah McCarthy, *Myself and My Friends* (London: Butterworth, 1933), p. 104. This distinction should be borne in mind, I think, in reading Larkin's description of Hardy's grief: 'Not till his first wife had died could Hardy's love poetry for her be written, and then it was mixed with a flood of regret and remorse for what he had lost. This kind of paradox is inseparable from poetic creation, and indeed from life altogether. At times it almost appears a sort of basic insincerity in human affection.' 'Mrs. Hardy's Memories', *Critical Quarterly*, 4 (1962), 75–9. Dylan Thomas drew a laugh from his audience when he said that Hardy grieved Emma's 'absence doublefold because he had never sufficiently valued her presence'; 'An Introduction to Thomas Hardy', *An Evening with Dylan Thomas* (Caedmon Records, 1963). The implication of the laughter is that Hardy decided to feel, for literary purposes, the love which he refused to feel, with good reason, during Emma's life. J. Hillis Miller finds through Hardy's work what he finds in *The Well-Beloved*: 'that law of mediated desire . . . which dictates that love will be inflamed by whatever separates the lover from his goal while at the same time providing him indirect access to her' (*Thomas Hardy*, p. 175). What is 'almost . . . insincerity' for Larkin has become a 'law of mediated desire' for Miller. This perhaps fits a symbolist or decadent tradition better than it fits Hardy. On the subject of lost opportunity, Hardy admired Browning's 'Too Late' theme: 'there's nothing to be said about procrastination that is not in that poem ['The Statue

and the Bust']', Felkin, p. 30. And there are many Hardy poems (45, 221, 270, 354, 424, 431, 355, 516, 544, 568, 577) which fulfil Pound's description of Hardy's philosophy: 'Carpe diem never so coupled to an almost surprise that it, the day, should have to be seized, and usually wasn't' (Confucius to Cummings, p. 325). But when the moment is seized in Hardy's poetry (211, 408, 759), it becomes a determining fate locking the lovers in a pattern which time and change overwhelm. Thus where Browning's lovers fail for lack of moral courage, Hardy's lovers fail ultimately because what they think and feel grows stealthily out of touch with what they are and become.

30 The Diary of Arthur Christopher Benson, ed. Percy Lubbock (New York: Longmans, 1926), pp. 260–1. Hardy made this comment on 2 November 1913. He may have been influenced by Barnes's approach to poetry: 'I saw all the dear scenes and well remembered events and beloved faces of youth all distinctly before me, and all I had to do was to write them down . . . the thoughts and words came of themselves.' Quoted by Trevor Hearl, William Barnes (Dorchester: Longmans, 1966), p. 178.

31 Pound, Confucius to Cummings, p. 328.

32 Thomas, 'An Introduction to Thomas Hardy.'

33 Paulin discusses the history of awkward attempts to resolve the question of the speaker of the poem, in Thomas Hardy: The Poetry of Perception, pp. 133–4.

34 Some of William Morgan's rather complex arguments about the temporal perspectives used in 'Poems of 1912–13' seem to parallel my interpretation. Cf. 'Form, Tradition, and Consolation in Hardy's "Poems of 1912–13"', PMLA, 89 (1974), pp. 496–505, esp. 496–7: the recriminations and guilt experienced in the recent past tend to be replaced by a vision of the distant past. Davie pushes such a view to an extreme in 'Hardy's Virgilian Purples', Agenda, 10 (1972), 138–56: 'the chilling achievement is on the contrary that remorse is excluded from them' (pp. 148–9). Davie believes that the image of early love in 'At Castle Boterel' represents a metaphysical reality which triumphs over time.

35 Quotations taken from J. I. M. Stewart, Thomas Hardy: A Critical Biography (London: Longman, 1971), pp. 225–6, 220; Hynes, pp. 151, 130.

36 Next to this sentence, from a 13 December 1917 review of Moments of Vision in Land and Water which Hardy included in his scrapbook, Hardy drew a line and wrote 'good!'.

37 Viola Meynell, ed., Friends of a Lifetime: Letters to Sydney Carlyle Cockerell (London: Jonathan Cape, 1940), p. 291.

38 Some of these points, I discovered, are made in an excellent short explication by Mordecai and Erin Marcus, 'Hardy's During Wind and Rain', The Explicator 19 (December 1960), No. 14.

39 On the subject of 'The Interloper', cf. Purdy, p. 200; Bailey, The Poetry of Thomas Hardy, pp. 386–8; also cf. below, Chapter 3, note 15; and Bjork, pp. 76, 302.

40 As Davie says, the poem 'was almost certainly written long afterwards, when the marriage had turned out badly': Thomas Hardy and British Poetry (New York: Oxford University Press, 1972), p. 18.

41 Thomas, 'An Introduction to Thomas Hardy'; Larkin, 'Wanted: Good Hardy Critic', Critical Quarterly, 8 (1966), p. 179. Interestingly, after announcing his conversion to Hardy in the preface to The North Ship, Larkin added: 'Many years later [after Larkin read 'Thoughts of Phena'], Vernon [Watkins] surprised me by saying that Dylan Thomas had admired Hardy above all poets of this century.' In Dylan Thomas's Letters to Vernon Watkins (New York: New Directions, 1957), pp. 17–18, Watkins, referring to Thomas, said: 'He understood . . . why I could never write a poem dominated by time, as Hardy could. This, in fact, was also true of Dylan.'

CHAPTER 2

1 Blackmur, 'The Shorter Poems of Thomas Hardy', *Southern Review* 6 (1940), pp. 22–3.

2 In 'A Critic's Job of Work', Blackmur contrasts imagination and thought: 'The tragic character of thought . . . is that it takes a rigid mold too soon; chooses destiny like a Calvinist, in infancy' (*Form and Value in Modern Poetry* [New York: Anchor, 1952], p. 343). For Hardy, this tragic plot also applies to imaginative experience.

3 Hopkins, letter to Alexander Baillie, 14 January 1883, *A Hopkins Reader*, ed. John Pick (Garden City, New York: Image Books, 1966), p. 177.

4 *Literary Notes II* [216]. The full quotation, from William James's 'Bergson and His Critique of Intellectualism', *A Pluralistic Universe* (London: Longmans, 1909), p. 244, is: 'We live forward, we understand backward, said a Danish writer [Kierkegaard?]; and to understand life by concepts is to arrest its movement, cutting it up into bits as if with scissors, and immobilizing these in our logical herbarium where, comparing them as dried specimens, we can ascertain which of them statically includes or excludes which other. This treatment supposes life to have already accomplished itself, for the concepts, being so many views taken after the fact, are retrospective and post mortem.' James's lecture begins by discussing the Zeno paradox as an example of the inability of concepts to mirror process.

5 *Life*, 352: the 'German author' to whom Hardy attributes the statement is Börne. Cf. *Literary Notes I*, 218. I assume this is Ludwig Börne, 1786–1837, German political writer and satirist.

6 In 'The Symbolism of Poetry', Yeats wrote a passage which is curiously similar to 'Copying Architecture in an Old Minster' and provides a good image for this chapter: 'I was writing once at a very symbolical and abstract poem, when my pen fell on the ground. . . . Had my pen not fallen on the ground and so made me turn from the images that I was weaving into verse, I would never have known that meditation had become trance, for I would have been like one who does not know that he is passing through a wood because his eyes are on the pathway.' Similarly Hardy will become more aware that as patterns weave unconsciously, they reveal themselves at moments when the trance of meditation breaks. Until this happens, we cannot see the pattern for the trees. For Yeats, the interruption serves to reveal the transcendent reality of his dreams and the magic liberation of symbols. For Hardy, such an interruption confirms a prison.

7 For somewhat similar approaches to intellectual history through images, cf. Stephen Pepper, *World Hypotheses* (Berkeley: University of California Press, 1961) and Arthur Lovejoy, *The Great Chain of Being* (Cambridge: Harvard University Press, 1936).

8 In 'A Wife Comes Back' (554), a man indulges in 'his life's one day of dreamery' and imagines that his estranged wife 'freshed back' to the young beauty he once loved. He discovers the tragic obsolescence of this dream pattern when he searches for her 'under the leafy pairs / Of the avenue elms' and finds only 'an ancient dame . . . with features frozen and numb'. 'The Ageing House' (435) describes where another beloved lived, where the wind 'blithely spoke . . . to the little sycamore tree': but now 'slow effacement / Is rife throughout, / While fiercely girds the wind at the long-limbed sycamore tree'.

Hardy may have remembered an image in Coleridge's 'The Three Graves' which impressed him as a 'morbid poem' (*A Pair of Blue Eyes*, 19, p. 203). We feel the coming doom of Coleridge's heroine as she 'stepped beneath the boughs / Into the mossy track': this image is repeated in various ways. In his preface to the poem, Coleridge himself uses the word 'morbid' in a specific sense when he says that his tale describes 'the morbid action on the fancy' resulting from 'an Idea violently and suddenly impressed on it'.

9 John Combs, 'Cleaving in Hardy's "The Convergence of the Twain"', *CEA Critic*, 37 (November 1974), 22–3, discusses Hardy's line: 'This creature of cleaving wing.' 'The two basic – and exactly opposite – meanings of *cleave* create an ambiguity perfect for this poem's purposes,' i.e. cleaving as dividing the water, cleaving as adhering to the iceberg. Once the pattern is realised by the ship, the ship is destroyed. William Hyde has a brief note on 'Hardy's Spider Webs', *Victorian Poetry*, 8 (1970), 265–8.

10 'On Sturminster Footbridge' (426) ends with the image: 'beneath the roof is she who in the dark world shows / As a lattice-gleam when midnight moans.' The image takes on an ominous weight from the earlier images of decaying networks: the 'reticulations' which 'creep upon the slack stream's face', the 'years of flood' which have scrabbled hollows in 'the pier's sodden base'.

11 Hardy often uses the word 'memoried' in the almost physical sense of engraved. A woman grows 'thin, thinner wrought' with an old 'memoried spot' (614). Hardy is bound to a 'memoried place' (839). A 'memoried reason' hurts like a 'pricking blade' (899). An old love stands evermore in his 'memoried passion' (541). The 'House with a History' (602) has a 'memoried face'. 'Memoried' means much the same as 'time-trenched' in 'The Maid of Keinton Mandeville' (513). Behind many of Hardy's images, of course, stands the classic Shakespearean image: 'Time . . . delves the parallels in beauty's brow.' But Hardy uses the image to create a dramatic coalescence of inner and outer worlds.

12 In the *Life*, Hardy notes a scenic effect: 'Winter. The landscape has turned from a painting to an engraving' (*Life*, 184). The opposite process is described in the spring growths in *The Woodlanders*, 20, p. 170: 'the woodland seemed to change from an open filigree to a solid opaque body.' Also, cf. 'Neutral Tones' and below, p. 65.

13 *Life*, 355. This enigmatic note is not explained in the *Life*, but seems relevant to the visit Hardy made to English cathedrals about the same time and described just previous to this note. While 'matrix' and 'mould' can be roughly synonymous terms, I assume that the distinction is one between the pattern and the object which is cast from the pattern. Hardy may be reminding himself to imagine the architect's design behind the finished work. This is how some architects I have consulted interpreted the phrase. On the other hand, it is barely possible that the distinction is just the reverse, that the matrix is the material in which the pattern or mould is implanted. I would be glad to be illuminated on this point by any current Gothic architect. In the draft for his *Life*, Hardy himself shows his perplexity: 'He makes only one note this spring, which is not very intelligible: "View the matrices rather than the moulds": T.H. Vol. II 1892 to [end] 2nd copy,' p. 503, *Drafts for Biography, Original Manuscripts*, Reel 7.

14 C. J. P. Beatty's introduction to *The Architectural Notebook of Thomas Hardy*, ed. Beatty (Philadelphia: Macmanus, 1966) notes many details of Hardy's architectural career and many specific technical connections between this notebook and architectural currents of the time. I have tried to treat some of the wider dimensions of the topic and to add additional information.

15 Frank Jenkins, 'The Victorian Architectural Profession', *Victorian Architecture*, ed. Peter Ferriday (Philadelphia: Lippincott, 1964). Hardy occasionally refers to the opposition

between the artistic amateur and narrow professional: for example, in *Desperate Remedies*, II, 2, p. 22.

16 Hardy and Pinion, *One Rare Fair Woman*, p. 169, quotes Hardy's discussion of this association and also the Architectural Association founded in 1847 to promote exchange of ideas among beginning architects.

17 Eastlake, p. 352. The original edition has been reprinted with an introduction by J. Mordaunt Crook (New York: Humanities Press, 1970).

18 According to Henry-Russell Hitchcock, 'High Victorian Gothic', *Victorian Studies*, I (1957), 47–71, High Victorian Gothic thrived because of 'the informality – not to say the amateurishness – of architectural education in Britain. This encouraged personal discipleship and the cultivation of individual expression rather than the continuation, as in France, of an established official tradition' (p. 50).

19 *Writings*, 147, 273 (where Orel tracks down the apparent reference. William Fredeman, *Pre-Raphaelitism, A Bibliocritical Study* (Cambridge: Harvard University Press, 1965), pp. 13–15. Hardy quotes from a Rossetti poem in *Literary Notes* II [79]. In a letter of 1906, Hardy notes that Rossetti had rechristened a painting 'Two on a Tower' after the appearance of Hardy's novel: cf. R. L. Purdy, *Thomas Hardy Memorial Exhibition* (New Haven: Yale University Press, 1928), p. 14.

20 On the emphasis on design in the 1850s and 1860s cf. Raymond Watkinson, *Pre-Raphaelite Art and Design* (London: Studio Vista, 1970), pp. 129–30. Also cf. Robert Peters, 'Algernon Charles Swinburne and the Use of Integral Detail', *Victorian Studies* 5 (1962), 289–302. Peters discusses the duality in Victorian aesthetics, 'the particular on the one hand, the encompassing whole on the other, and the difficulties of maintaining these in a meaningful aesthetic tension' (p. 302). Peters cites the detailed notebooks of Dobell, Hunt, Hopkins; Ruskin's descriptions of clouds and vegetable forms; Browning's oak-worts, honeycombs, finches, etc.; Tennyson's Arthurian detail; Meredith's nature passages; Rossetti's mannered sonnets; Swinburne's vignettes like the boar scene in *Atalanta in Calydon*; Arnold's flower stanzas. Kristine Garrigan, *Ruskin on Architecture* (Madison: University of Wisconsin, 1973), notes that Ruskin, like Walpole before him, emphasised surface pattern in the arts (pp. 8–9). She quotes Ruskin on his 'love of all sorts of filigree and embroidery . . .' (p. 47). John Unrau, *Looking at Architecture with Ruskin* (University of Toronto, 1978) argues persuasively that Ruskin's notion of ornament involves larger structural considerations, that for Ruskin minute surface ornament should be ideally consistent with the large-scale composition of the building (cf. p. 67 and *passim*).

21 Ruskin, *Works*, ed. Cook and Wedderburn (London: Allen, 1903–12), vol. 15, pp. 115–16.

22 Beatty, p. 14.

23 In his own idiosyncratic way, William Barnes expressed many of these aesthetic assumptions in his 'Thoughts on Beauty and Art', *Macmillan's Magazine*, 4 (1861), 126–37: 'Again, the beauty of a species is the full revelation of God's forming will – as, in an ash-tree, is shown the forming of one stem, with limbs, boughs, and twigs, of still lessening sizes.' This essay may have influenced Hopkins's fragment on 'Ash-Boughs'.

24 Eastlake, p. 352. At the same time, according to Peter Collins, *Changing Ideals in Modern Architecture, 1750–1950* (Montreal: McGill University Press, 1967), Blomfield was a traditionalist and did not share the Victorian anxiety about the need to find a new style. 'Such a thing as the creation of a new style would, he thought, be so complete a falsification of all history and all analogy that he advised his audience to disabuse their

minds of any such expectation. In architecture, at least, if nothing else, the development theory was the true one, and that development would have to be gradual, and, to a certain extent, almost unconscious' (p. 145).

25 'Music Books Painting and Drawings', Reel 10, *Original Manuscripts*, includes plans for a church, beautiful drawings of a transept and stair railings, plans for an extensive town house, designs for ornamental hinges (some of which seem to reflect the designs in Owen Jones), eight lovely designs for pew ends, and the original plans for Max Gate. The church design has been reproduced and discussed by Beatty in 'A Church Design by Thomas Hardy', *Thomas Hardy Yearbook*, 4 (1973–4), pp. 66–72. The University of Texas has twenty additional drawings: cf. Ann Bowden, 'The Thomas Hardy Collection', *Library Chronicle of the University of Texas*, 7 (Summer 1962), 6–14, for a Hardy drawing of a tower window.

26 Cf. Blunden's description of his visit in *The Great Victorians*, ed. H. Massingham (New York: Doubleday, 1933), p. 222. In *The Hand of Ethelberta*, Hardy associates Pugin's principles with 'the true and eternal spirit of art' (38, p. 329). Also cf. *Life*, 38.

27 Kenneth Clark, *The Gothic Revival* (New York: Holt, Rinehart, 1962, 3rd edition, p. 185).

28 This should be Arthur, whom Hardy is confusing with David Brandon, an important architect early in the Gothic Revival who worked largely with country mansions and designed Holy Trinity, Haverstock Hill, 1849–51. Cf. Eastlake, pp. 210, 301.

29 According to Garrigan, *Ruskin on Architecture*, p. 10, the Gothic Revival was greatly helped by 'the increasing number of relatively inexpensive books of engravings of England's Gothic buildings'.

30 '[H]e was a "literary architect" – a person always suspect in the profession in those days, Hardy used to say,' *Life*, 77. The Brandon books are *An Analysis of Gothick Architecture* (London: Pelham Richardson, 1847); *The Open Timber Roofs of the Middle Ages* (London: David Bogue, 1849).

31 Beatty, pp. 30–4; also cf. p. 4, and p. 16 (on the lack of originality in the published notebook).

32 In 1899 he wrote: 'Having used up all the cathedrals within 80 miles or so last year, it becomes difficult to decide on future ones.' Cf. Hardy and Pinion, *One Rare Fair Woman*, pp. 75–6. Also cf. *Life*, 295, 405, 420, and *passim*.

33 Cf. J. Hillis Miller's discussion, *Thomas Hardy*, pp. 205–7.

34 Cf. Eastlake's summary of the problem, pp. 233–4. Hardy probably knew well Hugo's description of Notre Dame as a 'transition edifice' representing 'the accumulations formed by ages; the residuum of the successive evaporations of human society – in short, a species of formations'. On Hugo and Hardy, cf. Björk, pt. ii, p. 350 and the translation published in London by Chapman & Hall, 1866, pp. 103–4.

35 *Life*, 357. A beautiful photograph of the south transept can be found in Timothy O'Sullivan's *Thomas Hardy: An Illustrated Biography* (London: Macmillan, 1975), p. 26. An illustration of the transept, by H. Emrich, was also included with the first publication of 'The Abbey Mason' in *Harper's Magazine* 126 (December 1912), pp. 21–4. Illustration 3 is adapted from *English Cathedrals*, introd. Martin Hürlimann (New York: Viking, 1961), revised edition, 103.

36 One guidebook, Edmund Foord's *Cathedrals* (London: Dent, 1925) cannot accept the truth of the historical record attributing the south transept to Wygmore's period.

37 Paley's *Manual*, 3rd edition, p. 11; Brandon's *Analysis*, p. 4. Reel 10, *Original Manuscripts*, includes several pages of tracings from Paley's mouldings. Rickman's

description is in *Attempt to Discriminate the Styles of Architecture in England*, published in 1817: cf. Paul Frankl, *The Gothic: Literature Sources and Interpretations Through Eight Centuries* (Princeton University Press, 1960), p. 507. The first division into phases had apparently been made by Thomas Warton (Frankl, p. 497).

38 Brandon's *Analysis*, pp. 2–3, 31, 41. Bond speaks of Gloucester's architectural style 'there elaborated in south transept and choir, between *c*. 1331 and *c*. 1350, when it was adopted at Winchester, Canterbury, and York, speedily overran England, superseded Late Decorated design, and became our one and only style till the very last days of English Gothic architecture. This is the famous Perpendicular or Rectilinear style.

The supreme importance of Gloucester in the history of the later Gothic has never been adequately recognized. She turned the current of English architecture in a wholly new direction. . . . [T]o the remotest corners of the land, to cathedral, abbey church, collegiate and parish church, there was brought the influence of Gloucester' (p. 134). Cf. Hardy's stanzas beginning: 'From Gloucester church it flew afar. . . .' The importance of the triangle shape was also emphasised by Pugin and given a pragmatic motivation: 'the most beautiful pitch of a roof or gable end is an inclination sufficiently steep to throw off snow without giving the slate or lead covering *too perpendicular a strain*, which is formed by two sides on an equilateral triangle.' Cf. *The True Principles of Pointed or Christian Architecture* (London: Bohn, 1858), pp. 10–11 (originally published 1841). In *The Hand of Ethelberta*, Christopher guides Ethelberta to a view of Salisbury Cathedral: 'We get the grouping of the chapels and choir-aisles more clearly shown – and the whole culminates to a more perfect pyramid from this spot' (39, p. 347).

39 Pound, *Confucius to Cummings*, p. 286. Hardy would have known Browning's 'Fra Lippo Lippi' which also uses a dialogue between artist and abbot in order to convey a personal aesthetic.

40 *Life*, 357. John Harvey, *Gothic England* (London: Batsford, 1948), 2nd edition, argues persuasively that the architect was William Ramsey, the king's chief mason at the Tower of London, who designed St Paul's chapter house and adapted the transept in a similar manner: 'The Gloucester work, adjacent to a royal castle in Ramsey's charge, and built around the tomb of the martyred Edward II, is too closely akin to the design of St. Paul's Chapter House and cloister arcades for this to be a matter of coincidence' (p. 51).

41 Reproduced nicely in Evelyn Hardy, *Thomas Hardy* (London: Hogarth, 1954), p. 224 (facing). See Illustration 4.

42 *Life*, 363; *Writings*, 121. Cf. also Hardy and Pinion, *One Rare Fair Woman*, p. 178: 'poetry must have symmetry in its form, and meaning in its content.'

43 *Writings*, 215; On such 'associationism' and Ruskin's promotion of it, cf. George Hersey, *High Victorian Gothic: A Study in Associationism* (Baltimore: Johns Hopkins University Press, 1972). It is interesting to parallel Hardy's response to old Gothic with Hawthorne's: cf. Maurice Charney, 'Hawthorne and the Gothic Style', *New England Quarterly*, 34 (1961), 36–49.

44 Beatty, 33. The quotation following is from *Writings*, 216.

45 Hardy was ambivalent about the success of Scott's restorations. In his *Wessex Poems* drawing of Salisbury Cathedral, Hardy draws the interior of the nave 'with Sir Gilbert Scott's iron screen still there to add mystery and depth to the choir and sanctuary', as Sir John Betjeman interprets the picture in 'Hardy and Architecture', *The Genius of Thomas Hardy*, ed. Margaret Drabble (London: Weidenfeld and Nicolson, 1976), p. 150. In later years Hardy wrote to Henry Newbolt: 'My interest in Salisbury Cathedral . . . has lasted ever since 1860. . . . At that time my interior, as arranged by Wyatt, was still

untouched by Scott, the organ being over the screen. The result was that a greater air of mystery and gloom hung over the interior than does now, and it looked much larger from the subdivision'. Quoted in Newbolt, *My World as In My Time* (London: Faber, 1932), p. 286.

46 Reproduced in O'Sullivan, *Thomas Hardy*, p. 52. Quotation taken from *Life*, 79. Stephen Smith also makes such drawings in *A Pair of Blue Eyes*, 7, p. 51. Betjeman claims that the seat-ends are 'still there' ('Hardy and Architecture', p. 153).

47 *Life and Art by Thomas Hardy*, ed. Ernest Brennecke (New York: Greenberg, 1925), p. 137.

48 Brandon, *Analysis*, p. 71.

49 *Rookwood* (London: Dent, 1931), III, 2, p. 174.

50 In his preface to *A Pair of Blue Eyes*, Hardy describes the way crude Gothic art harmonised with the wild Cornwall coastline. He places the story at a time of church-restoration which he associates with the attempt to 'restore the grey carcases of a mediaevalism whose spirit had fled'. 'Hence it happened that an imaginary history of three human hearts, whose emotions are not without correspondence with these material circumstances, found in the ordinary incidents of such church-renovations a fitting frame for its presentation.' Other influences of architecture on Hardy's descriptions of nature and character in the novels have been well discussed by Josef Hartmann, *Architektur in den Romanen Thomas Hardy's* (Pöppinghaus, 1934).

51 Hunt, 'The Pre-Raphaelite Brotherhood', *Contemporary Review*, 49 (1886), p. 740.

52 See Illustration 5. References in this paragraph are to *On the Origin of Species: A Facsimile of the First Edition*, introd. Ernest Mayr (Cambridge: Harvard University Press, 1964), 4, p. 130; 14, p. 489; 4, p. 84. The diagram is in Chapter 4, pp. 116–17 (insert).

53 *Origin* 4, p. 124; also cf. pp. 117, 120, 119.

54 C. W. Saleeby quotes this famous definition in 'The Apostle of Evolution', *Academy* 65 (12 December 1903), 673–4, a review from which Hardy quotes another part in *Literary Notes II* [173].

55 Lennart Björk, ed., *The Literary Notes of Thomas Hardy*, I, ii, p. 323. In *Far From the Madding Crowd* Hardy is perhaps thinking of Spencer when he describes the swarming of bees: 'A process somewhat analogous to that of alleged formations of the universe, time and times ago, was observable. The bustling swarm had swept the sky in a scattered and uniform haze, which now thickened to a nebulous centre: this glided on to a bough and grew denser till it formed a solid black spot upon the light' (27, p. 204).

56 *Natural Causes*, pp. 67–8. Hardy's notations from Maudsley are in *Literary Notes I*, 241–9.

57 Cf. Wright, pp. 35–6. In his conclusion, Morley quotes D'Alembert's comparison of the thinking man to 'a musical instrument', etc.

58 Pinion, *A Hardy Companion*, pp. 205–8. The *Agamemnon* describes the 'close net' which Jove threw over Troy, so that none could 'overleap the vast toil of slavery', that 'all-ensnaring bane' (ll. 358, 360–1). Cassandra is caught in the 'toils of destiny' (l. 1048). Contributing to the imagery is the crimson drape which Clytemnestra spreads for Agamemnon, and the fatal gown which Cassandra, punning, calls the 'net of Hades' (l. 1115). After Agamemnon lies dead, the images grow more elaborate: Clytemnestra describing her fatal snare of mischief, 'an endless net, as if for fishes' (ll. 1375, 1382) which the chorus later describes as 'this web of the spider' (ll. 1492, 1516); and Aegisthus describes Agamemnon 'lying . . . in the woven robes of the furies' (l. 1581). I am quoting Theodore Buckley's translation which Hardy used. Frank Hedgcock reported a conversation he had with Hardy in 1910: 'He never wearied of Aeschylus and

Sophocles. He found the Greeks stimulating and suggestive. they put their thoughts in a way that kindled thought in others. He often laid the book down and pondered what he had just read and, perhaps, linked it to some experience of his own. Sometimes these reflections led to his taking pencil and paper and jotting down suggestions for a poem or even a few lines of verse, to be worked up later'. Cf. Hedgcock, 'Reminiscences of Thomas Hardy', p. 291.

59 Tennyson's *In Memoriam* 3 ('A web is woven across the sky'); Swinburne on love's web in Laus Veneris, l. 41 and following; Shelley's 'web of being blindly wove' in 'Adonais'. Schopenhauer makes use of the image in *The World as Will and Idea* as does Carlyle in *The French Revolution*. Gibbon uses the web image more frequently as the *Decline* draws to its close with the final siege of Constantinople: cf. Heritage Press edition, ed. J. B. Bury, pp. 2255, 2341, 2348, 2355. Also see Symonds, *Studies of the Greek Poets* which contains the image Hardy copied in his *Literary Notes I*, 71. The Pater passage on the 'magic web' is from the 'Winckleman' chapter in *The Renaissance*.

60 *The Revolt of Islam*: Canto 3, stanza xxxiv; also 5, lii; 6, xxvii and xxviii; 7, xi and xxxii; 9, ii and xii; 10, xlii; 12, xxxiii and xxxix.

61 *Middlemarch* (Penguin Books, 1965): Chapter 15, pp. 177–8; also 12, p. 145; 36, p. 380; 18, p. 210; 68, p. 741; 27, p. 297; 32, p. 337; 29, p. 313; 58, p. 631; 61, p. 665; 15, p. 170.

62 Appleman, 'Darwin, Pater, and a Crisis in Criticism', *1859: Entering an Age of Crisis*, ed. Appleman, Madden, and Wolff (Bloomington, Indiana University Press, 1959).

63 Also cf. *Life*, 210. References in this paragraph are to Jones, *Grammar of Ornament*, p. 7; Paley, *Manual of Gothic Mouldings*, p. 13 (Paley is quoting an *English Review* article of December 1844) and p. 31; Ruskin, *Seven Lamps of Architecture* in *Works*, VIII, p. 118; *Modern Painters* in *Works*, III, p. 207; *Seven Lamps* in *Works*, VIII, p. 117.

64 Stewart M. Ellis, 'Thomas Hardy'; Some Personal Recollections', *Fortnightly Review*, 123 (1928), 393–406; Ellis, *Mainly Victorian* (London: Hutchinson, n.d.), p. 110. Carl Weber, 'Ainsworth and Thomas Hardy', *Review of English Studies*, 17 (1941), 193–200, cites some parallels but others are more striking. The storm and lightning scene in *Far from the Madding Crowd* was possibly influenced not only by the storm scene in *Rookwood* but by the Fire of London scene in *Old Saint Paul's* (V, 3). The last two pages of the story portion of *Windsor Castle*, where Henry views the Round Tower and waits for the signal of Anne Boleyn's execution, has several similarities to the end of *Tess*. Interestingly Hardy mentions *Windsor Castle* in the *Life*, 25, in the context of *Tess* and the damsels he had known in his youth. Another execution scene occurs at the end of Hugo's *Notre Dame*. *The Scottish Cavalier* (London: Colburn, 1850, 3 Vols.) may have sown hints for several scenes in Hardy's mind. The description of the malignant portraits of Lady Barbara and others in Lady Grizel's castle (I, pp. 61–2) forecasts the portraits of the d'Urberville ladies at Wellbridge in *Tess*. Grant's trio, Walter, Lilian, and Lord Clermistonlee closely parallel Clare, Tess, and Alec d'Urberville. Clermistonlee seduces Lilian into marriage by maligning the absent Walter. The novel also ends with an execution. In vol. 2, p. 184, Grant describes the grotesque visage of a fountain vomiting water while Walter and Lilian pledge their futile vows: compare 'The Gurgoyle: its Doings' in *Far from the Madding Crowd*. The scene of Scottish soldiers leaving for England (II, 224) may have been the germ of *The Trumpet-Major*. Chapter 4 of *The Scottish Cavalier* is entitled 'A Pair of Blue Eyes'. For later scenes using moon-lit Gothic silhouettes, also cf. I, 99; II, 83–7, 290 (a dawn scene).

65 These details are taken from various guidebooks, most notably Homan Potterton's *A Guide to the National Gallery* (London: Trustees, n.d.), and from David Robertson's

Sir Charles Eastlake and the Victorian Art World (Princeton: Princeton University Press, 1978). The South Kensington Museum opened in 1857.

66 Smart, 'Pictorial Imagery in the Novels of Thomas Hardy', *Review of English Studies*, N.S. 12 (1961), 262–80. Pinion, *A Hardy Companion*, pp. 193–200. Günther Wilmsen, *Thomas Hardy als impressionistischer Landschaftsmaler* (Marburg: G. H. Nolte, 1934) lists many Impressionist nature scenes in Hardy. Interestingly, Wilmsen's most frequent example is *A Pair of Blue Eyes* which Tennyson admired. Smart notes the influence of Impressionist colour theory (pp. 268, 278). Also cf. *Life*, 184: 'The impressionist school is strong. It is even more suggestive in the direction of literature than in that of art.' Penelope Vigar, *The Novels of Thomas Hardy* (London: Athlone, 1974) is also good on the painterly scenes in the novels. Norman Page, *Thomas Hardy* (London: Routledge, 1977) discusses the connection between Hardy's novels and Victorian genre painting (pp. 64–89).

67 Abate Luigi Lanzi, *The History of Painting in Italy*, trans. Thomas Roscoe (London, 1828), 6 volumes; revised in three volumes (London: Bohn, 1847) which I am citing here. Some of Hardy's notes are direct quotations, others close paraphrases, others summaries made in Hardy's own terms after he read Lanzi's sections. For quotes or paraphrases, cf. Hardy on Cimabue (Lanzi I, 42), Da Vinci (I, 126), Luca Giordano (II, 56), Giorgione (II, 133), Mazzuola (II, 406), Domenichino (III, 86). The observation Hardy adds to Lanzi's treatment of Correggio takes some elements from Lanzi (especially II, 389–91) but amounts to a new *aperçu*: 'An ideal beauty with not so much of heaven as in Raphael, yet surpassing that of nature, but not too lofty for our love'. The source of Hardy's notes for the other schools of painting still needs to be identified.

68 *Life*, 206. The painting is reproduced by Fanny Hering, *Gérôme: The Life and Works* (New York: Cassell, 1892), p. 24 (facing). See Illustration 6. Hardy has an intriguing entry for 1888 in the *Life*, p. 208: 'At the Salon. "Was arrested by the sensational picture called 'The Death of Jezebel' by Gabriel Guays [sic], a horrible tragedy, and justly so, telling its story in a flash."' A letter to me from René Le Bihan, curator of the musée de Brest, reports: 'Cette toile a hélas disparu dans l'anéantissement de notre musée en 1941 et nous n'en conservons ici aucune trace ni photographiée ou gravée ou dessinée.' Monsieur Bihan notes that the painting – 'La mort de Jezabel' by Julien Gabriel Guay – was exhibited in the Exposition Universelle of 1889. I have found no reproduction in guidebooks for the Exposition or for the Salons of the period. I would appreciate hearing from anyone who knows of a reproduction or has some memory of this painting.

69 *Tess*, 53, p. 470. Hardy also mentions Crivelli's skeletal hands in *Desperate Remedies*, IX, 4, p. 173.

70 Boldini: 'The Morning Stroll.' The only reproduction I have found is a small plate in Carlo Ragghianti and Ettore Camesasca's *L'Opera Completa di Boldini* (Milan: Rizzoli Editore, 1970), No. 22 D. The original is 'in collezione nordamericana non identificata'. Cf. Illustration 8.

71 Most of Strang's etchings are reproduced in *William Strang: Catalogue of His Etched Work 1882–1912* (Glasgow: Maclehose, 1912) and the *Supplement* (1923). They are described in David Strang's *William Strang: Catalogue of His Etchings and Engravings* (University of Glasgow, 1962). 'The Crucifixion' is Plate 664. 'The End', singled out 'for its force' in Laurence Binyon's preface to the *Supplement* is Plate 139 and is also reproduced in F. Newbolt's *Etchings of William Strang* (London: Newnes, 1907). See Illustration 10. Hardy cut out a review of Strang's etchings (cf. Chapter 3, p. 110) which may have influenced his later opinion. Strang's portraits of Hardy are dated as follows:

1893 'Portrait of Thomas Hardy', Catalogue No. 200, etching. This portrait was apparently finished in 1892 (Purdy, *Letters*, p. 284) and used as the frontispiece for Lionel Johnson's *The Art of Thomas Hardy* (London: Mathews and Lane, 1894). It was widely reproduced between 1895 and 1898 in the journals listed in the A.L.A. Portrait Index. Cf. Frontispiece.

1893 Pencil sketch for the above painting. In the Dorset County Museum.

1893 'Thomas Hardy', National Portrait Gallery 2929, oil painting. Reproduced as the frontispiece for *Thomas Hardy's Personal Writings*, ed. Harold Orel and *One Rare Fair Woman*, ed. Hardy and Pinion.

1894 'Portrait of Thomas Hardy', Catalogue No. 227, etching. Reproduced in Desmond Hawkins, *Hardy: Novelist and Poet* (London: David and Charles, 1976), p. 132 (facing).

1896 'Portrait of a Man', Catalogue No. 268, etching. This resembles the previous etchings, and is identified as Hardy's portrait by Laurence Binyon in his prefatory essay to the *Supplement*, p. xix.

1910 'Portrait of Thomas Hardy O. M.', Catalogue No. 517, dry point etching. Cf. Frontispiece.

1910 'Thomas Hardy', Fitzwilliam Museum No. 733, pencil drawing, dated 26 September 1910. Exhibited in the Royal Academy in 1911.

1910 'Thomas Hardy', Windsor Castle Inv. 13737, drawing. 'In September he sat to Mr. William Strang for a sketch-portrait, which was required for hanging at Windsor Castle among those of other recipients of the Order of Merit' (*Life*, 350–1). See Illustration 9.

1919 'Thomas Hardy', Catalogue No. 703, engraving on copper. Used as the frontispiece of the Mellstock edition of Hardy's works. Cf. Frontispiece.

1919 'Thomas Hardy', National Portrait Gallery 1922, pencil drawing. Reproduced as the frontispiece of the *Later Years*, and later as the frontispiece to E. R. Southerington's *Hardy's Vision of Man* (New York: Barnes and Noble, 1971); also in Hawkins's *Hardy: Novelist and Poet*, p. 153 (facing).

1920 'Thomas Hardy', Catalogue No. 710, engraving on copper based on the above drawing. Indeed these last three portraits seem practically identical. One is used as the frontispiece of William Rutland's *Thomas Hardy* (London: Blackie and Son, 1938).

The *Later Years* also reproduces a 1918 Strang drawing of Florence Hardy, p. 160 (facing), reproduced but unaccountably given a date of 1910 by Gittings, *The Older Hardy* (Plate 12). Strang also did famous portraits of Tennyson, Stevenson, Kipling, and others: cf. Binyon, *William Strang* (New York: Keppel, 1904). According to the *DNB*, Strang first made a name as 'an etcher of imaginative compositions, in which homeliness and realism, sometimes with a grim or fantastic element, were subdued to fine design and severe drawing'. The best bibliographies on Strang are in the *Allgemeines Lexikon der Bildenden Künstler* (Leipzig, 1967) and the Art Institute of Chicago's *Index to Art Periodicals*.

72 Smart, 'Pictorial Imagery in the Novels of Thomas Hardy', p. 277.

73 Hardy makes the traditional romantic association of the moon with the half-light of imaginative vision – in 'On Stinsford Hill at Midnight' (550), 'Imaginings' (477), and 'The Man Who Forgot' (490). But with Hardy the moon makes the imagination expand and then leads it into a stunned recognition of the loss of what is imagined. The moon is therefore a compound symbol both for the shaping of imaginative vision and the circumstance which imprisons vision. Thus the moon can, consistently, represent that

external fate which the romantic mind cannot see: 'The broad bald moon edged up where the sea was wide. . . . That, behind, / My fate's masked face crept near me I did not know' ('On the Esplanade' (682)).

74 In 1921 Hardy said that Charlotte Mew 'is far and away the best living woman poet' (Vere Collins, *Talks with Thomas Hardy at Max Gate, 1920–1922* [London: Duckworth, 1928], p. 49). 'It was discovered after Hardy's death . . . that he had copied out her poem "Fin de Fête". . . .' (Alida Monro, introduction to Charlotte Mew's *Collected Poems* [London: Duckworth, 1953], p, xv). 'Fin de Fête' (p. 55) ends: 'But now, / Oh, what a lonely head! / With just the shadow of a waving bough / In the moonlight over your bed.'

75 In her review of *Human Shows*, 'Memory's Immortal Gear', *Dial* 80 (1926), 417 – 21, Marianne Moor commented: 'The sense of masonry with shadows on it, of Gothic ogives and mullions, enriches what would without it, perhaps, still be poetry, but how insistent are these imagined interiors and exteriors.' In *Human Shows* Hardy describes 'mullioned windows' (709), 'mullioned shades' (726), and the 'mullioned pane' (719), which preside at the conclusion of tragic relationships. Hartmann, *Architektur*, p. 52, notes the many times mullions are cited in the novels.

76 In 'She Revisits Alone the Church of Her Marriage' (596), the woman returns to what was once her 'culminant crest of life' and as she broods in this obsolete scene, the 'chancel' of the first stanza becomes the 'check-floored chancel' of the second and then the 'fateful chancel' and finally 'this hoary chancel, / Where all's the same'. In 'The Church-Builder' (139) the suicide will soon 'cross the patterned floor'.

77 Influencing these *gestalt* transitions in Hardy may have been Schopenhauer and his version of the Platonic cave. Hardy's discovery of the complex inner–outer pattern is like Schopenhauer's discovery of the 'Will' in the self and the world. The following passage is taken from Hardy's copy of *On the Fourfold Root of the Principle of Sufficient Reason*, trans. Mme Karl Hillebrand (London: 1897), p. 317:

> In the Grotto of Pausilippo, darkness continues to augment as we advance towards the interior; but when once we have passed the middle, day-light again appears at the other end and shows us the way; so also in this case: just at the point where the outwardly directed light of the understanding with its form of causality, gradually yielding to increasing darkness, had been reduced to a feeble, flickering glimmer, behold! we are met by a totally different light proceeding from quite another quarter, from our own inner self, through the chance circumstance, that we, the judges happen here to be the very objects that are to be judged.

Hardy was also influenced by the *gestalt* effect in Tennyson's 'Tears, Idle Tears' (as the dying man makes the transition from life to death, the 'casement slowly grows a glimmering square') and Wordsworth's 'Intimations' ode: the light of vision fades into the light of common day. Most suggestive to Hardy were perhaps the framing images used in Arnold's 'The Scholar Gypsy', ll. 8–9 and 217. Pursuing his vision, the scholar must '[c]ross and recross the strips of moon-blanch'd green'.

78 *Origin* 4, p. 84; 9, p. 295; 4, p. 84.

79 Tate and Brady's translation of Psalm 90, which Hardy called one of his 'familiar and favourite hymns' (*Life*, 275). Psalm 39, which Hardy cites in 'After Reading Psalms XXXIX., XL., etc.' (661), says, in the King James version: 'thou hast made my days as an handbreadth; and mine age is nothing before thee.' 'In Tenebris I' (136) cites Psalm 101 (Latin numbering) which says: 'My days are consumed like smoke.' In *Life*, 393, Hardy quotes the Tate and Brady stanza from Psalm 90, beginning, 'For in Thy sight a

thousand years / Are like a day that's past', and ending, 'Thou sweep'st us off . . .' etc.

80 Hardy wrote to Edward Clodd in 1916: 'My suspicion is that when people say they have been 'reading Gibbon' they have not gone much further than those chapters [xv and xvi], though there are so many equally interesting . . . I have always rather delighted in it [Gibbon's style].' Ashley Catalogue, x, p. 77.

81 Hardy also knew well Jeremy Taylor's exploration of the Jeremiah theme in *Holy Living and Dying*: cf. *Chapter 1*, pp. 5–6. For Hardy's markings in his Bible, cf. Kenneth Phelps, *Annotations by Thomas Hardy in His Bibles and Prayer Book* (Guernsey: Toucan Press, 1966).

82 Lowes, 'Two Readings of Earth', *Essays in Appreciation* (Boston: Houghton Mifflin, 1936), p. 125.

83 *Far from the Madding Crowd* also describes snow-light: 'The moon shone to-night, and its light was not of a customary kind. His window admitted only a reflection of its rays, and the pale sheen had that reversed direction which snow gives . . .' (14, p. 114).

84 Hardy's 'underthought' of light patterns, like his meditative structures, language, and metres, has a way of making seemingly mediocre poems become curiously interesting. One of the Hardy poems Blackmur attacks, as symptomatic of Hardy's obsessive formulas, is 'The Telegram' (323). The poem, however, is *about* the growth of a formula, the bride's formula of sentimental nostalgia, the bridegroom's formula of self-pitying bitterness. This pattern of their mentalities creates the 'long lane overhung / With lovelessness'. That the obsessive pattern is not Hardy's is vividly illustrated when we discover to our surprise in the last stanza that the narrator is not 'Hardy' but the bridegroom. The setting, which Blackmur finds extraneous, in fact provides Hardy's characteristic context for the tragic process:

> – The yachts ride mute at anchor and the fulling moon is fair,
> And the giddy folk are strutting up and down the smooth parade,
> And in her wild distraction she seems not to be aware
>   That she lives no more a maid. . . .

These movements are meshed. The moon is fulling, the folk are strutting, *and* her wild distraction, shadowed by the swelling resentment of her companion, grows. The moon symbolises the 'honeymoon' of the couple, its expanding 'distraction'. Yet the 'fulling moon' is also external to the honeymoon and even opposed to it for the couple endures what is now a 'waning honeymoon'. Thus the moon represents a complex fulling of a pattern which is a human pattern within the larger pattern of reality, two patterns, one fulling, one waning, which will jar when consummation comes.

85 Hopkins may have been influenced by a passage in *Far from the Madding Crowd*: 'The road stretched through water-meadows traversed by little brooks, whose quivering surfaces were braided along their centres, and folded into creases at the sides; or, where the flow was more rapid, the stream was pied with spots of white froth, which rode on in undisturbed serenity' (6, p. 46). Compare 'Inversnaid'. In October 1886, Hopkins wrote Bridges: 'How admirable are Blackmore and Hardy! . . . Do you know the bonfire scenes in the *Return of the Native* and still better the sword-exercise scene in the *Madding Crowd*, breathing epic? or the wife-sale in the *Mayor of Casterbridge* (read by chance)?' In November 1887, Hopkins again wrote Bridges: 'It is in modern novels that wordpainting most abounds. . . . Wordpainting is, in the verbal arts, the great success of our day.' Hopkins seems to be thinking primarily of Hardy here for in May 1888, he writes Coventry Patmore: 'I lately read Blackmore's last book. . . . I am a devoted

admirer of his descriptions, his word-painting, which is really Shakesperian. Otherwise this book is disappointing. . . . Hardy is a finer man.' Cf. *Letters . . . to Robert Bridges*, ed. Claude Abbott (London: Oxford University Press, 1955), revised impression, pp. 239, 267; *Further Letters . . .*, ed. Abbott (London: Oxford University Press, 1956), 2nd edition, p. 390. The serial publication of *The Return of the Native* was illustrated by Hopkins' brother, Arthur (Purdy, 25). In the novel, Hardy describes the heron which Mrs Yeobright watches: it

> . . . flew on with his face toward the sun. He had come dripping wet from some pool in the valleys, and as he flew the edges and lining of his wings, his thighs, and his breast were so caught by the bright sunbeams that he appeared as if formed of burnished silver. Up in the zenith where he was seemed a free and happy place, away from all contact with the earthly ball to which she was pinioned; and she wished that she could arise uncrushed from its surface and fly as he flew then. (IV, 6, p. 343)

Should not this passage be added to the list of probable influences on 'The Windhover'? Another possible influence on Hopkins's poem was the two paragraphs beginning, 'All by the hedge ran a little stream', in *Lorna Doone*, Chapter XXXVIII. This passage is also remarkably similar to the one quoted above from *Far from the Madding Crowd*. Hardy greatly admired Blackmore's book and noted parallels between the two novels (Purdy and Millgate, *Letters*, pp. 37–8).

86 Wright, 80.
87 *Literary Notes IV*, 33; cf. Björk, *The Literary Notes*, vol. 1, p. 175.
88 Cf. Eastlake, *Gothic Revival*, p. 132, for a summary of the theory. A more recent discussion is W. D. Robson-Scott's *The Literary Background of the Gothic Revival in Germany* (Oxford: Clarendon Press, 1965), especially pp. 5, 27. Ruskin's discussion is in *The Stones of Venice* II, vi, 'The Nature of Gothic'. Hartmann, *Architektur*, pp. 59–60, cites twelve other such images in Hardy's novels.
89 Paulin, *Thomas Hardy*, p. 24, has a different, but quite interesting interpretation, of this drawing.
90 *Complete Poems*, 9, 49, 742; 62, 70, 75, 122, 123, 130, 139, 152, 667; 156, 314, 323, 332.
91 Holloway, *The Victorian Sage* (London: Archon, 1962), p. 259; also cf. p. 252. The pattern image is also used in Ian Gregor's *The Great Web: The Form of Hardy's Major Fiction* (London: Faber, 1974).
92 *Mayor of Casterbridge*, 21, p. 160. *Under the Greenwood Tree* I, 1; IV, 2 (also note the great branches of the greenwood tree overspreading the wedding), *A Pair of Blue Eyes*, 2; 6; 25, pp. 273–4 (at a key moment of discovery, Stephen watches his friends in the summer-house 'through the horizontal bars of wood work, which crossed their forms like the ribs of a skeleton'); 39, p. 423 (the novel ends as it began, with silhouettes 'become black disks van-dyked against the sky'). In *The Return of the Native*, the pattern images describe both the subjective world of Eustacia Vye and the objective world of the heath. Hartmann relates Hardy's silhouette imagery to his architectural background.
93 *Woodlanders*, cf. *passim* chapters 1, 3, 4, 6, 7, 9, 10, 19: most of these chapters are rich in several examples.
94 Thus when Hardy says that Grace 'traced the remainder of the woodland track, dazed by the complications of her position' (29, p. 251), the early images fill in the bare remark. Several pages later, Hardy seems positively to assert the connection between abstract and concrete complications: 'This track under the bare trees and over the cracking sticks,

screened and roofed in from the outer world of wind by a network of boughs, led her slowly on' (33, p. 283). I cannot seem to find such images later in the novel, except perhaps for the mantrap, 'a cobwebbed, object curiously framed in iron' (46, p. 423), whose melodramatic relevance to the pattern is obvious. Interestingly, Hardy said that he did not end the novel well. Cf. Purdy and Millgate, *Letters*, pp. 149, 191.

95 In *Tess*, cf. especially Chapters 2, 4, 11, 20, 25, 32, 42.

96 While Pugin's towns are largely imaginary, he may himself have been thinking of this ancient capital of King Alfred and the home of Arthur's Round Table. In the second edition of *Contrasts* (1841), Pugin added two illustrations, one of contrasting poorhouses, and the other of contrasting towns. The ancient poorhouse is evidently modelled after St Cross Hospital in Winchester (noted by Nikolaus Pevsner in *Some Architectural Writers of the Nineteenth Century* [Oxford: Clarendon, 1972], p. 106). The new poorhouse is practically identical with the prison which dominates the contrasting town of 1840. Other details in the contrasting towns are similar to details in views of Winchester which I have seen in guidebooks, though I am not native enough to know how unique these details are. The Gothic architecture of Winchester is, however, generally more Norman than Pointed: if Pugin was thinking of Winchester, he 'improved' it.

If Pugin gave Hardy the idea of viewing Winchester in this contrasting way, nevertheless many of Hardy's specific details – especially the broad tower and Norman windows of the cathedral, the tower of the hospice (a reference to St Cross's with its Norman chapel attached), and certain details of the prison built in 1848 – are drawn from Winchester rather than Pugin. There are a few discrepancies between Hardy's picture and Winchester: St Thomas's (now the Hampshire Record office) has only one spire, and the roofs of the prison are pitched. Mr F Liesching, Governor, HM Prison, Winchester Hants, kindly sent me information on the prison and its prospect. There is also some doubt whether the prospect could ever have been seen as Hardy described it. Hermann Lea, in *Thomas Hardy's Wessex* (London: Macmillan, 1913), written over a twenty-year period and with occasional advice from Hardy himself, notes that the prospect was obscured – 'at least . . . when the present writer was there – by trees which have grown up in later years' (p. 31). In my own visit to Winchester, and after scaling a forty-foot tower on the grounds of Montgomery of Alamein nearby, I found it unlikely that Hardy could literally have seen his prospect from the first milestone (labelled '1 to West Gate Winton') on Romsey Road. The brow of a broad and heavily treed hill would have to have been closely shaved. Even then, the cathedral points more or less toward the milestone so that the 'immense length' of the nave could not well be seen.

An important passage in *A Laodicean* (I, 2, pp. 11–13) suggests tht Hardy was well aware of Pugin's *Contrasts*. Somerset views a Baptist chapel: 'The chapel had neither beauty, quaintness, nor congeniality to recommend it: the dissimilitude between the new utilitarianism of the place and the scenes of venerable Gothic art which had occupied his daylight hours could not well be exceeded. . . . Being just then *en rapport* with ecclesiasticism . . . he could not help murmuring, "Shade of Pugin, what a monstrosity!"' In Pugin's *Contrasts*, the 'Baptist Chapel', number 8 in the New Town, has replaced 'St. Edmunds', number 10 in the Old Town. In *Real Conversations*, p. 49, Hardy regrets 'that Winchester did not remain, as it once was, the royal, political, and social capital of England'. London, by contrast, is 'so monstrously overgrown'.

Pugin's identifying numbers are very hard to discern in the published version, though I think I have made out all except number 15, the 'Socialist Hall of Science', in the town of 1840. I have correlated the published version with Pugin's original version which is reproduced by Phoebe Stanton, *Pugin* (New York: Viking, 1972), pp. 90–1. The 'Socialist Hall' in the original version becomes Mr Evans Chapel in the published version. In turn, Mr Evans Chapel becomes the New Christian Society (which is not mentioned in the original). The left-most portion of the long industrial mill is labelled Messrs. Toppings Workhouse in the original; it seems to be unlabelled in the published version though Kenneth Clark says that the right-most portion is the 'Socialist Hall of Science' (*The Gothic Revival*, p. 186). If this architectural drawing is indeed one of England's most famous, it is remarkable that Pugin's labels have never been clearly identified. Many are wrongly identified by Clark. On Pugin's plate, therefore, I have juxtaposed clearer numbers placed just under the pictures in vertical alignment with what seem to be Pugin's numbers.

97 *Life*, p. 258. I recently obtained a microfilm of C. J. P. Beatty's *The Part Played by Architecture in the Life and Work of Thomas Hardy (with particular reference to the Novels)*, a Ph.D dissertation for the University of London, 1963. The thesis contains a voluminous number of quotations of architectural scenes from the novels and reproduces many letters and documents relating to the models for these scenes. Of particular interest to me were: (1) Sir Albert Richardson's interview of Hardy: 'Hardy said architecture had taught him to place one thing upon another, the value of order and sequence' (p. 2); (2) Henry-Russell Hitchcock's evaluation of two Hardy church designs as 'better than Blomfield' and 'in a class with the top architects of High Victorian Gothic' (p. 604); (3) Beatty's underlinings of silhouette and architecture images which should be added to those listed by Hartmann; (4) Hardy's detailed reading of John Hutchins's *The History and Antiquities of the County of Dorset*, 3rd edition, and Hardy's marginalia changing Hutchins's description of Stinsford Church from 'Early-English or First Pointed style' to 'Transition from the Norman to Early-English or First Pointed style' (p. 612), and (5) Beatty's identification of the grotesque clockwork in *Far from the Madding Crowd* (in the scene where Troy waits to marry Fanny) as the Wimborne clock of 'Copying Architecture from an Old Minster' (pp. 267–9).

98 In the *Fourfold Root*, p. 276, Schopenhauer writes: 'the will did not first cherish the intention . . . and then adapt the means to it . . . its willing was rather immediately the aim and immediately the attainment of that aim.' Consciousness discovers the Will's aim only after the aim is achieved. This idea influenced Hardy's notion of patterns which control consciousness and become visible to consciousness only after they are completed.

99 To illustrate the difference between Northern and Southern countries, Ruskin describes 'the variegated mosaic of the world's surface which a bird sees in its migration', then adopts an even higher satellite view of the planet, ending with an acknowledgement of 'the great laws by which the earth and all that it bears are ruled throughout their being' ('The Nature of Gothic'). Also cf. Darwin above, p. 60. On the paintings, cf. Smart, pp. 267–8.

CHAPTER 3

1 *Land and Water*, 13 December 1917, and *Westminster Gazette*, 8 December 1917. Hardy wrote his replies in the margins of the columns of the latter. The word 'stalk' has continued to be controversial: cf. Marsden, p. 150; also James Southworth, *The Poetry of Thomas Hardy* (New York: Columbia University Press, 1947), p. 153.

2 As in Hardy's description of Tess and Angel falling in love at Dairyman Crick's dairy:

'something had occurred which changed the pivot of the universe for their two natures; something which, had he known its quality, the dairyman would have despised, as a practical man; yet which was based upon a more stubborn and resistless tendency than a whole heap of so-called practicalities' (*Tess*, 24, p. 194).

3 The work seems to make conscious use of *A Pair of Blue Eyes*: cf. Reginald Snell, 'A Self-Plagiarism by Thomas Hardy', *Essays in Criticism*, 2 (1952), 114–17. In 1923, the year he finished the *Queen of Cornwall*, Hardy said *A Pair of Blue Eyes* was his favourite novel: Roy McNutt, 'A Visit to Mr. Thomas Hardy', *Dalhousie Review*, 6 (1926), 51–5.

4 In the *London Mercury*, 6 (1922), 631–2, Hardy published a poem by Moule which presumably contains the view Moule developed in his articles: 'Ave, Caesar Imperator! . . . Dying men salute thee, Caesar'. A newspaper clipping of this poem is pasted in the back of Hardy's copy of Palgrave's *Golden Treasurey* (at the Dorset County Museum) and dated by Hardy '1862'. I have not seen the newspaper articles by Moule. In a letter to Hardy dated Thursday, 1870 (transcribed in the Dorset County Library), Moule said that he had two articles in that day's *Echo* – an allusion to a London journal founded in 1868.

  Horace's phrase intrigued Hardy and he returned to it often. Cf. below, p. 138. In his signed copy of Smart's translation of Horace (London: Bohn, 1859), in the Colby College Library Collection, Hardy underlined Smart's translation: 'The Greeks suffer for what their princes act foolishly.' Hardy crossed out 'princes act' and wrote 'kings *do*' in the margin. At the top of the page he put the original Latin.

5 The *Life* ms. ('T.H. Vol 1, 1840 to 1891', *Original Manuscripts*, Reel 8) shows that the first paragraph is a late addition.

6 Jacqueline Bratton's *The Victorian Popular Ballad* (London: Macmillan, 1975) reveals that the term 'ballad' covers many more types and inter-relationships than I have distinguished here. Good discussions of Hardy's ballads can be found by Douglas Brown, Paul Zietlow, Jean Brooks, and others, but their insights still need to be integrated with Bratton's historical research. In his *Life*, p. 359, Hardy quotes from an important article on the ballad, 'Modern Developments in Ballad Art', *Edinburgh Review*, 213 (1911), 153–79. Hardy quotes the article's opening statement on the difficulty of classifying poems. The article then notes the wide use of the term 'ballad' as a description of story-telling poems, certain verse metres, songs, non-narrative lyrical ballads, etc.

7 *CP*, 157, 163, 894, 198, 162, 228, 47

8 *CP*, 194, 195, 164, 619, 52, 135, 156, 165, 261.

9 *Real Conversations*, pp. 32, 37.

10 *Colby Library Quarterly* (November 1954), pp. 262–4. A good example of Hardy's personalising the principle of memory in these years can be seen in another set of poems. Before 1900, Hardy wrote some historical epiphanies: 'In the Old Theatre, Fiesole' (67), 'Rome: On the Palatine' (68). In the 1900s he wrote some more: 'By the Barrows' (216), 'The Roman Road' (218), 'The Roman Gravemounds' (329). In the earlier poems, the historical past and present are brought together in grandiose ways: 'her act flashed home . . . The power, the pride, the reach, of perished Rome'; 'in Caesar's house . . . Time seemed fiction, Past and Present one.' In the later poems, the imperial theme is recanted in favour of more personal themes: while 'thoughtful men / Contrast its days of Now and Then . . . Visioning on the vacant air / Helmed legionaries . . . Uprises there / A mother's form upon my ken, / Guiding my infant steps.'

11 Lawrence, *Letters*, ed. David Garnett (London: Cape, 1938), p. 429.

12 *Writings*, p. 40; also cf. *Life*, pp. 284, 298.

13 In 'Modern Developments in Ballad Art', the writer distinguishes 'the early descriptive ballad and the advanced pictorialism of the latter decades of the century', i.e. in Tennyson and the Pre-Raphaelites (p. 166).

14 In the modern ballad, 'the story-teller shares with the story told the interest of the reader. . . . Ethical and psychological complexities have undoubtedly encroached upon an art of which simplicity was once the hall-mark of merit' (*ibid*, pp. 174, 178).

15 The poem has an unhappy likeness to Hardy's personal situation. During the early 1900s Emma Hardy's mental disturbance grew and expressed itself as a regressive nostalgia for her girlhood. When Hardy read her *Recollections* shortly after her death, he was profoundly affected by her description of her Cornwall days and shared this throe of the past in his love elegies. Thus, 'The Satin Shoes' describes the bride: 'From her wrecked dream, as months flew on, / Her thoughts seemed not to range.' And the narrator concludes by repeating the poem's second stanza, conventional there but strangely insistent when repeated: 'Yet she was fair as early day . . .' (334). An important letter by Hardy on Emmas 'aberration' and 'childlike' character is quoted by Henry Gifford, 'Thomas Hardy and Emma', *Essays and Studies*, 19 (London: Murray, 1966), p. 117.

16 'We sang the Ninetieth Psalm to her – set to Saint Stephen's tune' (212). Placed just before 'The Rash Bride' is 'A Church Romance' which ends with a similar allusion: 'Bowing "New Sabbath" or "Mount Ephraim."' Here the detail seems deliberately meant to symbolise the moment of vision which fixed itself on the bride 'long years thence'. John Betjeman imitates the ending effect of 'The Rash Bride' in 'Exeter'.

17 *CP*, 153. The formal tableaux correspond beautifully, if obscurely, with the automatism which drives the narrator to her perverse mistake and now drives her under memory's control. It is as though she is driven to make her life into a tragic ballad. Tom Beresford, a psychologist, compares this to 'headline thinking'.

18 *CP*, 331. Another possibility is that the second narrator starts suddenly to refer to himself in the third person – as though his life were forever defined by that moment and thus made 'distant'. Compare Hardy's other plays on the identity of narrator and participant in 'The Telegram' (323), 'Beyond the Last Lamp' (257), 'The Phantom Horsewoman' (294). Gordon Gerould notes that in some traditional ballads 'an attempt to tell the story in the first person . . . fades out after a few stanzas into the normal objectivity of the third': *The Ballad of Tradition* (New York: Gordon reprint, 1974). Stephen Dedalus notes a similar phenomenon in 'that old English ballad *Turpin Hero*' and makes it illustrate his stages of art advancing toward godlike epic impersonality (*Portrait of the Artist as a Young Man*, v, 214–15, Viking edition). Hardy's interest in the self-distancing spell of memory should be distinguished from Dedalus' triumphant aestheticism.

19 *Literary Notes II*, [117]. Hardy is quoting from 'At the Sign of the Ship', a regular feature, this one from *Longman's Magazine*, 36 (May 1900), 88–96. Lang refers to the 'traditional version' of the 'old song', 'The Bonny Bonny Banks o' Loch Lomond'. Interestingly, Hardy adds the word 'ballad' to Lang's account. The first three words and the italics of the entry are Hardy's.

In making the ballad's form explicitly consistent with its subject matter, Hardy also represents an interesting fusion of two traditions, supposedly opposed: the Romantic tradition of the subjective speaker, the ballad tradition of the objective story. Attacking Hardy's ballads, Howe notes: 'Hardy was trying something that may well be impossible: he was trying to give a personal flavour to a form that achieves its finest effects through impersonality': 'The Short Poems of Thomas Hardy', *Southern Review*, N.S. 2 (1966), p. 888.

20 *CP*, 213, 796, 642, 489. Compare Wordsworth, *The Excursion*, I, II, 614–19: '. . . the things of which he spake / Seemed present; and, attention now relaxed, / A heart-felt chillness crept along my veins.' In 1880 Hardy had his own personal version of this affective drama: 'You would talk to her . . . and believe you were talking to a person of the same date as yourself, with recent emotions and impulses: you would see her sideways when crossing the room to show you something, and realize her, with sudden sadness, to be a withered woman whose interests and emotions must be nearly extinct (*Life*, p. 136).

21 *CP*, 288, 630, 289, 611, 526, 483.

22 *CP*, 396, 542, 383, 416, 523, 550.

23 Lawrence, *Letters*, p. 474; Woolf, quoted in Blunden, *Thomas Hardy* (London: Macmillan, 1942), p. 173; *CP*, 548, 538. Also see Blunden's testimony in 1922, 'Thomas Hardy', *The Great Victorians*, ed. H. Massingham (New York: Doubleday, 1933), p. 222; Felkin in 1919, p. 32; Hamlin Garland in 1923, *Afternoon Neighbours* (New York: Macmillan, 1934), p. 92; at least four such witnesses are cited by D. F. Barber, ed., *Concerning Thomas Hardy* (London: Skilton, 1968), pp. 98, 85, 128, 118. Edith Wharton's testimony is very similar but I cannot discover the date of her visit: *A Backward Glance* (New York: Appleton, 1934), pp. 215 – 16. In a letter of 1923, Hardy said he suffered from an 'overclouding' of his mind: Gittings, *Young Thomas Hardy* (Boston: Little, Brown, 1975), p. 4. In 1919, Florence Hardy noted: 'He forgets things that have happened only a day or two before . . . though of course the memory of his early life is miraculous' (*Friends of a Lifetime*, p. 302).

24 Purdy, p. 266; *Life*, pp. 378, 302, 405.

25 *CP*, 722; *Life*, 389; *CP*, 723, 722; Margaret Carter, letter of 2 December 1925, in Purdy's *Memorial Exhibition*, p. 37.

26 Thus we must qualify David Perkins's generalisation about Hardy that the Romantic 'subjective sources of true insight and knowledge' in the visionary imagination 'were not available to him'. His 'obsessive attention to the whole context of experience . . . strips and disintegrates the momentary assertions of the imagination, converting what seemed to be a vision into an illusion'. 'Hardy and the Poetry of Isolation', *ELH*, 26 (1959), 253–70. Perkins has some good remarks on Hardy, Proust, and memory.

27 *CP*, 644, 401, 393, 422, 358, 359, 523, 550.

28 *Life*, p. 55; *CP*, 85; *Real Conversations*, pp. 45 – 6; *CP*, 87, 151; *Life*, 368; *CP*, 464, 419, 697, 695, 722, 723.

29 *Friends of a Lifetime*, p. 284; Alfred Noyes, *Two Worlds for Memory* (Philadelphia: Lippincott, 1953), p. 148; *Queen of Cornwall*, pp. 40, 69, 77.

30 *CP*, 370, 413; Collins, *Talks*, p. 66 (Hardy said that Blake, like Wordsworth, benefits by selection); *Friends of a Lifetime*, p. 284; *CP*, 507, 467, 641, 553, 512, 372, 683, 581, 599.

31 Stephen, 'Dreams and Realities', *Fortnightly Review*, 30 (1878), p. 348.

32 Arthur Clayborough, *The Grotesque in English Literature* (Oxford: Clarendon Press, 1965), p. 1, summarising the *OED* account. Of all the traditions associated with Hardy, the tradition of the grotesque is the most difficult to define. A good bibliography of works on the grotesque was distributed at the 1977 MLA section, 'The Form and Function of the Comic Element in Twentieth-Century Grotesque', led by Rainer Sell, *PMLA*, 92 (1977), 1134.

33 Margot Northey attempts a brief summary of the relationship between the terms, 'Gothic' and 'grotesque', in her introduction to *The Haunted Wilderness: The Gothic and Grotesque in Canadian Fiction* (University of Toronto Press, 1976). Two strong recent trends in modern criticism, studies in the grotesque and studies of the Gothic novel,

seem unaware of each other's existence. Devendra Varma, *The Gothic Flame* (London: Barker, 1957), touches on the relationship between Gothic architecture and the Gothic novel. It is interesting that Hardy's formative years were characterised by the greatest of the Gothic revivals and the most active critical discussion of the term 'grotesque'.

34 Hardy later read Symonds's 'Caricature, the Fantastic, the Grotesque', in *Essays Speculative and Suggestive* (London: Chapman, 1890). Symonds (in 1890) sees the grotesque as a combination of the distortion of caricature and the ideality of fantasy. The fantastic is produced by the 'excited imagination' showing its 'independence of fact and external nature'. 'The grotesque is a branch of the fantastic', with an element of caricature added. An example was medieval Teutonic art: 'The free play of the Northern fancy ran over easily into distortion, degradation of form, burlesque.' Earlier, in *The Mayor of Casterbridge* and *The Woodlanders*, Hardy had shown his interest in the grotesque images of Norse mythology.

35 Bagehot, *Literary Essays*, vol. 2, *Collected Works*, ed. N. St John-Stevas (Cambridge: Harvard University Press, 1965), pp. 359, 354. Bagehot also associates grotesque art with the imperfect nature of the universe: 'It deals . . . not with what nature is striving to be, but with what by some lapse she has happened to become' (p. 353). Bagehot (and Browning) may have influenced Hardy's description of the 'Unfulfilled Intention' in *The Woodlanders* (7, p. 59): 'The leaf was deformed . . . the taper was interrupted,' etc. Five paragraphs later, Hardy describes the woodlanders' walking-sticks, wrought into monstrous vegetative corkscrew shapes 'by the slow torture of an encircling woodbine during their growth, as the Chinese have been said to mould human beings into grotesque toys by continued compression in infancy'. Bagehot may have also influenced Hardy's earlier statement in the *Life*, p. 124: 'A perception of the FAILURE OF THINGS to be what they are meant to be, lends them . . . a new and greater interest. . . .'

36 The grotesque in Hardy's fiction has been widely noted but by no means exhaustively treated. Richard Carpenter, 'Hardy's Gurgoyles', *Modern Fiction Studies*, 6 (1960–1), 223–32, is a good summary of some of the grotesque images in the novels. Penelope Vigar, *The Novels of Thomas Hardy*, also gives many illustrations. On Hardy's use of Gothic elements, with a brief reference to the grotesque, cf. James Scott, 'Thomas Hardy's Use of the Gothic: An Examination of Five Representative Works', *Nineteenth-Century Fiction*, 17 (1963), 363–80; S. F. Johnson, 'Hardy and Burke's Sublime', *Style in Prose Fiction*, ed. Harold Martin (New York: Columbia University Press, 1959). Also cf. J. O. Bailey, 'Hardy's Mephistophelian Visitants', *PMLA*, 61 (1946), 1146–84; Emma Clifford, 'The Child: The Circus: And Jude the Obscure', *Cambridge Journal*, 7 (1954), 531–46; Albert Guerard, *Thomas Hardy* (Norfolk, Conn.: New Directions, 1964), *passim*. Also cf. Smart, 'Pictorial Imagery in the Novels of Thomas Hardy', p. 269.

37 Ruskin, *Works*, XI, 171–2. Ruskin cites Dickens as an example of satiric grotesques.

38 Cf. above pp. 58, 66, 70. Also cf. Millgate, p. 289, on the influence of 'Alonzo the Brave'.

39 Archer, *Real Conversations*, pp. 45–6.

40 *CP*, 30; *Real Conversations*, p. 37; Barber, *Concerning Thomas Hardy*, p. 107; *Friends of a Lifetime*, p. 305; *Life*, pp. 427–8, 440–1. On the subject of Hardy and ghost folklore, see Firor, *Folkways in Thomas Hardy* (Philadelphia, University of Pennsylvania Press, 1931), Chapter 3; Pinion, *A Hardy Companion*, pp. 152–61; J. O. Bailey, *Thomas Hardy and the Cosmic Mind* (Chapel Hill, University of North Carolina Press, 1956), pp. 4–5.

41 *CP*, 222, 32, 153, 261, 62, 36, 284, 286, 289, 396, 542.

42 *CP*, 428, 518, 549, 546, 580, 410, 580.

43 *Life*, p. 287; *The Well-Beloved*, II, 6, p. 93; III, i, p. 150; III, 7, p. 202; *Life*, p. 286. J. Hillis

Miller, *Thomas Hardy*, p. 214, reproduces the original conclusion of the novel. In *Far from the Madding Crowd* Hardy associates a grotesque image with a similar psychological discovery. Chapter 46 opens with the image of gurgoyles and their grotesque desecration of Fanny's grave: this is the setting for Troy's discovery that the 'illusion' of his invincibility had long since been undermined and that nature had circumvented his sentimental gesture: 'A man who has spent his primal strength in journeying in one direction has not much spirit left for reversing his course.' After Proust read *The Well-Beloved*, he reported in 1909: 'I have just read something very beautiful which unfortunately resembles what I am doing (only it is a thousand times better). . . . It doesn't even lack that slight touch of the grotesque which is an essential part of all great works.' *Letters*, trans. Mina Curtiss (New York: Random House, 1966), p. 204.

Hardy's exploration of 'exhumed emotion' and Proust's exploration of involuntary memory have striking similarities. Indeed, the publication dates of the volumes of *A La Recherche* (1913–27) closely parallel the publication dates of Hardy's last five volumes of poetry (1914–28). By 1926 Hardy realised the close connection between Proust and the theme of *The Well-Beloved* (cf. above, Chapter 1, p. 55); whether he realised other connections, like that which Proust readers notice in 'Under the Waterfall' (probably written in 1913 when Proust's first volume of *A la Recherche* was published), is unknown. Both men explore the surprising power and 'cruel anachronism' (Beckett, *Proust* [New York: Grove, 1931], p. 28) which memory represents. But for Proust the anachronism can be overcome and the past recaptured. While Hardy is attracted by this possibility, his more characteristic position is that the past can only be 'exhumed' and is thus essentially grotesque. L. A. Bisson makes good connections between the two novelists in 'Proust and Hardy, Incidence or Coincidence', *Studies in French Language, Literature and History*, ed. Mackenzie (New York: Cambridge University Press, 1950), pp. 24–34.

44　*William Strang: Catalogue*, No. 311: see Illustration 17. Roger Bodart, *Antoine Wiertz* (Anvers: Sekkel, 1949), No. 13. Hardy may also have been aware of the symbolist movement in art in the 1890s, and its exploration of dream and nightmare: cf. Philippe Jullian, *The Symbolists* (London: Phaedon, 1973).

45　*CP*, 595. According to Hillis Miller, this wish reflects Hardy's ultimate assumption, which Miller defines elsewhere, 'that time is an illusion. For him everything already exists before it happens and goes on existing after it has happened in history' (*Thomas Hardy*, p. xi; also cf. pp. 231, 241). A distinction must be made contrasting Hardy with Proust and Schopenhauer (the figures with whom Miller most associates Hardy). Miller is very good on Hardy and the tragedy of belated recognitions (especially pp. 203, 210, 245), but like Proust tends to convert such belatedness into the eventual triumph of poetic detachment. On Hardy and Schopenhauer, cf. below, p. 121 and Note 70. Allowing for this distinction, I find Miller very valuable on the relation of lyric speaker to novel narrator (p. 194), on the lifelong spell of brief images (p. 120), and on the Hardy–Proust relations.

46　*Literary Notes II*, 71. The review from which this is taken, in *The Spectator*, 68 (1892), 431, is critical of Strang's stock figures, the 'intruders' cited in the sentence. Hardy cut the review off just at this point. 'Danse Macabre' is reproduced in *William Strang: Catalogue*, No. 172.

47　Hardy describes Eustacia in a scene characterised by Browningesque grotesques and Burkean sublimity: 'Never was harmony more perfect than that between the chaos of her mind and the chaos of the world without' (*Return of the Native*, v, 7, p. 421). In the mature lyric poem, such 'harmony' is, in fact, a deep disharmony.

48　Lowell's poem on Hardy, 'The Lesson', also captures well the Hardyesque sense of being split between present and past: 'the child's boat luffs in the same dry chop, / and we are where we were. We were!' Compare Hardy's ghosts who 'feel the energy again / That made them what they were!' (410).

49 *Friends of a Lifetime*, p. 284. This print is beautifully reproduced in O'Sullivan's *Thomas Hardy*, pp. 150–1. Another colour reproduction is in Darrell Figgis's *The Paintings of William Blake* (London: Benn, 1925), Plate 74; and in *Newsweek*, 27 March 1978.

50 *Friends of a Lifetime*, p. 287; Felkin, p. 27. In 1909 Hardy had related another dream: 'I am pursued, and I am rising like an angel up into heaven, out of the hands of my earthly pursuers. . . . I am agitated and hampered, as I suppose an angel would not be, by – a paucity of underlinen.' Reported by Violet Hunt, *I Have This To Say: The Story of My Flurried Years* (New York: Boni, 1926), p. 76, noted by Hynes, p. 184.

51 These differences are very difficult to formulate and would have to be based on the writers' ultimate assumptions about will and world. Michael Steig follows Freud's lead in 'Defining the Grotesque: An Attempt at Synthesis', *Journal of Aesthetics and Art Criticism*, 29 (1970), 253–60: 'in the grotesque the threatening material is distorted in the direction of harmlessness without completely attaining it.' This theory tends to be in the tradition of Ruskin's ignoble grotesque, where the caricaturist deliberately distorts reality, rather than the sublime grotesque, where reality overwhelms the visionary. The former might be illustrated in Browning's wilful and partly playful distortions; the latter might be illustrated in Hardy's lyric grotesques which are beyond play and signify the point where the mind has lost control of its world. Lee Byron Jennings remarks on a perennial confusion in discussions of the grotesque, namely 'the difficulty of distinguishing between the depiction of a chaotic world and the willful production of chaos for other reasons'. *The Ludicrous Demon: Aspects of the Grotesque in German Post-Romantic Prose* (Berkeley: University of California Press, 1963), p. 158.

52 *CP*, 603, 649, 906, 604, 439. On the Zeno paradox, cf. *Chapter 2*, Note 4.

53 Philip Jason suggests that this image reflects the Norse myth of Hamlet's Mill which grinds out time and decay: *Victorian Poetry*, 14 (1976), 262. We have already cited the image of Skrymir in 'The Wind's Prophecy'. Skrymir was a giant, full of protean changes and disguises, who poses impossible tasks to Thor and his companions: to drink the sea, to outeat fire, to outrun thought (*Larousse Encyclopedia of Mythology*). Pinion notes Hardy's reference to Skrymir in the story, 'Interlopers at the Knap', Chapter 1. There Hardy associates the snoring giant with 'the ironical directing-post . . . holding out its blank arms to the raw breeze'.

54 Thomson, *The Speedy Extinction of Evil and Misery: Selected Prose*, ed. William Schaefer (Berkeley: University of California Press, 1967), p. 314: 'A Lady of Sorrow.' Cf. Hardy, *Literary Notes I*, 208.

55 Stephen, 'War', *Cornhill Magazine*, 37 (1878), 478–89; 'Dreams and Realities', p. 345.

56 Tolstoy, 'Bethink Yourselves!' trans. V. Tchertkoff and I.F.M., *The Times* (27 June 1904), pp. 4–5.

57 Herbert Read, quoted by Arthur Lane, *An Adequate Response: The War Poetry of Wilfred Owen and Siegfried Sassoon* (Detroit: Wayne State University Press, 1972), p. 69.

58 Vivian de Sola Pinto, *Crisis in English Poetry: 1880–1940* (London: Hutchinson, 1967), fifth edition, p. 121.

59 Fussell, *The Great War and Modern Memory* (New York: Oxford University Press, 1975), p. 175.

60 The *TLS* article to which Hardy refers in *Life*, p. 373 (cf. below, p. 132) claimed that the Prussian victory in 1870 affected 'their whole conception of the nature of life', tempted them to militarism and war romance, and was thus a major factor in the coming

of the First World War. I. F. Clarke's *Voices Prophesying War: 1763–1984* (London: Oxford University Press, 1966) is a good account of the apprehensiveness, propaganda, chauvinism, idealism, and caricatures which lead to war. It begins: 'In the early summer of 1871 an anonymous story [George Chesney's 'Battle of Dorking' in *Blackwood's*] about a successful German invasion of the United Kingdom alarmed the nation. . . .' Bernard Bergonzi's *Heroes' Twilight* (New York, Coward-McCann, 1965), Chapter 2, discusses the fear of foreign invasion which was felt after the Franco-Prussian war of 1870. When the Great War finally came, Sassoon said, looking back at the summer of 1914: 'It seemed almost as if I had been waiting for this thing to happen.' Quoted by Lane, p. 87.

61 *French Revolution*, II, 3, vii. In *Signs of the Times* in 1829, Carlyle had written: 'How often have we heard, for the last fifty years, that the country was wrecked, and fast sinking.' But the sense of apprehensiveness perhaps takes on a new intensity in the Victorian period: W. L. Burn, *The Age of Equipoise* (London: Allen, 1964), says that the Victorian 'would have appreciated a painting of the urchin hurrying up the avenue with the fatal telegram, *What Does It Say?* or *What Will Happen Now?*' (p. 30). Charles Kingsley's reaction is quite common: 'I cannot escape that wretched fear of a national catastrophe, which haunts me night and day.' Cf. Margaret Thorp, *Charles Kingsley* (Princeton University Press, 1937), p. 125. Blunden, a fine war poet, was sensitive to this dimension in Hardy: 'Before his death Hardy, with something like the additional sense of a master mariner in a fog, was constrained to think that he had been dreaming; he knew in his own way that there was a fresh and appalling disaster ahead' (*Thomas Hardy*, p. 257).

62 Fussell, p. 23. Also, cf. Lane, p. 87.

63 Gosse, 'War and Literature', *Inter Arma* (New York: Scribner, 1916), p. 3.

64 Geoffrey Harpham, 'The Grotesque: First Principles', *Journal of Aesthetics and Art Criticism*, 34 (1975–6), p. 463.

65 Orel, *The Final Years of Thomas Hardy, 1912–1928* (London: Macmillan, 1976), p. 129.

66 Hardy and Pinion, *One Rare Fair Woman*, pp. 85, 92, 99; Orel, *Final Years*, p. 130; Hardy and Pinion, p. 99; M. van Wyk Smith, *Drummer Hodge: The Poetry of the Anglo-Boer War* (Oxford: Clarendon Press, 1978), pp. 55, 74, and *passim*; *CP*, 64, 44.

67 Hardy and Pinion, p. 89; *CP*, 59; *Life*, p. 311; Archer, *Real Conversations*, p. 47. Fussell, p. 21, notes how the Christian vocabulary of the First World War had been nurtured especially by 'the Arthurian poems of Tennyson and the pseudo-medieval romances of William Morris'. In 1903 Hardy wrote Quiller-Couch: 'The romance of *contemporary* wars has withered for ever, it seems to me: we see too far into them – too many details. Down to Waterloo war was romantic, was believed in.' F. G. Atkinson, ' "Yours Very 'Truly Thomas Hardy" ', p. 62.

68 *Dynasts*, Fore Scene, p. 9; I, 1, ii, p. 16; I, 2, v, p. 71; II, 3, i, p. 263.

69 *Dynasts*, p. xii; also Fore Scene, *passim*; I, 5, IV, p. 128; II, 4, v, p. 306; II, 1, iii, p. 196; III, 6, v, p. 192. The 'unnatural Monster' image culminates earlier observations Hardy made about the grotesque shapes of crowds, 'a monster whose body had four million heads and eight million eyes' (*Life*, p. 137; also cf. 131). Hardy's later personification may also owe something to the influence of James Thomson's grotesque personifications of the blind soulless universe: cf. Peter Noel-Bentley, ' "Fronting the Dreadful Mysteries of Time": Dürer's Melencolia in Thomson's City of Dreadful Night', *Victorian Poetry*, 12 (1974), 193–203.

70 Hardy's attitude to Schopenhauer seems curiously ambivalent. On three widely separate occasions, in 1902, 1914, and 1922, he includes Schopenhauer in a list of philosophers

he respects: *Life*, p. 315; *CP*, 'Apology' to *Late Lyrics and Earlier; Friends of a Lifetime*, p. 280. Yet when Helen Garwood sent Hardy her thesis on the subject, her delight at receiving a reply from the master himself must have been tempered by its contents: 'My pages show harmony of view with Darwin, Huxley, Spencer, Hume, Mill, and others, all of whom I used to read more than Schopenhauer': cf. Pinion, *Hardy Companion*, p. 106. In a letter of 1909, Gosse said that Hardy 'n'admet pas que Schopenhauer ait exercé une influence sur son oeuvre': quoted by F. A. Hedgcock, *Thomas Hardy Penseur et Artiste* (Paris: Librairie Hachette, 1911), p. 499. In 1920, Gosse repeated his assertion, as quoted in the *Literary Review* section of the *New York Evening Post*, 3 (9 September 1922), p. 18: 'To this day he is very slightly and superficially acquainted with the writings of Schopenhauer.' On Hardy's notations from Schopenhauer's works, cf. Wright, pp. 39–56. On Hardy and Schopenhauer, also see Gittings, *The Older Hardy*, p. 114.

71 Cf. above, Note 6.

72 Cf. David Thatcher, *Nietzsche in England 1890–1914* (University of Toronto Press, 1970) and Patrick Bridgwater, *Nietzsche in Anglosaxony* (Leicester University Press, 1972). The attacks followed the lead of Max Nordau's *Degeneration*, translated in 1895, a critique of *fin de siècle* writers which attacked Nietzsche for his megalomania and mysticism. His books, Nordau said, are 'a succession of disconnected sallies, prose and doggerel mixed. . . . rarely are a few consecutive pages connected by any unity of purpose or logical argument' (Thatcher, p. 28). A few works, including *Thus Spake Zarathustra*, had been translated in 1896; *The Genealogy of Morals* appeared in translation in 1899, *Beyond Good and Evil* in 1907.

73 Ernest Brennecke quotes this in *Life and Art by Thomas Hardy*, p. 139. This is the only compliment Hardy ever pays Nietzsche, but it may be a significant one in showing Hardy's ability to empathise with Nietzsche's critique of contemporary values. Hardy's summaries of Nietzsche's thought suggest he was acquainted with *Zarathustra*, the first translation of which appeared in 1896.

74 Hardy notes Nietzsche's views on the Greek chorus, and on the Apollonian – Dionysian conflict, which he takes from Arthur Symons's article 'Nietzsche on Tragedy', *The Academy and Literature* (30 August 1902): cf: *Literary Notes II*, [153]. Wright notes an entry in *Literary Notes II*, [100], *c.* 1898, in which Hardy approvingly notes a newspaper article on Nietzsche's 'insanity' (Wright, p. 38). But Hardy also, a few pages later, quotes Nietzsche on the artist and his age (*Literary Notes II*, [105]). Other Hardy references to Nietzsche cited below are from *Friends of a Lifetime*, p. 280 (note the similar language in Wilfrid Blunt's letter of 1915, p. 194); Brennecke, *Life and Art*, pp. 137–9; *Life*, p. 364. Also cf. *Life*, p. 315.

75 Thatcher, p. 42.

76 Hardy's remarks in letters to the *Manchester Guardian* started a dispute in the pages of the *Manchester Guardian*, *Daily News and Leader*, and *Daily Chronicle* between 8 October and 12 October 1914. In the *Manchester Guardian*, Bernard Gilbert replied on 8 October and noted Nietzsche's attack on German materialism. Thomas Beecham followed the next day by noting Nietzsche's hatred of jingoism and Treitschke (with whom Hardy had associated Nietzsche). Beecham also compared Nietzsche's celebration of the superman to Carlyle's celebration of Frederick the Great. Hardy was supported by the editorial for 10 October and in turn replied on 13 October, quoting *Zarathustra*: 'I do not counsel you to conclude peace but to conquer. . . . Beware of pity.' These last five items are in Hardy's scrapbook, 'Personal Reviews', *Original Manuscripts*, Reel 6. Hardy was again supported by the editorial, and by a further article on 15 October. On 17 October, Beecham and Ananda Coomaraswamy replied, the latter comparing Nietzsche to Blake.

On 20 October, the great Nietzsche translator, Oscar Levy, replied and noted that 'seven years ago . . . Nietzsche was practically unknown'. Articles on 21 and 22 October again attacked Nietzsche for being self-contradictory; the series ended after an acknowledgement that the correspondence had become voluminous. Oscar Levy looked back at the dispute, in 'Thomas Hardy and Friedrich Nietzsche', *Outlook* (London), 61 (1928), 217–18. He noted other responses of the time. After comparing the two writers – both are 'aware of tragic circumstances of life' – Levy then stressed their difference: 'Hardy has the *horror fati*, Nietzsche proclaims the *amor fati*.' Patrick Bridgwater suggests that Hardy was a major factor in reversing the rising estimates of Nietzsche in Britain and in associating Nietzsche's name with the causes of war: cf. *Nietzsche in Anglosaxony*, pp. 132, 143.

77 *CP*, 493, 494; also quoted in this paragraph are *CP*, 50, 498, 495, 504.

78 Sassoon, *Siegfried's Journey 1916–1920* (New York: Viking, 1946), Chapters 6–7, pp. 96, 104.

79 Letter to Arthur Symons, 13 September, quoted in *Colby Library Quarterly*, 4 (1956), 115–16. In 1916 Hardy wrote Henry Newbolt that he had read Newbolt's heroic account of the Battle of Mons and congratulated himself on being able to keep down 'boyishness in relishing it'; letter of 3 December, Colby College Library Collection. I assume Hardy is referring to the account which would appear in Newbolt's *Tales of the Great War* (London: Longmans, 1917). Newbolt was 'the leading exponent of the public school soldier' (van Wyk Smith, p. 57). In 1922 Hardy noted a crowning irony, that the romantic image of Napoleon may have been a prime influence on German militarism: 'What a Nemesis for the French nation!' (*Life*, p. 418).

80 *Final Years*, p. 129; *Writings*, p. 247; Frédéric Lefèvre, 'An Hour with Thomas Hardy', *Living Age*, 325 (11 April 1925), 100.

81 *CP*, 503, 496, 368, 499, 495, 918, 545, 696. In 1918, Sassoon asked Hardy if he believed in the League of Nations 'or any such design for the prevention of war. Rather diffidently, he expressed his view that wars came about almost like atmospheric disturbances, adding that he had sometimes felt that they were caused by supernatural agencies and were beyond human control.' *Siegfried's Journey*, Chapter 8, p. 120. The diffidence, the words 'almost' and 'sometimes', the irony, are important qualifications.

82 Fussell, p. 75. Charles Sorley's 'When you see millions of the mouthless dead' is a celebrated war poem describing dreams haunted by 'pale battalions' of the slain: cf. Lane, p. 82. Commenting on '"And There Was a Great Calm"', Blunden said that Hardy's lines 'catch the peculiar life of the war of 1914–1918 as in an eternal transparency' (*Thomas Hardy*, p. 257). Blunden's own vision of men 'meditating war with which the world still bleeds' ('Uneasy Peace'), the grotesque imagery which accompanies this meditation (as in 'January Full Moon, Ypres', 'The Zonnebeke Road', and others), show the influence of Hardy in ways which need to be examined.

83 Wright, p. 15, notes Hardy's annotation in Dryden – *Absolom and Achitophel*, l. 752. For a related idea, cf. 'What is Militarism', above, p. 132. For a later explication of this Orwellian irony, cf. Eric Voegelin, *The New Science of Politics* (Chicago: University of Chicago Press, 1952): 'In an age when war is peace, and peace is war, a few definitions will be in order . . .' (p. 171). Voegelin has beautifully expressed the central insight of Hardy's war vision. The last two sentences may remind readers of Hardy's 'Apology' to *Late Lyrics and Earlier*:

> With radical immanentization the dream world has blended into the real world terminologically; the obsession of replacing the world of reality by the transfigured

dream world has become the obsession of the one world in which the dreamers adopt the vocabulary of reality, while changing its meaning, as if the dream were reality. . . . As a consequence, types of action which in the real world would be considered as morally insane because of the real effects which they have will be entirely moral in the dream world because they intended an entirely different effect. The gap between intended and real effect will be imputed not to the Gnostic immorality of ignoring the structure of reality but to the immorality of some other person or society that does not behave as it should behave according to the dream conception of cause and effect. The interpretation of moral insanity as morality, and of the virtues of *sophia* and *prudentia* as immorality, is a confusion difficult to unravel. (pp. 167–70)

'No one . . . can predict what nightmares of violence it will take to break the dream' (p. 173).

84 Inge, *Outspoken Essays*, 27, 27, 30, 33, 23–4, 25, 8, 40, 52.
85 Huxley, 'The Evolution of Theology: An Anthropological Study', written in 1886 and included in *Science and Hebrew Tradition* (1893). Lang reviewed the essay in 'The Witch of Endor and Professor Huxley', *Contemporary Review*, 66 (1894), 165–76.
86 *Ashley Library Catalogue*, vol. 10, letter of 27 February, insert between pp. 126–7. Clodd, *Thomas Henry Huxley* (London: Blackwood, 1902).

EPILOGUE

1 Bergson, *Creative Evolution*, trans. Arthur Mitchell (New York: Modern Library, 1944; originally, Holt, 1911), p. 54. Hardy's translations are not identical with Mitchell's. Other passages from Bergson quoted below are on pp. 99, 53, 194, 342. Hardy was thinking about Bergson, in connection with the Zeno paradox, as early as 1909: cf. Chapter 2, Note 4.
2 Hardy also quotes Bergson's distinction between the 'inert' and the 'living' – an apparent reference to *Creative Evolution*, pp. 215–17. This chapter also contains some famous statements of particular relevance to the romantic pastoral hope: 'Philosophy can only be an effort to dissolve again into the Whole. Intelligence, reabsorbed into its principle, may thus live back again its own genesis' (p. 210). A page after that which Hardy cited, Bergson writes:

Let us seek, in the depths of our experience, the point where we feel ourselves most intimately within our own life. It is into pure duration that we then plunge back, a duration in which the past, always moving on, is swelling unceasingly with a present that is absolutely new. . . . We must, by a strong recoil of our personality on itself, gather up our past which is slipping away, in order to thrust it, compact and undivided, into a present which it will create by entering. Rare indeed are the moments when we are self-possessed to this extent: it is then that our actions are truly free. (pp. 218–19)

Later Bergson says: 'The object of philosophy would be reached if this intuition could be sustained. . . . To that end a continual coming and going is necessary between nature and mind' (p. 261). Again: 'Install yourself within change, and you will grasp at once both change itself and the successive states in which *it might* at any instant be immobilized' (p. 334).

3 Earlier Bergson recommends a language that would reconcile the hypothetical nature of the intellect's abstractions with the fixed object references which he associates with instinct (p. 175).

4 *Writings*, pp. 98, 95–6, 95. Cyril Clemens, 'My Chat with Thomas Hardy', *Dalhousie Review*, 22 (1943), 87–94.

5 Other traditions of pastoral, its complex relation to city life, social life, and the realities of rustic life, have been discussed and applied to Hardy's novels by various writers, for example, Harold Toliver, *Pastoral Forms and Attitudes* (Berkeley: University of California Press, 1971); Mervyn Williams, *Thomas Hardy and Rural England* (London: Macmillan, 1972); Raymond Williams, *The Country and the City* (London: Chatto and Windus, 1973). For my purposes I have found the most useful of books on pastoral to be Laurence Lerner's *The Uses of Nostalgia: Studies in Pastoral Poetry* (New York: Schocken, 1972).

6 3, p. 21. Hardy wrote *The Trumpet-Major* (1879–80) about the same time he wrote the review on Barnes quoted above. What he felt toward Barnes may have been like what the soldiers felt toward Overcombe Mill.

7 *Friends of a Lifetime*, p. 307.

8 Williams, *A Preface to Hardy* (London: Longmans, 1976), p. 155.

9 Lewis, 'The Shorter Poems of Thomas Hardy', *The Bell*, 8 (1944), 513–25. Lewis is quoting Grierson on Donne.

10 Ransom, 'Honey and Gall', *Southern Review*, 6 (1940), p. 5.

11 *CP*, 184, 163, 280, 367, 562, 548. The influential argument is Hynes's, pp. 69–70.

12 *CP*, 675, 673, 791, 730, 786, 681, 704, 743; *Woodlanders*, 28, p. 246; 38, p. 335; 28, p. 247; *Jude*, IV, 1.

13 *CP*, 700, 708, 679, 705, 672.

14 *CP*, 675, 698, 703.

15 *CP*, 675, 663, 664.

16 *CP*, 818, 816, 820, 829.

17 *CP*, 844, 846, 907, 910, 918; *Life*, p. 15; *Jude*, I, ii, p. 15; *Under the Greenwood Tree*, I, iv.

Bibliography

LIST OF WORKS CITED MORE THAN ONCE

Ainsworth, William Harrison. *Rookwood*. London: Denton, 1931. Originally published 1834.

The Ashley Library: A Catalogue of Printed Books, Manuscripts and Autograph Letters, vol. x. London: Dunedin, 1930.

Bagehot, Walter. 'Wordsworth, Tennyson, and Browning; or, Pure, Ornate, and Grotesque Art in English Poetry'. In *Literary Essays*: vol. 2. *Collected Works*. Ed. N. St John-Stevas. Cambridge: Harvard University Press, 1965.

Bailey, James O. *The Poetry of Thomas Hardy*. Chapel Hill: University of North Carolina Press, 1970.

Barber, D. F., ed. *Concerning Thomas Hardy*. London: Skilton, 1968.

Beatty, C. J. P., ed. *The Architectural Notebook of Thomas Hardy*, Philadelphia: Macmanus, 1966.

Bergson, Henri. *Creative Evolution*. Trans. Arthur Mitchell. 1911; rpt. New York: Modern Library, 1944.

Betjeman, Sir John. 'Hardy and Architecture'. *The Genius of Thomas Hardy*, ed. Margaret Drabble. London: Weidenfeld and Nicolson, 1976.

Björk, Lennart, ed. *The Literary Notes of Thomas Hardy*. vol. 1, pts. i and ii. Göteborg: Acta Universitatis Gothoburgensis, 1974.

Blunden, Edmund. *Thomas Hardy*. London: Macmillan, 1942.

_____. 'Thomas Hardy', in *The Great Victorians*, ed. H. Massingham. New York: Doubleday, 1933.

Bond, Francis. *Gothic Architecture in England*. London: Batsford, 1905.

Brandon, Raphael and Brandon, David. *An Analysis of Gothick Architecture*. London: Pelham Richardson, 1847.

_____. *The Open Timber Roofs of the Middle Ages*. London: David Bogue, 1849.

Brennecke, Ernest. *Life and Art by Thomas Hardy*. New York: Greenberg, 1925.

Clark, Sir Kenneth. *The Gothic Revival*. 3rd edition. New York: Holt, Rinehart, 1962.

Collins, Vere. *Talks with Thomas Hardy at Max Gate, 1920–1922*. London: Duckworth, 1928.

Darwin, Charles. *On the Origin of Species: A Facsimile of the First Edition*. Introd. Ernst Mayr. Cambridge: Harvard University Press, 1964.

Eastlake, Charles L. *A History of the Gothic Revival*. London: Longmans, 1872. Reprinted with an introduction by J. M. Mordaunt Crook. New York: Humanities Press, 1970.

Fayen, George. 'Hardy's *The Woodlanders*: Inwardness and Memory', *Studies in English Literature*, I (1961), 81–100.

Felkin, Elliott. 'Days with Thomas Hardy', *Encounter*, 18 (April 1962), 27–33.

Friends of a Lifetime: Letters to Sydney Carlyle Cockerell. Ed. Viola Meynell. London: Jonathan Cape, 1940.

Fussell, Paul. *The Great War and Modern Memory*. New York: Oxford University Press, 1975.

Garrigan, Kristine. *Ruskin on Architecture*. Madison: University of Wisconsin Press, 1973.

Gerber, Helmut and Davis, Eugene. *Thomas Hardy: An Annotated Bibliography of Writings About Him*. De Kalb, Illinois: Northern Illinois University Press, 1973.

Gibbon, Edward. *The Decline and Fall of the Roman Empire*. Ed. J. B. Bury. New York: Heritage Press, 1946

Gittings, Robert. *The Older Hardy*. London: Heinemann, 1978.

_____. *Young Thomas Hardy*. Boston: Little Brown, 1975.

Gosse, Edmund. 'Mr. Hardy's Lyrical Poems', *Edinburgh Review*, 207 (1918); rpt. in *Thomas Hardy: The Critical Heritage*. Ed. R. G. Cox. New York: Barnes and Noble, 1970.

Grant, James. *The Scottish Cavalier*. London: Colburn, 1850. 3 vols.

Hardy, Evelyn and Gittings, Robert, eds. *Some Recollections of Emma Hardy*. London: Oxford University Press, 1961.

Hardy, Evelyn and Pinion, F. B. *One Rare Fair Woman: Thomas Hardy's Letters to Florence Henniker 1893–1922*. London: Macmillan, 1972.

Hardy, Thomas. *Complete Poems*. Variorum Edition. Ed. James Gibson. London: Macmillan, 1979.

_____. *The Early Life . . . By Florence Emily Hardy*. New York: Macmillan, 1928.

_____. *The Famous Tragedy of the Queen of Cornwall*. London: Macmillan, 1923.

_____. *The Later Years . . . By Florence Emily Hardy*. New York: Macmillan, 1930.

_____. *The Life of Thomas Hardy . . . by Florence Emily Hardy*. London: Macmillan, 1962.

_____. *The Original Manuscripts and Papers*. Wakefield, Yorkshire: EP Microform Ltd., 1975:

    Reel 5: *Poetry, Essays and Short Stories*.

    Reel 6: *Scrapbooks* ('Personal Reviews', etc.).

    Reels 7 and 8: *Drafts for Biography*.

    Reel 9: *Memoranda, Diaries, and Notebooks* (Literary Notes, I, II, etc; Schools of Painting, etc).

    Reel 10: *Music Books, Paintings, and Drawings*.

_____. *The Works of Thomas Hardy in Prose and Verse*. Wessex Edition. London: Macmillan, 1912–1931.

_____. Writings. *Thomas Hardy's Personal Writings*. Ed. Harold Orel. Lawrence: University of Kansas Press, 1966.

Hartmann, Josef. *Architektur in den Romanen Thomas Hardy's*. Pöppinghaus, 1934.

Hedgcock, Frank. 'Reminiscences of Thomas Hardy', *National and English Review*, 137 (1951), 220–8, 289–94.

Hynes, Samuel. *The Pattern of Hardy's Poetry*. Chapel Hill: University of North Carolina Press, 1961.

Inge, William. *Outspoken Essays*. 2nd edition. London: Longmans, 1921.

Jones, Owen. *The Grammar of Ornament*. 1856; 2nd edition, 1865; rpt. London: Quaritch, 1868.

Lane, Arthur. *An Adequate Response: The War Poetry of Wilfred Owen and Siegfried Sassoon*. Detroit: Wayne State University Press, 1972.

Larkin, Philip. *The Less Deceived*. 1955; rpt. New York: St Martin's Press, 1965.

Lawrence, T. E. *Letters*. Ed. David Garnett. London: Cape, 1938.

Marsden, Kenneth. *The Poems of Thomas Hardy*. New York: Oxford University Press, 1969.

Maudsley, Henry. *Natural Causes and Supernatural Seemings*. London: Kegan Paul, 1886.

Miller, J. Hillis. *Thomas Hardy: Distance and Desire*. Cambridge: Harvard University Press, 1970.

Millgate, Michael. *Thomas Hardy: His Career as a Novelist*. New York: Random House, 1971.

'Modern Developments in Ballad Art', *Edinburgh Review*, 213 (1911), 153–79.

Murry, John Middleton. 'The Poetry of Thomas Hardy', *Athenaeum* (1919); rpt. in *Aspects of Literature*. London: Collins, 1920.

Orel, Harold. *The Final Years of Thomas Hardy, 1912–1928*. London: Macmillan, 1976.

O'Sullivan, Timothy. *Thomas Hardy: An Illustrated Biography*. London: Macmillan, 1975.

Paley, F. A. *A Manual of Gothic Mouldings*. 3rd edition. London: John Van Voorst, 1865.

Paulin, Tom. *Thomas Hardy: The Poetry of Perception*. London: Macmillan, 1975.

Pinion, F. B. *A Hardy Companion. A Guide to the Works of Thomas Hardy and their Background*. London: Macmillan, 1968.

Pound, Ezra. *Confucius to Cummings: An Anthology*. New York: New Directions, 1964.

Pugin, A. Welby. *Contrasts: or, A Parallel Between the Noble Edifices of the Middle Ages and Corresponding Buildings of the Present Day; Shewing the Present Decay of Taste*. 2nd edition. London: Charles Dolman, 1841. Rpt. New York: Humanities Press, 1969. Intro. H. R. Hitchcock.

Purdy, Richard. *Thomas Hardy: A Bibliographical Study*. London: Oxford University Press, 1954.

_____. *Thomas Hardy Memorial Exhibition*. New Haven: Yale University Press, 1928.

_____, and Millgate, Michael, eds. *The Collected Letters of Thomas Hardy*. Oxford: Clarendon Press, 1978.

Real Conversations. Recorded by William Archer. London: Heinemann, 1904.

Ruskin, John. *Works*. Ed. E. T. Cook and Alexander Wedderburn. 39 vols. London: Allen, 1903–12.

Sassoon, Siegfried. *Siegfried's Journey 1916–1920*. New York: Viking, 1946.

Schopenhauer, Arthur. *On the Fourfold Root of the Principle of Sufficient Reason*. Trans. Hillebrand. London: 1897.

Smart, Alastair. 'Pictorial Imagery in the Novels of Thomas Hardy', *Review of English Studies*, N.S. 12 (1961), 262–80.

Southern Review, Thomas Hardy Centennial Issue, 6 (Summer 1940).

Stephen, Leslie. 'Dreams and Realities', *Fortnightly Review*, 30 (1878), 334–52.

_____. 'War', *Cornhill Magazine*, 37 (1878), 478–89.

Stewart, J. I. M. *Thomas Hardy: A Critical Biography*. London: Longmans, 1971.

William Strang: Catalogue of His Etched Work 1882–1912. Glasgow: Maclehose, 1912. *Supplement*. Glasgow: Maclehose, 1923.

Taylor, Richard H., ed., *The Personal Notebooks of Thomas Hardy*. London: Macmillan, 1979.

Thatcher, David. *Nietzsche in England 1890–1914*. Toronto: University of Toronto Press, 1970.

Thomas, Dylan. 'An Introduction to Thomas Hardy', *An Evening with Dylan Thomas*. Caedmon Records, 1963.

Tolstoy, Leo. 'Bethink Yourselves!' Trans. V. Tchertkoff and I.F.M. *The Times* (27 June 1904), pp. 4–5.

van Wyk Smith, M. *Drummer Hodge: The Poetry of the Anglo-Boer War (1899–1902)*. Oxford: Clarendon, 1978.

Vigar, Penelope. *The Novels of Thomas Hardy*. London: Athlone, 1974.

Weber, Carl. *Hardy and the Lady from Madison Square*. Waterville, Maine: Colby College Press, 1952.

'What is Militarism?' *Times Literary Supplement* (27 July 1916), pp. 349–50.

Wright, Walter. *The Shaping of The Dynasts*. Lincoln: University of Nebraska Press, 1967.

Index